THE ENDURING INDIANS
OF KANSAS

THE ENDURING INDIANS
OF KANSAS

*A Century and a Half
of Acculturation*

JOSEPH B. HERRING

UNIVERSITY PRESS OF KANSAS

© 1990 by the University Press of Kansas
All rights reserved

Published by the University Press of Kansas (Lawrence, Kansas
66045), which was organized by the Kansas Board of Regents and is
operated and funded by Emporia State University, Fort Hays State
University, Kansas State University, Pittsburg State University,
the University of Kansas, and Wichita State University

Library of Congress Cataloging-in-Publication Data

Herring, Joseph B., 1947–
The enduring Indians of Kansas : a century and a half of
acculturation / Joseph B. Herring.
p.   cm.
Includes bibliographical references.
ISBN 0–7006–0469–3 (alk. paper)
1. Indians of North America—Kansas—History—19th century.
2. Indians of North America—Kansas—Government relations.
3. Indians of North America—Kansas—Cultural assimilation.
I. Title.
E78.K16H47   1990
978.1'00497–dc20
90–32766
CIP

British Library Cataloguing in Publication Data is available.

Printed in the United States of America
10   9   8   7   6   5   4   3   2   1

For Margie and Jack Herring

CONTENTS

ILLUSTRATIONS AND MAPS

Maps

ACKNOWLEDGMENTS

Since I began my research on the Indians of Kansas several years ago, there have been many people who have gone beyond the call of duty to ensure the successful completion of the project. Perhaps the person who stands out above the rest is my wife, Karen Capell, who has offered her understanding, compassion, and help when I needed them the most. She has also assisted in the writing and editing, as well as lending constructive criticisms; she is my toughest critic. To Karen, along with our children, Meghan and Kelly, I offer my sincerest thanks.

Many others deserve thanks as well. During my graduate school days at Texas Christian University, R. David Edmunds made sure that I gained a firm grasp of American history, especially American Indian history. Dave was instrumental in my receiving the Walter Rundell Fellowship, which provided funds that helped me complete my research. It was a great honor to receive an award named after my former mentor at the University of Maryland, the late Walter Rundell, Jr. I wish to thank the Western History Association and Westerners International for making the Rundell Award available.

I also would like to extend my sincerest thanks to those who helped with the manuscript; they include William Unrau, Jeanne Cardenas, Raymond Wilson, James Ronda, and Michael Green. I thank them for reading and editing chapters and offering advice on additional research possibilities.

Many archivists and librarians deserve credit for helping me with the research. These include Barbara Rust, Margaret Hacker, Kent Carter, Beverly Moody, Barbara Leahy, Overnice Wilks, and Margie Jenkins of the National Archives, Southwest Region, at Fort Worth, Texas. Others from the National Archives who deserve mention are Alan Perry of the Central Plains regional office at Kansas City, Missouri, and Richard Crawford of the Washington, D.C., office. Also lending a hand were Joseph Forte, Sister Mary Delores Strunk, and Mary Richardet of the Kansas Newman College Library; Linda Lombard, also of Kansas Newman; and Sandy Echt, Mary Charlotte Ferris, Janna Ferguson, Sally Brady, Brenda Barnes, and Ruth Ross of Mary Couts Burnett Library at Texas Christian University. My mapmaker, Rick Floyd of Dallas, Texas, has done his usual fine work.

Finally, special mention goes to Donald E. Worcester and James Kettle, who read the manuscript several times and helped improve it greatly. Don and Jim are still the two best editors in the Southwest.

1

INTRODUCTION

The forced migration and "Trail of Tears" of the Cherokees, Choctaws, and other southern tribes during the 1830s and 1840s was the most dramatic result of President Andrew Jackson's Indian removal policy. Less well known is that the tribes of the Old Northwest—Ohio, Indiana, Illinois, Michigan, and Wisconsin—were also coerced into surrendering their lands and moving beyond the Mississippi River. Many of these tribes emigrated to a place that came to be called Kansas. During the 1820s, 1830s, and 1840s more than ten thousand displaced Indians settled "permanently" along the wooded streams and rivers of eastern Kansas, at the edge of the western prairie. By the early 1870s, however, there remained only several hundred Kickapoos, Potawatomis, Chippewas, Munsees, Iowas, Sacs, and a few others.

These Indians were still in Kansas because they had managed to walk the fine line between their traditional ways and those of the whites.[1] Although the Kickapoos, Potawatomis, and others had acculturated, they had not assimilated into the dominant American culture. They may have spoken English, farmed individual plots of land, donned overalls or calico dresses, and taken on other trappings of white society, but they never completely abandoned their traditional customs, kinship networks, and religions and never forgot that they were Indians.[2]

By outwardly adapting to Euro-American ways, they won the grudging respect of whites, who accepted them as members of the larger Kansas farming community. Other tribes who had refused to make any accommodation had lost their lands and were forced to move to Oklahoma, then known as Indian Territory. Most of those who assimilated, accepting the individualistic and materialistic values that white society forced upon them, met the same fate.

This study defines the processes of acculturation and assimilation as two separate concepts.[3] The latter involves the complete absorption of a minority people—Indian tribe or immigrant group—into the traditional and cultural mainstream of a larger and more powerful society. Those who have assimilated into the dominant society (this includes, for example, most Irish and German Americans) have given up or forgotten most elements of their former cultural heritage and have lost their earlier identity. In contrast, acculturation is the intercultural borrowing that takes place when two or more diverse peoples come into close contact. Each adopts certain cultural traits of the other, resulting in new and blended forms; yet each retains a certain degree of cultural autonomy.

In the case of the Indians, of course, acculturation has been a largely one-sided process; they have adopted far more Euro-American cultural traits than vice versa. Nevertheless, the Indians who remained in Kansas acculturated on their own terms; to them, acculturation was a defense mechanism that proved crucial to their survival. Despite their acculturative concessions to the new ways, they avoided eviction from Kansas while remaining, at heart, Indians who identified with their respective tribes, bands, and clans. They resisted governmental demands that they abandon their tribes for uncertain lives as individual family farmers.

Their acculturation without assimilation was a lengthy process that began long before the tribes were moved to the West. As was true of the southern Indians, the traditional political, economic, and social practices of these tribes had already been altered by years of interaction with whites. Although most Indians benefited little by these changes, several bands of Kickapoos, Chippewas, Munsees, Iowas, Sacs, and Potawatomis had at least learned how to deal with whites. Members of these bands had developed creative strategies to cope with the problems caused by an influx of white settlers onto their new lands. They managed to forestall efforts to remove their people from Kansas. With few exceptions, their bands had leaders who effectively resisted efforts by Indian agents and missionaries to change their ways. These bands were able to remain in Kansas by adapting to the dominant society as necessary, but at their own pace and by passive, nonviolent resistance.

All of the emigrant tribes that settled in nineteenth-century Kansas faced a constant struggle to keep their possessions and to maintain their cultural integrity. Immediately after the first significant number of émigrés began arriving in their new homes during the 1820s, Indian agents and other federal employees, traders, and missionaries appeared to minister to their needs. Although many of these whites had honest intentions, their efforts to help Indians were generally more harmful than beneficial.

Most whites, convinced that Indians must either abandon their "heathen" ways or perish, scorned tribal customs and religions. Indian agents, therefore, worked to remake their unwilling wards into yeoman farmers and to bring them "up to the standard of morals and intellectual and religious cultivation, that would gladen [sic] the hearts of all lovers of their country and its institutions." The whites believed that federal officials should furnish European-style clothing to the Indians, whose breechcloths, blankets, paints, bear-claw necklaces, ear-bobs, bracelets, and other jewelry reinforced "their ancient traditions, superstitions and customs, which has [sic] so long and so effectively interfered with their advancement in civilization."[4] Few whites seemed to realize that that very fabric of custom and religion sustained the Indians in their bitter struggle to survive.

The leading advocates of change for Indians were the Protestant and Catholic missionaries, most of whom were sincere and interested primarily in winning Indian souls. Especially confident of success were the Jesuits, most of them recent arrivals from Belgium, France, and other European countries. The Jesuits worked among several Kansas tribes, including the Potawatomis and Kickapoos. They knew that they held several advantages over their Baptist, Presbyterian, Methodist, and Moravian counterparts. The Jesuit order's bureaucracy mobilized missionaries on a grand scale, and their well-rounded classical education gave the priests a facility with languages that Protestant ministers generally lacked. In addition, priests were unhindered by family affairs or financial worries, and many Indians appreciated their chastity, a practice many whites failed to observe.

Experience had taught the Jesuits, moreover, to make concessions to local customs and to begin serious proselytizing only after mastering the Indians' languages and understanding their folkways. While others may have condemned traditional dancing, games, and festivals, the "blackrobes" wisely tolerated these ceremonies. Rather than trying to eradicate existing Indian practices, they sought to adapt them to Catholicism. By giving Christian meaning to tribal ritual, as they did with the Vermillion Kickapoos and others, the Jesuits sometimes inadvertently helped create a cultural blend dominated by the native contribution rather than the European.[5]

Regardless of their religious affiliation, the Catholic and Protestant missionaries were firm believers in the American melting pot, and they were convinced that accepting Christ's teachings would radically improve the Indians' way of life. The preachers optimistically believed that conversions would come quickly and easily. But in 1837, when the Baptist missionary John G. Pratt first arrived at the Shawnee Mission near the mouth of the Kansas River, he was shocked by the Indians' indifference to his preaching. He wrote to a superior that it was "truly painful to notice the stupidity of these 'sons of the forest,' in the reception of religious instruction." He was sure, nevertheless, that the Indians, "wandering they know not where," would soon "embrace the same Savior, and become heirs, also, of the kingdom of Heaven." Pratt believed that God had directed him to this "land of darkness" and had blessed him with an "abundant opportunity" to save the souls of those "without the Gospel and destitute of its sanctifying influences."[6]

Expecting their charges to embrace the Gospel, to adopt white ways, to give up hunting for farming, and to reject polygamy, gambling, and alcohol, Pratt and other missionaries established missions and schools on tribal lands. Both the Protestants and the Catholics were, however, nearly always disappointed; for although Indians were willing to incorporate selected aspects of Christianity, they had practiced their traditional religions for centuries and were reluctant to reject the rites of their ancestors in favor of the beliefs of whites.

Even more distasteful, missionaries often found themselves competing unsuccessfully with traditional religious leaders for the hearts and minds of the people. The Methodist minister Jerome Berryman complained that Kenekuk, the Kickapoo prophet, had thwarted his conversion efforts. The Methodist insisted that such "impostors must be held in check by the counteracting influences of popular virtue, or they will in time barbarize the world."[7]

But as one Kickapoo man explained, the band's moral code had already approximated that of the preachers, and the Indians were satisfied that they had found the true path. The Kickapoos did not need to become Methodists or Catholics. "We are happier and more flourishing here. . . . It is only a few years since we learnt [God's] will and commands" through the prophet Kenekuk, but if "[we] obey him, we shall daily grow wiser and happier." The Kickapoos' devotion to their own religious leader was unquestioning; the prophet's charismatic hold over his band was something that Berryman and other missionaries could hardly understand, let alone appreciate.[8]

The Jesuit Christian Hoecken discovered that Indians generally feared, "respected and revered" their own religious leaders, believing that they could "kill or cure and make their patients suffer or pine away."[9] This reverence and fear proved a major obstacle to mission work. "The superstitions of the Indians lie at the foundation of much of their barbarity," wrote Charles F. Coffin, clerk for the Committee of Friends (Quakers) on Indian Affairs. The tribespeople, Coffin asserted, were under the spell of an Indian "priesthood whose spiritual knowledge does not rise above the simplest arts of necromancy and soothsaying, and we can well understand how capricious and unsatisfactory must be the workings of a polity resting upon such a basis."[10]

Although they resisted conversion efforts, most tribes allowed the missionaries to set up stations among them and preach. When the eastern Indians arrived in Kansas, they hoped to quickly reestablish their former way of life, and they shrewdly realized that missionaries could be useful as intermediaries between themselves and a government slow in providing promised treaty monies, food, clothing, and farm implements. Missionaries could protect their charges from unscrupulous traders, and by witnessing contracts and other transactions they could also counteract whites who attempted to usurp Indian lands.

By the 1840s several religious groups had established missions in Kansas. The Methodists worked among the Shawnees and other tribes, while the Baptists preached to the Delawares and Ottawas; the Catholics built St. Mary's Mission for the Potawatomis; the Moravians proselytized among the Munsee Delawares; and the Presbyterians spread the Gospel among the Iowas and Sacs. As advocates of the government's civilization program, the preachers agreed that Indians should assimilate, and they promoted educational and farming opportunities for their charges. At the Baptist Manual Labor School, for example, Superintendent Johnston Lykins established a model farm to help "Americanize the Indians, and attach them to our country and institutions."[11]

Such attempts to Americanize Indians, however, were destined for failure. Preferring their own ways, most tribespeople refused to become assimilated. Racism on the part of settlers, businessmen, federal agents, and other whites, moreover, made it extremely difficult for whites and Indians to live as neighbors. This fact proved unfortunate for most of the Indians of Kansas. Although governmental officials had assured the tribes that the Kansas lands were theirs forever, by the late 1840s white settlement had reached the Missouri River and pressures mounted to move the Indians out of the way of progress. The Mexican War ended in 1848, opening California and other western territories to settlement.

As a result, Illinois Sen. Stephen A. Douglas and others argued that the Indian lands posed a barrier to United States expansion. "How are we to develop, cherish and protect our immense interests and possessions on the Pacific," Douglas proclaimed, "with a vast wilderness fifteen hundred miles in breadth, filled with hostile savages, and cutting off all direct communication. The Indian barrier must be removed."[12] Politicians and businessmen pressured federal officials to open the lines of communication to California by creating a right-of-way through Indian country. In response, officials began plotting a new general Indian policy because the removal of Indians to isolated areas was no longer an option. For the sake of American progress and development, the reservation system became a necessity.[13]

The emigrant Indians of Kansas would be among the first to feel the effects of the new reservation policy. They had lived under federal supervision within set geographical boundaries since they first arrived in the West; their lands were, in effect, already considered reservations. But businessmen and settlers in Missouri and other states were clamoring for access to Indian lands, and Senator Douglas was championing construction of the transcontinental railroad.

In 1853 Commissioner of Indian Affairs George Manypenny began negotiating with the Kansas bands to sell a portion of their lands. By the following year, he had convinced most of them that if they expected to remain in Kansas they would have to confine themselves within even narrower geographical boundaries. Manypenny believed that close federal supervision of the Indians on their reduced reservations would be to the tribes' benefit. He was certain that if Indians were assimilated into American society they would be able to live in peace with the settlers, and he accordingly strove to bring them the benefits of white civilization. To hasten the process, he sought to break up tribal cohesiveness and authority, to give individual Indians owner-

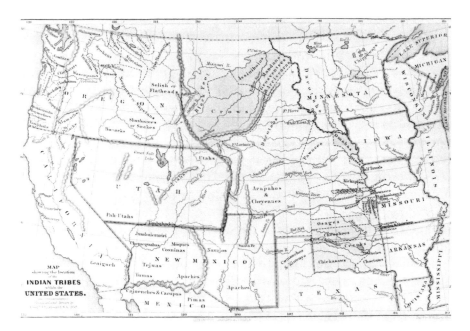

The locations of Indian tribes west of the Mississippi, including those in Kansas, as shown on Capt. Seth Eastman's 1852 map. (Courtesy of the Wichita State University Library)

ship of farms, and to sell "surplus" reservation lands to businessmen and settlers. Manypenny thought that the reservations could adequately support the tribes as independent family farmers; to him, the reservation policy was only a temporary measure.

Unfortunately for the Indians, Congress passed the Kansas-Nebraska Act of 1854 just after Manypenny and his subordinates had concluded treaty negotiations with the various tribes. This new law, introduced and promoted by Senator Douglas, had been enacted in response to overwhelming political and economic pressures to organize Kansas and Nebraska. Both territories were opened to white settlement, with no provision prohibiting the extension of slavery into either; southerners hoped to bring slavery to Kansas. When news of the act's passage reached the West, settlers, speculators, railroad agents, and other opportunists rushed to stake claims in the new Kansas Territory. Within a short time, proslavery and abolitionist forces had turned the territory into a battleground and Bleeding Kansas gained national attention.

The future looked hopeless for the Kansas tribes. "Trespasses and depredations of every conceivable kind have been committed on the Indians," Manypenny lamented. "They have been personally maltreated, their property stolen, their timber destroyed, their possessions encroached upon, and divers other wrongs and injuries done them."[14] Thomas H. Gladstone, a correspondent reporting on Bleeding Kansas for the London *Times*, observed in 1856 that the rapid immigration of whites into the area would soon result in the dispossession of the Indians and "cause their transference once more to a district further West."[15] Alarmed Indians throughout the region feared that whites were again "preparing to drive them . . . away from the graves of their fathers, kindred and children."[16] Hoping to bring order out of chaos, the Delawares and others sold railroad rights-of-way across their lands, trusting the railroad companies to reimburse them handsomely. The Indians were sadly mistaken.

In their book *The End of Indian Kansas: A Study of Cultural Revolution, 1854–1871*, H. Craig Miner and William E. Unrau describe the distressing events that followed. Throughout the late 1850s, increasing numbers of whites moved to Kansas Territory, and competition between settler organizations and railroad officials for control of tribal lands intensified. Loose coalitions called "Indian rings" formed to fight for corporate dominance. These Indian rings included various combinations of Washington bureaucrats, congressmen, businessmen, army officers, Indian agents, and even tribal "chiefs" who joined forces to dispossess the Indians. Under the banner of "popular sovereignty" (a catch phrase of the day, meaning let the people decide), businessmen also secured political and economic control of Kansas. Preoccupied first with slavery, then with the Civil War and Reconstruction, successive Washington administrations were unwilling or unable to protect the Indians from the forces arrayed against them.[17]

Even some missionaries plotted against the Indians as Catholic and Protestant preachers fought for control over the various tribes. Once missions were established, the preachers set to work acquiring large blocks of valuable land from their neophytes. Touring Kansas and Nebraska just prior to the Civil War, ethnologist Lewis Henry Morgan observed that "all of these missions look out well for themselves when a reservation is broken up and a band is moved to a new home." Morgan discovered that Methodist, Quaker, and Presbyterian missionaries had each procured several sections of land from the Indians. "How this was done," he wrote, "I do not know." Noting that the Indians resented the preachers' actions, Morgan found it "painful to hear and see so many and such constant evidences of mistrust in the Indian mind, of white people and their motives."[18]

Although arguments that they needed title to the lands in order to carry out mission work were usually based on honest intentions, some men of the cloth engaged in blatant fraud. Members of the Baptist Home Mission Society, for example, conspired with Agent Clinton C. Hutchinson to cheat the Ottawa Indians out of their Kansas lands. In 1860 Hutchinson and the Baptists arranged a deal with Ottawa leaders willing to accept bribes in exchange for tribal property. Two years later twenty thousand acres, a fourth of the reservation, were set aside to build a "university," ostensibly to benefit the Indians. But by 1864 white men were speculating freely in Ottawa University lands, and lots had been laid out to build a new town. Although federal officials later ruled that Hutchinson and his cohorts had acted improperly, by 1870 the swindle had taken its toll on the Indians. Overmatched by their enemies and torn by internal squabbles, most of the Ottawas had agreed to move to Indian Territory; very few ever attended the school built in their name.[19]

Throughout this period, individual Indians played vital roles in the exploitation of the tribes.[20] Indeed, without the cooperation of certain Indians, as Miner and Unrau point out, the businessmen and others would have had difficulty convincing eastern politicians or concerned humanitarians and philanthropists that their actions were justifiable.

But when legitimate tribal elders sought to defend the interests of their people against the chicanery, businessmen and missionaries persuaded Indian agents to replace these leaders with others who were more amenable. The Moravian minister Joseph Romig, for example, noted that Chippewa Chief Eshtonoquot's actions hindered conversion efforts because the people were afraid that the chief was "an old witch." Romig demanded that governmental officials punish Eshtonoquot, who was "very illiterate or ignorant, and a bigotted [sic] Catholic." A short time later, Agent Henry Martin ordered the tribe to dismiss the "old and childish, and totally unfit" chief. The new Chippewa leaders proved more receptive to financial inducements and other favors in return for their lands. Martin also dismissed the Sac leader Mokohoko from his band's government-recognized council, because the Indian refused to sell tribal lands and "bids defiance" to education and mission work. Even though most Sacs continued to follow Mokohoko's advice, the agent ignored him and turned to Moses Keokuk, who was willing to comply with Martin's instructions.[21]

Similar instances occurred on almost every Kansas reservation. During the 1840s, for example, the Iowas had been divided into factions, one led by the traditionalist White Cloud, the other by the more flexible No Heart. Agents and missionaries praised No Heart as a "friend to the mission" who encouraged others to remain "sober and peacible [sic]" and "to stay at home and go to work."[22] White Cloud, on the other hand, frequently incurred the wrath of Indian agents who failed to appreciate Iowa customs. In the spring of 1848, White Cloud led a war party seeking revenge against Pawnee horse thieves. When the returning warriors celebrated the taking of Pawnee scalps, an outraged agent, Alfred Vaughn, rejected their contention that they had as much right to fight their enemies as did the United States Army. Vaughn dismissed White Cloud as a government-recognized leader.[23]

Later that year the agent had White Cloud and two others arrested for harassing the missionaries. One of the accused had pulled a Presbyterian minister's hair during Sunday services; another allegedly killed mission cattle. Vaughn ordered White Cloud detained because of "his conduct towards the missionaries" and for "threats against myself & the whites generally. Besides his attempts to induce the children to leave the school, he is guilty of almost continual drunkenness."[24]

Among the Indians who incurred the most vehement wrath of federal agents was a Prairie Potawatomi leader named Wahquahboshkuk. During the late nineteenth century, Wahquahboshkuk helped the Potawatomis in resisting formal education, Christianity, and the allotment of their reservation into individual family farms—the major provisions of the federal civilization program. "This man is and has been for a number of years, in open declared opposition, not only against allotments, but all other reform . . . for the benefit of the Indians," wrote Agent J. A. Scott in 1893. "He has so persistently opposed law and regulation, has shown such an evil and malicious disposition, and is so clearly guilty of a purpose to create discord" that he should be expelled from the reservation.[25]

Under Wahquahboshkuk, the Prairie Potawatomis held together as a cohesive group despite the efforts to undermine their solidarity. Most bands, however, were unable to resist such constant pressures and resignedly agreed to leave Kansas. Weakened by intratribal factionalism, the Weas, Miamis, Delawares, Ottawas, Shawnees, and most others abandoned Kansas during the nineteenth century. The actions of various federal officials, missionaries, and certain tribal leaders gave a fiction of legality to the great land dispossession that contributed to the virtual end of Indian Kansas.

In their book, Miner and Unrau emphasize the actions of whites who victimized Kansas tribes; the authors never intended to focus on the Indians' strategies to save their Kansas homes. Their "study of cultural revolution" is, therefore, more an analysis of unscrupulous business activities and the demographic changes that resulted than of cultural revolution among the Indians. After 1870 there remained in the state nearly one thousand stubborn Indians who still refused to give up their lands or to become imitation white farmers. Those steadfast Indians—groups of Kickapoos, Chippewas and Munsees, Iowas, Sacs, and Potawatomis—are the subjects of this study.

Although each of the surviving groups faced similar obstacles and had similar experiences, each of their stories is unique. Because of the complexities involved in meshing their stories together in a coherent fashion, a note on the organization of this study is in order. Chapter 2 describes the environment of Kansas, discusses the background to the Jacksonian Era Indian removal, and delves into the settlement of Kansas by Indians from the East.

Subsequent chapters focus individually on the Vermillion Kickapoos, who under the religious leadership of the prophet Kenekuk remained a unified people who resisted conversion to Christianity and individual land allotment; the Chippewas and Munsee Delawares, who also retained their Kansas homes but gave up their identity as Indians in the process; the Iowas and the Missouri Sacs, who followed a successful strategy of peaceful coexistence with their often hostile white neighbors; and the Prairie Potawatomis, who took the lead among Kansas Indians in resisting formal education, Christianity, and land allotment.

There is also a chapter on a group of Sac Indians—sometimes called the Mississippi Sacs and Foxes—under the leadership of Mokohoko. These Sacs failed in their efforts to remain in Kansas, but their story is one of courage and determination; their methods of passive resistance to governmental policies and their adherence to traditional ways appeared to be the correct prescriptions for success. Simple bad luck prevented them from achieving their goals.

The concluding chapter attempts to tie together the experiences of those intrepid Kickapoos, Chippewas, Munsees, Iowas, Sacs, and Potawatomis and brings their story up through to the present. The narrative that follows sheds light on their legacy of persistence—the Indians' enduring struggle to retain their Kansas lands and to hold on to their distinct and cherished tribal cultures.

2

REMOVAL TO "KANSAS"

The courageous pioneers of the nineteenth century are usually described as self-reliant Euro-Americans who made their way west in covered wagons. These pioneers carved homes and farms out of the prairie, braved the forces of nature in a strange new land, and fought off fierce Indians to bring the fruits of American civilization and democracy to the wilderness. For Kansas and most of the West, however, this is both an exaggerated and a distorted picture. Indian peoples had settled in Kansas centuries before the first Europeans ever saw the land. The Spanish explorer Francisco Vasquez de Coronado and his expedition, while wandering through southern Kansas in 1541 in a futile search for the fabulous kingdom of Quivira, encountered several villages of Wichitas, an agricultural people.

By the eighteenth century, the Kaws (Kansa Indians), the Osages, the Pawnees, and others were settling and hunting in the area. Then, some sixty years before Kansas was opened to white settlement in 1854, Indians from the East infringed on the hunting grounds of the indigenous tribes, exploring, hunting, and settling in what would later become Kansas. These intruders, who had a long history of interaction with the French, the British, and the Americans, brought with them syncretic cultures that often included the English language, Christianity or Christian-like religions, modern farming techniques, and sophisticated tools and weapons.

Among the intruders were small groups of Iowas and Missouri Sacs who had crossed the Missouri River as early as the 1790s to gather food and to hunt in the region between the Nemaha and Kansas rivers.[1] Following the War of 1812, bands of Shawnees, Delawares, Kickapoos, and other easterners also arrived, and by the late 1820s many were making Kansas their permanent home. By 1854, when the territory was opened to white settlement, thousands of other Indian immigrants had flocked into Kansas. These acculturated tribespeople had adopted many aspects of the dominant Euro-American culture, and when they arrived with their wagons and belongings in Kansas, they continued their accustomed ways of living. Free of interference from white settlers, some of them built lodges of animal hides or bark; others constructed log cabins. They planted corn, squash, beans, and melons; raised pigs and cattle; collected nuts and berries, and hunted buffalo, deer, and other game.

Like the later American pioneers, they fought off Indians who resented the intrusion on their lands. Years of interaction with eastern whites had given these transplanted Indian pioneers a sophistication that most of the resident Osages, Kaws, Pawnees, and Sioux lacked. The indigenous tribes found it difficult to compete with the better armed and equipped easterners, who infringed on their hunting and gathering grounds, introduced smallpox and other diseases that devastated their populations, and brought whiskey that demoralized their people. The eventual winner in this cultural conflict was a foregone conclusion.[2] The intruders, who had faced pressure from whites invading their eastern lands and destroying their game, were well aware that Kansas was an ideal location. The rich soil, numerous streams, sufficient timber, and abundant wildlife made eastern Kansas especially attractive; anyone who had inspected the region thoroughly realized that it was not part of the mythical Great American Desert.

Critics of the government's Indian removal policy have expressed the opinion that nineteenth-century federal officials intended to resettle the tribes on lands considered worthless by whites. It was never the expressed intention of Washington bureaucrats or politicians, however, to exile Indians to desert wastelands. Although those involved in the removal process had varied and often questionable motives, some were sincerely concerned for the Indians' welfare. Men such as the famous explorer William Clark and the Baptist missionary Isaac McCoy believed that Indians were capable of advancing to a level of civilization comparable to whites. If these "red savages" could only be exposed to the proper agrarian environment, they might be individually assimilated into mainstream American society.[3]

Since each assimilated Indian family would need only a small farm when the tribes were dissolved, there would be vast "surplus" lands available for white settlement. If civilizing the eastern Indians proved difficult, their removal west to provide more time for assimilation might be necessary. In the West, Indians could be resettled on fertile lands, instructed in agriculture, and isolated from the "vices" of white society.[4] The area just beyond Missouri and Arkansas, in present-day eastern Kansas, Nebraska, and Oklahoma, seemed a perfect place for "civilizing" America's original inhabitants. How tribes who were far removed from white settlements would learn to live like whites was never satisfactorily explained, and Kansas could not remain out of the public's eye for long. Businessmen, speculators, and settlers would soon appreciate the vast potential of Kansas.[5]

That Kansas was more than a desert wasteland became more obvious as the years went by. Meriwether Lewis and William Clark, on their expedition to the Pacific in 1804, were among the first Anglo-Americans to record observations of the region. Favorably impressed with the land along the Missouri River and its tributaries, the explorers noted the flourishing game and vegetation on the Kansas side. Crossing Kansas in 1806, Zebulon Montgomery Pike observed numerous "buffaloes, elks, deer, cabrie [antelope], and panthers" along the Cottonwood and other rivers. But Pike doubted that white settlers would find the prairie of the more western region desirable. "These vast plains of the western hemisphere," he wrote, "may become in time equally celebrated with the sandy deserts of Africa." His views contributed to a growing belief that an immense wasteland lay between Missouri and the Rocky Mountains.[6]

When visiting the Kaw (Kansa) Indian village near present-day Manhattan, Kansas, five years later, trader George C. Sibley was more favorably impressed. Sibley observed numerous deer, elk, and antelope on his journey from Fort Osage, Missouri. "This [is] a very wild but extremely beautiful and high prairie country," he wrote, "pretty well watered and variegated with strips of woodland, ranges of lofty rugged, naked hills, overlooking extensive tracts of meadow ground." He found the land "delightful to the eye of the mere rambler, and [it] may at no distant period offer inducements even for Christian settlements."[7]

In 1819 Maj. Stephen H. Long led an expedition up the Missouri River en route to the Rockies. Edwin James—a botanist, geologist, and surgeon who accompanied the group—noted the rich soil, lush forests, and wild animals along the Missouri between the Kansas and Nemaha rivers. A separate exploring party trekking westward toward the Kaw village, however, reported a "want of trees, these being confined to the margins of the watercourses, while tracts of valuable soil

... have not a single tree or bush upon them." This led James to speculate that white settlers would avoid the region until forests could be planted, it being a common misconception of the day that treeless land was not arable. Maps published after Long and James's expedition invariably labeled the lands west of the one hundredth meridian the "Great American Desert." Although only the western part of Kansas fell within this category, many easterners remained convinced that the entire region was desolate.[8]

Long and James did not explore the Kansas hinterlands personally, but other whites as well as Indians were aware of its tremendous agricultural potential. If the indigenous Kaws, Osages, and others could be persuaded to move farther west, the way would be clear for the eastern tribes to emigrate. All that remained was finding a sufficient moral justification for the federal government to set in motion a general removal policy. The Indians' future would be decided in the East; policies evolved there by men who may never have seen an Indian would profoundly affect their fate.

Determined to get control of the Indians' domain, politicians and settlers in the plantation South and the farmlands of the Old Northwest argued that Indian hunters did not use the land as God had intended. Truly civilized people, the argument continued, were self-sufficient and farmed intensively, whereas "red savages" remained idle or lurked menacingly in the forest. Whites also asserted that because of the Indians' alliance with Great Britain in the War of 1812, the tribes should be removed beyond the Mississippi. But even those Indians who had been neutral or allied with the United States must go, for they also wasted land and hindered the growth of the nation.[9]

Federal officials sympathized and sought ways to solve the Indian "problem." Although treaties of peace signed by tribes in the Old Northwest following the War of 1812 did not call for land cessions, they helped pave the way for an eventual mass Indian removal to the West. Between 1815 and 1818, several tribes settled their differences with the United States and agreed to reject British influence. Peace assured, governmental agents immediately urged them to sell part of their lands. In response, cession treaties were signed by the Shawnees, Delawares, Miamis, Weas, Wyandots, Potawatomis, Kickapoos, and others in 1818 and 1819. These agreements were among the first of many that would result in the resettlement of thousands of Indians in Kansas.[10]

Although most of the treaties allowed the tribes to retain reduced reservations in the East, their eventual removal had already been decided. In October 1817 President James Monroe informed General Andrew Jackson, then in charge of the United States Army's southern division, that Indian removal was a governmental priority. "The hunter or savage state," Monroe wrote, "requires a greater extent of territory to sustain it, than is compatible with the progress and just claims of civilized life, and must yield to it." Two years later Secretary of War John C. Calhoun stressed the urgency of placing Indians "where a more extensive scope is afforded for the indulgence of their barbarous propensities and habits."[11]

These pronouncements signified that the government's long-standing policy of obtaining lands for an expanding nation while gradually absorbing Indians into the dominant society was nearing an end. In fact, by the 1820s acquiring lands to satisfy the needs of white settlers far outweighed the importance of "uplifting the savage."[12] Under the banner of states' rights, Georgia, Alabama, and Mississippi began to clash with the federal government over jurisdiction in Indian matters. Southern politicians charged that Indians controlled too much valuable territory and demanded immediate removal of all tribes.

When President John Quincy Adams took office in 1825, he was acutely aware that the removal issue was more complex than most people realized or would admit. The government's civilization program had proven embarrassingly successful in the South, where many Cherokees, Creeks, and others had taken on the trappings of white society. These tribes employed modern agricultural methods, sent their children to school, and adopted white models for their tribal governments. A prosperous few owned plantations and slaves. Since these tribes were rapidly becoming acculturated, President Adams could find no reasonable grounds to justify their forced removal. Indeed, he should have protected them, but because of demands by southern politicians, he reluctantly adopted a policy of persuading and pressuring the Indians to move voluntarily. He refused to eject them by force even to please southern voters.[13]

President Adams's liberal approach angered the Georgia and Alabama legislators who wanted to abolish tribal governments, deal with Indians individually, and place them under the jurisdiction of state laws. Intent on taking over Indian holdings, state leaders criticized Adams's diffident course of action. They began looking to the 1828 election for a candidate who would take the steps they demanded. Farther west, pressures to remove the Indians were also mounting. The growing populations of Indiana, Illinois, Michigan, and Missouri were eager to rid themselves of Indians and to divide their lands. As in the South, impatient officials demanded federal action, arguing that federal policymakers were duty-bound to move the tribes before war broke out between Indians and the settlers.

In St. Louis, the superintendent of Indian affairs, William Clark, the erstwhile explorer of Lewis and Clark fame, realized that he had to act soon to avoid a possible outbreak of violence against the Indians. Clark began to apply gentle pressure on the eastern tribes to abandon their homes. But before removal plans could proceed, the superintendent had to soften the resistance of the western tribes who were reluctant to sell their lands or to share their hunting grounds with outsiders, even if those outsiders were Indians. Fortunately for Clark, the Kaws and the Osages had already indicated a willingness to negotiate. George Sibley reported that the Kaws were ready to part with thousands of acres "for a mere trifle as compared with the immense value of the land, and I am very sure there can be no good reason urged why the govt. should refuse to purchase it."[14]

By early June 1825, Clark had persuaded representatives of the Kaws and Osages to meet with him in St. Louis for treaty negotiations. In exchange for annuities, agricultural implements, and other considerations, the two tribes agreed to relinquish claims to their lands in Missouri and Arkansas. They also ceded much of eastern Kansas, paving the way for the relocation of thousands of Indians. That fall the superintendent induced the Shawnees of southeastern Missouri to move farther west; they were among the first newcomers to arrive in Kansas.[15]

Over the next several years, bands of Delawares, Piankashaws, Weas, Peorias, Miamis, and others relinquished their eastern holdings and resettled in Kansas. Many tribal leaders had agreed to take their people west only after federal officials offered bribes of land and money in exchange for their signatures on removal treaties. Miami Chief John B. Richardville, for example, received title to over twenty thousand acres as well as thirty-one thousand dollars for selling his band's valuable lands in Indiana.[16]

Despite such tactics, some bands still refused to move, asserting their legal and moral right to remain. The Rock River, or Mississippi, Sacs and Foxes of Illinois, for example, insisted that they would never leave, and they justifiably denounced an 1804 treaty that called for their eventual removal to Iowa. They pointed out that federal officials had negotiated that agreement with Indians who had no right to speak for the tribe. Filled with deep resentment, the resolute Sacs and Foxes vowed to expel white intruders from their territory.[17]

In central Illinois, a Prairie Band Kickapoo leader named Mecina also refused to bow to the wishes of federal officials. When an Indian agent demanded that the band move to Missouri in accordance with its 1819 treaty, Mecina responded that he had never placed his mark on a paper to sell Kickapoo lands. Those who did, he said, had violated the commands of the Great Spirit, who had caused an earthquake to show his displeasure with the treaty.[18] Along the Wabash River near the Indiana-Illinois border, Kenekuk, the prophet of the Vermillion Kickapoos, also cited divine strictures against selling tribal possessions. The Great Spirit owned the earth, the prophet insisted; mere men were forbidden to buy or sell any part of it. "When I talked to the Great Spirit," Kenekuk told Superintendent Clark, "he did not tell me to sell my lands."[19]

While tribal leaders were resorting to moral suasion to save their homes, many whites sought ethical justifications for the tribes' removal. Self-appointed humanitarians, many of them New Englanders with little firsthand knowledge of Indians, were sincerely concerned for the Indians' welfare. Some demanded that the United States abide by its treaties; others advocated isolating the tribes from the "vices" of white society by removing them to a separate colony in the West, where they could slowly become assimilated, Christian citizens. This solution was supported by several missionaries, including Isaac McCoy, a Baptist preacher from Michigan who would play a leading role in determining the future of the Indians of the Old Northwest.

A staunch removal advocate who was also dedicated to improving the Indians' way of life, McCoy had gained influence among politicians and federal officials by the mid-1820s. He championed the establishment of a separate Indian colony outside the limits of American states and territories. In such a colony, isolated from white society, missionaries could help resettle, educate, and Christianize the emigrant tribespeople. "Indians are not untamable," McCoy asserted. "Give them a country of their own, under circumstances which will enable them to feel their importance, where they can hope to enjoy, unmolested, the fruits of their labours, and their national recovery need not be doubted."[20]

In June 1828 McCoy secured orders from Commissioner of Indian Affairs Thomas McKenney to lead a party of eastern Indians in a search of suitable land for a colony in the West. With six Potawatomis and Ottawas and two white assistants, McCoy left St. Louis in August, headed for the territory directly beyond the Missouri line. He was pleasantly surprised by what he found. "Timber is in plenty to admit a tolerably dense population for 75 miles west of Missouri state, afterwards more scarce," he wrote. "The soil is almost universally fertile, and the whole supplied abundantly with limestone ... the most sightly country I ever saw." After a return visit late in 1828, McCoy was sure he had found his "Indian Canaan."[21]

For McCoy's plans to become reality, the federal government would have to make Indian removal mandatory; the Adams administration's cautious approach would not produce the desired result. As the 1828 election neared, the appeal of Democratic presidential candidate Andrew Jackson became irresistible to the advocates of removal. Citizens of Alabama, Mississippi, Georgia, the Carolinas, Ohio, Indiana, Illinois, and Michigan knew that with "Old Hickory" in office, Indian lands would surely be opened to white settlers. The South and the West, therefore, rallied to the Jackson banner. With only New England voters supporting Adams, a Democratic victory was assured.

Jackson's victory signaled bad times for eastern Indians, for his administration immediately developed strategies for pushing all of them west of the Mississippi. In his March 1829 inaugural address, Jackson asserted that he would never abuse Indian rights and maintained that he intended to follow a liberal and humane Indian policy. The president realized, however, that the source of his political power was centered in the South and West. To retain the loyalty of those voters, he appointed John H. Eaton secretary of war and John M. Berrien attorney general; both were outspoken advocates of removal.[22]

In the South, the Cherokees, Creeks, and others actively opposed all attempts to evict them from their farms and plantations. Because Georgia, Alabama, and Mississippi had already passed laws of questionable constitutionality assuming state jurisdiction over Indians, Jackson acted quickly to avoid trouble. Seeking universal support for an aggressive removal policy, his first step was to ask the popular Thomas McKenney to continue as head of the Indian Office. McKenney agreed and enthusiastically assumed the task of winning approval of the proposed Indian removal bill, for he firmly believed that the survival of Indians depended upon their separation from whites. To achieve his goals, he organized the New York Board for the Emigration, Preservation, and Improvement of the Aborigines of America, which pledged full cooperation with the administration.[23]

As the chief disseminator of governmental removal propaganda, the board immediately sought endorsements from church leaders, newspaper editors, and concerned citizens. It achieved considerable success even in the Northeast, and several missionaries became active in the movement. Isaac McCoy, for one, proved a valuable ally. In May 1829 he made a tour of eastern states to rally public support for removal. Many other men of the cloth firmly believed that Indian contact with lower-class whites hindered education and Christianization efforts. In the West, Indians would be free of white "vices" and other harmful influences and, under the tutelage of missionaries, could become educated Christians.[24]

President Jackson insisted that removal was the only way to save the Indians from destruction, and he asked Congress to set aside "an ample district west of the Mississippi" and outside of the states and organized territories. It was "to be guaranteed to the Indian tribes as long as they shall occupy it, each tribe having a distinct control over the portion designated for its use."[25]

The debate on removal was brief. Soon after it began in April 1830, Congress voted in favor of the removal legislation. On May 28 Jackson signed into law a bill that would open to white settlers "large tracts of country now occupied by a few savage hunters." The president announced that the new law would

separate the Indians from immediate contact with settlements of whites; free them from the power of the States; enable them to pursue happiness in their own way and under their own rude institutions; will retard the progress of decay, which is lessening their numbers; and perhaps cause them gradually, under protection of the Government, and through the influence of good counsels, to cast off their savage habits, and become an interesting, civilized, and Christian community.

More to the point, it would allow the states "to advance in population, wealth, and power." The president ignored the fact that many eastern Indians had already "cast off their savage habits."[26]

Ostensibly, the removal bill did not force Indians to relinquish their lands, for the lawmakers had stipulated that treaty agreements must be negotiated before removal could proceed. But the subsequent treaty process had the same result. Federal agents resorted to deception, threats, bribery, and other devious methods to cajole Indians into accepting land cessions and removal. Treaty commissioners signed agreements with pro-removal elements of a tribe, ignoring legitimate tribal elders who opposed land cessions, then declared the agreements binding on all.

Because federal administrators awarded contracts for food and transportation services to the lowest bidder, many Indians suffered from improper diet and exposure on their removal to the West, and hundreds died.[27] Such hardships were of little concern to most Americans; the Indian question, it was assumed, was forever settled to the satisfaction of those who wanted their lands as well as those who believed removal was the first step toward civilization.

While McCoy hailed removal as the "first efficient step" toward tribal colonization, this solution to the Indian "problem" encountered difficulties from its very inception.[28] Most Indians resented the plan and resisted deportation. As a result, the process took more than twenty years, and when it ended there were still Indians in the East. Lack of foresight coupled with governmental ineptitude, moreover, doomed the civilization program that removal was supposed to facilitate. Most important, the trans-Mississippi country set aside for a "permanent" Indian home—the area beyond Arkansas, Missouri, and Iowa, west to the Rockies—blocked the natural lines of American expansion to the Pacific. Frustration over any obstruction to expansion had already begun to appear. With the entire continent as the ultimate prize, the cries of "Reannexation of Texas!" and "54-40 or fight!" soon made it obvious that federal Indian policy conflicted with the forces of Manifest Destiny.[29]

Meanwhile, despite the new removal law, most Indians stubbornly insisted on their rights and refused to leave their ancestral homes. It would take coercion or the threat of violence to convince the tribes of Indiana, Illinois, and other Old Northwest states that it was in their best interest to leave before they were crushed. The Black Hawk War provided the catalyst needed to make those Indians amenable to governmental demands. In May 1832 war erupted between the followers of a Sac warrior named Black Hawk who were determined to stay in Illinois and state militia and United States Army troops bent on evicting them. Black Hawk's followers hoped that other tribes and the British from Canada would come to their support, but they were sadly disappointed. Although the white troops lacked field experience and effective leadership, they quickly routed Black Hawk's poorly armed warriors—but not before the Indians had aroused considerable hysteria among settlers from Missouri to Michigan.[30]

This episode prompted angry demands from citizens in Illinois, Indiana, Missouri, and Michigan for the immediate removal of all Indians. By the fall of 1832, the shock of the Black Hawk War, together with the pressures of the removal bill, began to overwhelm Indians who were determined to stay in the East.[31] In October Superintendent Clark summoned leaders of both the Prairie and Vermillion Kickapoo bands to his St. Louis home to negotiate their removal to Kansas. Clark advised them not to "neglect this opportunity of leaving a country where you have long been looked upon with suspicion, and where you will shortly be treated as enemies."[32]

Clark assured the Kickapoos that although he had not visited Kansas personally, he knew it was ideal for resettlement. "Your Great Father, the President, does not wish your people to be permanently placed on land incapable of supporting them comfortably," he intoned. "He wishes to see his Red Children contented and happy."[33] With whites clamoring for their removal, the Kickapoos signed the Treaty of Castor Hill on October 24; the Prairie Kickapoos relinquished their Missouri lands and the Vermillion people gave up their homes on the Wabash.[34] Later, their advance parties found acceptable locations near Fort Leavenworth, and in early 1833 the first Kickapoos began arriving at their new Kansas reservation.

The Potawatomis, with over fifty villages in Wisconsin, Michigan, Illinois, and Indiana, also faced intense pressure to abandon their lands for homes in the West. It mattered little that several bands, including the Prairie Potawatomis, had fought alongside American troops

A sketch of a Potawatomi man, woman, and child made on May 21, 1851, by the Swiss artist Rudolph Friederich Kurz. (Courtesy of the Smithsonian Institution, National Anthropological Archives)

against Black Hawk's warriors. It was of no consequence either that most sought only a peaceful accommodation with white neighbors and were willing to share their lands with the increasing numbers of Americans. To whites, the Potawatomis would always be Indians with "savage" habits and "red" skins. Intent on taking their lands, whites would never accept them as equal members of the same social system; nothing could stop the process of removal.

In the summer of 1833, over six thousand Potawatomis assembled outside Chicago to face the inevitable. Meeting with governmental commissioners on September 14, Potawatomi chiefs at first insisted that they would not move before inspecting the lands west of the Mississippi. After stalling for several days, however, the leading spokesmen for the Indians agreed to relinquish an immense territory in Wisconsin, Michigan, and Illinois. In exchange, they were to receive five million acres of the Platte region just northeast of Fort Leavenworth. Unfortunately, Missouri politicians and settlers wanted this area, and they were able to annex it as part of their state. In 1834, therefore, federal officials substituted lands in the present state of Iowa for the Indians' future home. Many Potawatomis, however, shunned Iowa and moved in with the Kickapoos near Fort Leavenworth, while others claimed lands to the southwest of the fort along the Marais des Cygnes River.[35] In 1847 those who had settled in Iowa would sell their lands and move to Kansas.

Meanwhile, in 1834 several small Potawatomi bands still holding out in northern Indiana also faced eviction, but it took three years for officials to badger them into giving up their homes. Finally, in February 1837, the last of the treaties was signed and the Indiana Potawatomis began their trek to new homes along the Marais des Cygnes.[36] Blatant fraud and deception marked the Potawatomi negotiations, as officials ignored many of the legitimate tribal elders who opposed land cessions. Chief Menominee of the Indiana bands best expressed the feelings of the elders. "The President does not know the truth," he said. "He does not know that your treaty is a lie. He does not know that you made my chiefs drunk, got their consent, and pretended to get mine." Insisting that he would never leave, Menominee was certain that President Martin Van Buren "would not by force drive me from my home, [or] the graves of my tribe and children, who have gone to the Great Spirit." On August 29, 1838, the chief's faith in the president's sense of justice was shattered when troops arrived to escort his band to Kansas, whether they were willing to go or not.[37]

The experience of the Sacs and Iowas, longtime residents in the Platte region, was much less traumatic. Although the Sacs and Iowas came from different cultural backgrounds, they had been closely allied for many years and both had adopted the characteristic traits of the Plains Indians. The Sacs, known as the Sacs and Foxes of the Missouri, had already separated from Black Hawk's people by the turn of the century. Since that time, they had explored and hunted in Kansas, and a few bands had even established villages south of the Great Nemaha, near the eastern border of present-day Kansas and Nebraska. By the 1820s, their bark wickiups sat on the Kansas lands later deeded to the Kickapoos. The young Mokohoko, one of those independent Sac pioneers, eventually arose as a dynamic leader who would have a lasting impact on the entire Sac and Fox tribe.

In September 1836 the Sacs and Iowas met William Clark at Fort

Leavenworth to cede claims to the Platte country in exchange for small reserves on the present-day Kansas-Nebraska border.[38] By the following year, most had migrated across the Missouri and reestablished themselves on long-familiar territory. Over the next several years, the two bands developed a deep fondness for Kansas that made them stubbornly resist all future efforts to dislodge them from their lands.

While the Sacs and Iowas signed their treaties, federal authorities attempted to pressure the Michigan Chippewas to move west of the Mississippi. Most of the Indians refused and some fled to Canada; but a tiny band of Swan Creek and Black River Chippewas who lived near Detroit succumbed to governmental persuasion. Their leader was the opportunistic Eshtonoquot, known to whites as Francis McCoonse.

Touting himself as spokesman for all Michigan Chippewas, Eshtonoquot had traveled to England in 1835 to ask Parliament for compensation for dubious claims to Canadian lands. Insufficient funds forced the chief and his party to perform "shuffling dances" at the Victoria Theater in London to raise money. Later, one of Eshtonoquot's wives and a nephew died of "pulmonary disease" and were buried in England. The chief himself was allegedly found cavorting with a London prostitute, but the *Times* assured readers that he appeared to be "entirely innocent" of that "infamous charge." Nevertheless, the mission failed, for Parliament refused even to consider Eshtonoquot's claim.[39]

Returning to Michigan, Eshtonoquot became a favored "treaty chief" of federal officials intent on removing the Chippewas. Because he spoke English, other chiefs occasionally asked him to intervene with white authorities, but the tribe never considered him a chief. Accepting bribes and other concessions, Eshtonoquot agreed to sell tribal lands. When the Chippewas finally started for Kansas in 1839, however, the government's promises of money had been withdrawn because Eshtonoquot could persuade only sixty Indians to accompany him. Those gullible Chippewas found no money or provisions waiting for them at the new reserve in present-day Franklin County. "How are we to live," Eshtonoquot wondered in November. "We have no guns [and] no shoes to keep our feet from freezing. . . . These things make me sick in my Heart. We have nothing left to sustain life."[40]

But Eshtonoquot and the Chippewas were resourceful, and within a few years they had developed relatively prosperous farms. The chief missed few opportunities to enhance his personal wealth and prestige, and his followers soon learned how to fend for themselves. White settlers would find the sophisticated Chippewas difficult to swindle; these Indians also successfully resisted all efforts to expel them from their adopted land.

The Chippewas' defense of their possessions met its most serious challenge after a treaty allied them with a small band of Munsee Delawares, or Christian Indians, whose culture and religion differed radically from those of the Chippewas. The Munsees began migrating from Canada in 1837. Most continued to associate with the Delawares, but a small number, adherents of the Moravian Church, eventually severed their tribal affiliations. Although they retained many of their traditional ways throughout the 1840s and 1850s, widespread intermarriage with whites led to rapid acculturation. Like the Kickapoos, Potawatomis, Iowas, Sacs, and Chippewas, members of this small Munsee band were obstinate in their resolve to retain their Kansas farms.[41]

By 1850 Kansas had become home to thousands of Indian immigrants. The Missouri Sacs, Iowas, and Kickapoos had been given separate reservations between Fort Leavenworth and the Great Nemaha River; the Delawares and Shawnees each had their own reserves just southwest of the fort. During the mid-1840s the Sacs and Foxes of the Mississippi, then under Black Hawk's arch-rival Keokuk, had exchanged their Iowa holdings for 430,000 acres in present-day Franklin and Osage counties. The Potawatomis also relinquished Iowa lands during the 1840s to resettle on an immense tract west of the Delaware reserve; they were joined by kinfolk who had lived along the Marais des Cygnes for many years. The Chippewas, Ottawas, Munsees, Kaskaskias, Peorias, Piankashaws, Weas, and others lived south of the Kansas River.

The immigrants, as well as the indigenous Osages and Kaws, faced troubled times by mid-century. The Mexican War had opened California to American settlement, and with the discovery of gold there, hordes of gold-seekers passed through Indian country on their way west. As a result, Jesuit missionary Pierre Jean De Smet predicted that the Indians would soon be removed from Kansas. "As the white population advances and penetrates into the interior," wrote De Smet in 1851, "the aborigines will gradually withdraw. Already, even, it is perceptible that the whites look with a covetous eye on the fertile lands of the Delawares, Potawatomies, Shawnees, and others on our frontiers, and project the organization of a new Territory—Nebraska." Federal officials had already mapped plans for a new general policy that would confine all the Indians of the West to reservations; as a result of this new policy, the Indians of Kansas would be expected to sell much of their lands to the government.[42]

By the 1850s, therefore, these Indians again had to protect their homes from invading whites. How well they had prepared themselves for this eventuality would have a profound impact on the success or failure of their struggles to survive. Although those living in Kansas shared many outward cultural characteristics, and most were of the Algonquian linguistic family, there were distinct differences between the bands. Most were unable to adapt to changing conditions and quickly succumbed to white demands; but a few had mastered the techniques for survival and had the will to remain in their adopted homeland. Although whites held the upper hand in the ensuing struggle, those Indians who survived did so on their own terms, not those dictated by missionaries or Indian agents. For the small bands who were able to retain their lands and resist all efforts at forced removal, their triumph would prove a remarkable achievement.

3

THE VERMILLION KICKAPOOS

Among the Kansas bands who never capitulated to the forces of removal were the Vermillion Kickapoos. In the spring of 1833, about four hundred of these émigrés from Illinois settled near the west bank of the Missouri River a few miles north of Fort Leavenworth. Joined there by several Potawatomi families attracted by the religious teachings of Kenekuk, the Kickapoo prophet, the Indians immediately set about building new homes and preparing fields for planting. These Indians were used to hard work and were determined to be successful in Kansas. They had been defeated in their long struggle to keep their homes in Illinois; following the recent Black Hawk War they had been forced to surrender their lands between the Vermillion and Wabash rivers under tremendous pressure from federal officials and white settlers. Under the leadership of Kenekuk, they would be successful in their efforts to remain in Kansas. They would owe their survival in part to their acceptance of Kenekuk's insistence that men farm the fields—a radical departure from the Kickapoo belief that farming was women's work. They would owe it even more to their devotion to the prophet's religious tenets stressing peace, temperance, and land retention.[1]

Kenekuk first gained influence over his people after the War of 1812, which had proven disastrous for the Kickapoos and other tribes of the Old Northwest. During the late 1810s and into the 1820s, these Indians faced constant assaults on their lands and way of life. Against imposing odds, the Vermillion Kickapoos managed to hold on to their Illinois lands long after most other bands had been forced from the area. They were fortunate, for their leader, Kenekuk, worked to shore up the band's defenses against those who wanted to evict them from Illinois. By the early 1830s, the charismatic prophet had won the devotion of nearly four hundred Indians, who followed his advice and obeyed his commands. He evoked a religious fervor and piety among his people,

Kenekuk, the Kickapoo prophet, by George Catlin. (Courtesy of the National Museum of American Art, Smithsonian Institution; gift of Mrs. Joseph Harrison, Jr.)

who were convinced that he was indeed the special messenger of the Great Spirit.[2]

Kenekuk's rise to an influential position among the Indians was particularly surprising, for according to the oral history of his descendants, he had once been a drunken troublemaker. Cast out by his people after he had murdered a fellow Kickapoo, he wandered through the white settlements of Indiana and Illinois, begging for food and shelter and occasionally finding odd jobs. Fortunately, a Protestant minister took him in and taught him about Christianity and the ways of the whites. Under the minister's influence Kenekuk decided to change his sinful life and take the word of God to his people. The Kickapoos welcomed him back, and by 1816 Kenekuk, then in his mid-twenties, had emerged as a leader of the Vermillion Band.[3]

The young Indian brought his own version of religion to his people, however, not that of the kindly minister. His religion was not Christian but, rather, a message of peace and love that merged with traditional Kickapoo beliefs. In an era when whites constantly demanded and took Indian lands, the prophet's new faith provided an inner strength for the beleaguered Kickapoos. Blending evangelical Protestantism, Catholic ritual, and traditional Kickapoo beliefs, the prophet helped create a new Indian society. Far from causing the erosion of Kickapoo ways, this syncretism was a pragmatic accommodation to Euro-American culture that revitalized and strengthened the band's societal bonds. This voluntary acculturation helped the Vermillion Kickapoos and their allies adjust to rapidly changing conditions and enabled them to resist repeated attempts to dispossess them.[4]

Although he held a position of reverence among the Vermillion Kickapoos, Kenekuk was not considered a chief until years after he had returned from his exile. Traditionally, the right to call oneself a chief among the Kickapoos, as well as the Sacs, Foxes, and most other Central Algonquian tribes, was based on heredity—unless rejected by fellow tribe members, a chief's son assumed leadership upon his father's death. The Kickapoo tribe was divided into band and clan groups; historically, the clans had names such as Eagle, Raccoon, Bear, Water, Tree, Buffalo, Fox, Wolf, Turkey, and Thunder. The tribal chief of the Kickapoos usually came from the Eagle clan, with the Raccoon clan sometimes providing a second chief whose function was that of a speaker (it is not clear to which clan Kenekuk belonged). Because the Kickapoo bands had been widely scattered since the early 1700s, there was no one chief of the entire tribe; each band had its own head chief—who represented the village peace organization—its own lesser chiefs, and various assistants and speakers. Each band also had its war chief and his warriors.[5]

Kenekuk was a religious leader who attracted a following to his teachings. He eventually assumed the role of head chief of the Vermillion Kickapoos, combining the responsibilities of both peace and war chief, although he broke with tradition by refusing to revere warfare as a symbol of Kickapoo honor.[6] In the 1820s he instructed his growing flock that the Great Spirit wanted them to lay aside their tomahawks and extend the hand of friendship to other Indians as well as to whites. "We are all God's children," he advised followers. "Like sheep—some white, some red, some black; but all eat together. No fight[ing]—all love one another."[7]

Kenekuk's philosophy and teachings invariably confused outsiders. Most white observers assumed that he led his followers in some muddled form of Christianity. Presbyterian missionary William Smith thought the prophet's religion bore a "striking resemblance" to Catholicism. Kenekuk's adherents, Smith and other whites noted, faithfully attended church services on Sundays and holy days, believed in heaven, hell, and purgatory, and they worshipped Jesus, the Virgin, and the saints. One witness observed that as in the New England churches, men carried long rods at religious assemblies "to keep order among the children and dogs, and to see that each person was in his proper place." Adherents to the prophet's religion publicly confessed their sins on Fridays, but unlike Catholics they required physical evidence that God had given them absolution. Wrongdoers, therefore, submitted willingly to the whip. Another witness saw Kickapoos voluntarily accepting "lashes on their bare backs, so well laid on as to cause the blood to run freely. Many of them bore visible scars on their backs, caused by former flagellations." After the ordeal, the penitents shook hands with their flagellators and declared themselves "relieved of a heavy burden."[8]

Although such practices strengthened tribal unity and maintained discipline, Kenekuk's emphasis on peaceful coexistence with whites as well as abstinence from intoxicating drink proved even more important. The prophet knew that the violent anti-American policies of Black Hawk and the Mississippi Sacs had been disastrous, and he was determined that his people be spared a similar fate. Believing that white settlers might tolerate peaceful, sober Indians living near them, he commanded his followers to love their neighbors and to turn the other cheek when wronged. He warned drunks that they would "go into a place prepared for the wicked, and suffer endless days and nights of grief."[9] The Delawares, Ottawas, Shawnees, and other bands eventually disintegrated and lost their Kansas lands because of factionalism, drunkenness, or hostility; but Kenekuk's temperate and peaceful band avoided such pitfalls.

Recognizing that his followers belonged to various clans and that the clans were breaking up by the 1830s, the prophet urged the people to pledge allegiance to the band first and assign clan membership a secondary status.[10] Kenekuk's followers, therefore, threw away their clan medicine bundles—small pouches of sacred objects that possess spiritual power—which had been the central element of their traditional religion. They also stopped painting their bodies and abandoned other traditional practices distasteful to whites. But they clung to the basic Kickapoo beliefs that lay behind these rituals. They used only Indian languages, refusing to speak English or even to acknowledge any understanding of it, and they always performed their customary music and dances at religious ceremonies.[11]

Their reverence for their unique beliefs disturbed many whites, and the band's trust in the prophet instead of a priest or a minister confused and frustrated the missionaries. The Presbyterian William Smith, for one, noted that although Kenekuk ruled "in a manner which would reflect honor on an enlightened statesman," his teachings, which Smith found objectionable, "would be impossible to break down." For these and other reasons, many whites considered Kenekuk's people to be "wholly heathen."[12]

Because the Indians could not read the Bible, Kenekuk provided them with prayer sticks—wooden boards twelve to twenty inches long, on which appeared three sets of five traditional Algonquian figures. The prophet asserted that the prayer sticks meant to Indians what the Bible meant to whites. By means of these devices, the Kickapoos learned the teachings and wishes of the Great Spirit. The Methodist missionary William W. Redman saw Kenekuk's followers "looking steadfastly on small boards which they held in their hands." The minister learned that of the five characters inscribed on the boards, the "first represents the heart, the second the flesh, i.e., the passions and appetites; the third their life, i.e., all their acts and doings; the fourth their names, i.e., their Christian character; the fifth their kindred, i.e., all mankind." Although Redman looked favorably on such devices, a Methodist colleague, William Patton, warned that Kenekuk's faith was not Christian. "Let the [Methodist] Church

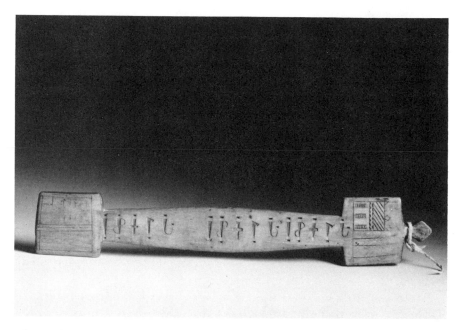

The Kickapoo prayer stick. (Courtesy of the Denver Art Museum)

awake to their duty," Patton proclaimed, "and in every reasonable way labor to dispel these dark clouds of superstition, sin and delusion."[13]

To many outsiders, the prayer sticks resembled the rosary, for the Kickapoos manipulated these devices while chanting like Catholics at prayer. Redman was told by the Kickapoo interpreter that the chants translated into English meant: " 'O Jesus, come into my heart'; or, 'Come and possess my heart.' " Other observers simply assumed that the Indians were copying the rosary. William Smith admitted, however, that he was somewhat mystified by the fascinating pieces of wood that the Indians used "like Roman beads." Isaac McCoy, after listening to the Kickapoos reciting "in a monotonous sing-song tone," also compared the devices to the rosary. To McCoy, however, the Indian chants showed little resemblance to Christian prayer.[14]

Although meaningless to most whites, the prayer sticks were important to Kenekuk's followers. The prayers as well as the other aspects of the prophet's faith helped reinforce tribal solidarity and gave adherents not only the courage and conviction to defend their rights but also taught them to avoid conflict with the more numerous settlers. As the band's leader in the 1820s, Kenekuk had led his people in a determined defense of their lands along the Wabash River in eastern Illinois. His efforts failed because of the combined pressures of President Andrew Jackson's Indian Removal Act and the 1832 Black Hawk War that raged in the western part of the state and aroused the settlers against all Indians.

After settling in Kansas, however, Kenekuk vowed never to abandon his adopted home; the Great Spirit owned the earth, he proclaimed, and mere men were forbidden to buy or sell it. The prophet would protect his people from any future land cessions by strengthening their social and cultural integrity. He knew that it was only a matter of time before whites began pressuring the Indians again, but he was determined that his people would be better prepared to defend themselves in the future. Unfortunately, the Vermillion people found that they had their hands full as soon as they arrived in Kansas. Initially, though, the difficulty was with their troublesome Indian kinfolk rather than with whites.

About one mile upriver from their new village lived a band of Prairie Kickapoos who had recently moved from Missouri. Federal officials thought that the Vermillion and Prairie bands should be thankful for the "benefits" generously bestowed upon them in the Treaty of Castor Hill, and bureaucrats assumed that the two factions would live in harmony. Commissioner of Indian Affairs Elbert Herring had little doubt that the Indians would "remain at peace, cultivate the arts of social life and advance in civilization."[15] Kenekuk's followers were indeed content in their new homes; their fertile lands along the Missouri more than satisfied their modest needs. They had no trouble complying with the commissioner's pronouncement.

While the prophet's men farmed and remained near their village, the Prairie Kickapoos clung to their traditional customs and shunned farming and sedentary life. They also rejected Kenekuk's religion, preferring to deal with their traditional manitous (supernatural forces that pervade the natural world). The Great Manitou, or Creator, stood at the top of their spiritual hierarchy, which also included the four winds, the sky, the moon and stars, and grandmother earth. These Indians also continued to revere their clan bundle rites and other traditional religious ceremonies. They rejected Christianity and resisted any Christian infusion into their traditional ceremonies.[16]

Often away from their village hunting or trading, the Prairie Indians enjoyed drinking and gambling; to the regret of federal officials, these

Kickapoos had their own methods of cultivating the arts of social life. Comparing the two bands, a Presbyterian missionary reported that although the Prairie Kickapoos frequently "get drunk and gamble," few of Kenekuk's people indulged in such activities. Sometimes Prairie Kickapoos physically attacked Kenekuk's sober followers, who feared that their women would be molested while the men were out working in the fields. The two bands quarreled constantly over moral, financial, and legal matters.[17] Chief Kishko of the Prairie Kickapoos complained, furthermore, that his new home was "not equal to his expectations," for game was scarce and Pawnee and Sioux enemies numerous. When Kishko's complaints reached Washington, Elbert Herring ordered Special Commissioner Henry Ellsworth "to visit those lands and make alterations as you may find just."[18]

In the late summer of 1833, Ellsworth left Fort Leavenworth on horseback to visit the nearby Kickapoo villages. With him was writer John Treat Irving, Washington Irving's nephew, who was eager to see how the Kickapoos lived. The men rode through forest and prairie, crossing several streams until they topped a high bluff overlooking the villages. The view below seemed idyllic. On three sides of the Kickapoo camps, timber-covered ridges bracketed a lush prairie. Dense woods bordered the Missouri River.[19]

As the men rode along the trail to the villages, they carried with them typical nineteenth-century notions that tribal culture and traditions were inferior and that all Indians were lazy and shiftless. A meeting with Kenekuk, "a tall bony Indian, with a keen black eye, and a face beaming with intelligence," forced Irving to modify his own opinions somewhat. The writer discovered "an energy of character" in Kenekuk that lent "much weight to his words, and has created for him an influence greater than that of any Indian in the town." Through an interpreter, the white men engaged the prophet in conversation. Irving believed, erroneously, that this was unusual for Kenekuk, who "generally kept aloof from intercourse with the whites." Because Kenekuk preached a strict religious moral code, moreover, Irving assumed he must be a Christian.[20]

On September 2, Ellsworth met with both Kickapoo bands to discuss their situation in Kansas. He pointed out that the Missouri River allowed them access and transport for agricultural and other trade goods; nearby Fort Leavenworth would, moreover, protect them from their Sioux and Pawnee enemies. The commissioner admonished them to learn to live together, for he would never "approve of the tribe ever being separated."

When Ellsworth had finished speaking, a Prairie Kickapoo rose to complain that his new village was too close to white settlements and many of the young men had become addicted to the whiskey they acquired across the river in Missouri. He also pointed out the difficulties of living near Kenekuk's people, who disapproved of the Prairie Band's traditional ways. "Our young men and chiefs do not agree as they did some time ago," he railed, because the prophet exercised a confusing influence that had caused factional strife.[21]

In contrast, Kenekuk's people were satisfied with the new land. The fertile soil produced abundant corn, beans, and pumpkins; the rich pastures supported large numbers of ponies and cattle; and there was enough wood for fuel and building purposes. For these reasons, Kenekuk announced that the Kickapoos would remain where they were.[22]

When Ellsworth called the two bands together again the following month, he warned the Prairie Kickapoos that their excellent lands were not to be abandoned. Chief Kishko replied that if he left, it would only be to go hunting; he did not plan to return to his former home in Missouri. Sometime later, however, a disgruntled Kishko and many followers trekked south to Indian Territory and never returned, giving the prophet's followers a numerical advantage in Kansas. When Kenekuk announced that he would "accept the land and say no more about it," Ellsworth informed his superiors in Washington that Kickapoo "dissatisfaction with the land is removed."[23]

Ellsworth was mistaken in believing that the matter had been solved. After Kishko's departure, a man named Pashishi assumed leadership of the remaining Prairie Kickapoos, who were still angry that federal officials had forced them to settle in what they considered unsuitable country. They asserted that Kansas lacked sufficient timber and game; they resented governmental interference in their affairs and rejected every attempt to change their traditions. Unlike Kenekuk's followers, they steadfastly refused to modify their traditional ways to please white men. A traveler described them as a "forlorn-looking set," with "swarthy features and dingy blankets contrasting strikingly enough" with "civilized" society.[24]

Despite their differences, neither Kickapoo band had any intention of accepting Christianity. Nevertheless, over the next several years numerous missionaries made attempts to convert them. The missionaries, who thought the prophet's religion halfway between paganism and Christianity, reasoned that after a little religious instruction the Vermillion Band would submit to conversion. Kenekuk's powerful influence over his people proved a hindrance at times, but the missionaries were sure they could overcome it and any other obstacle.[25]

The Kickapoos, for their part, had good reason for trying to make a favorable impression on the missionaries. Because repeated requests for the government's promised treaty assistance had gone unheeded, both Kenekuk and Pashishi realized that it was to their advantage to allow the Catholics and Protestants to come among them—maybe the preachers could help loosen federal purse strings. Although the Indian leaders realized that missionaries would try to undermine their authority, they believed that the advantages outweighed the risks.

Among the first missionaries to visit Kenekuk's village was Jesuit Father Benedict Roux. The priest made a brief stop in November 1833 but found that Kenekuk was away and would not return in time to meet him. Roux was not discouraged, for the Kickapoos treated him as if he were "an angel sent from heaven." He was deeply impressed that the sober and industrious Indians refrained from lying, stealing, and fighting. Because Kenekuk's two "docile" sons appeared to desire religious instruction, the Jesuit thought that "mighty conquests" could be won "if God would call one of the sons to the priesthood."[26]

Soon after Roux departed, Methodist missionary Jerome C. Berryman arrived at Kenekuk's village. Pleased by the band's sober and peaceful ways, Berryman decided that this was an ideal location for a Methodist mission. The preacher informed church superiors that although Kenekuk's faith had many "peculiarities foreign to Christianity," the Indians were "truly pious" and ready for conversion. He was greatly encouraged when, after an initial coolness, Kenekuk allowed him to preach. When the prophet instructed his followers to begin learning the tenets of Methodism, Berryman was fully convinced of the Indian leader's sincerity. The missionary was so confident about his prospects for winning converts that he hired Kenekuk as an assistant at an annual salary of two hundred dollars. Before long the Methodist preacher had baptized over four hundred Indians, including the prophet himself.[27]

But Berryman's expectations were not fulfilled. By 1835 it dawned on

him that Kenekuk rarely allowed him to officiate at religious ceremonies. The prophet explained that his people were unable to understand the white man's words. He promised to ease them gradually into
Christianity, but by now Berryman was dubious. Methodist Superintendent Thomas Johnson, on the other hand, remained optimistic.
Kenekuk's "peculiar" methods, including the use of flagellation, considerably hindered mission work, Johnson admitted. But although they
had encountered some difficulties, these were being overcome, "and I
think our prospects of ultimate success are as good as they have
been."[28]

Methodist hopes were severely dampened on July 4, 1835, when
Jesuit Father Charles F. Van Quickenborne arrived to follow up on
Roux's glowing reports of Kickapoo piety and to facilitate the band's
conversion. After spending the night with a local trader, Van Quickenborne met with the Kickapoo prophet. Following a brief exchange of
pleasantries, the two began discussing theology. When Kenekuk asked
for an explanation of Catholicism, the priest replied that "every man
must believe in God, hope in God, love God above all things, and his
neighbor as himself; those who do this will go to heaven, and those
who do not will go to hell."

When Van Quickenborne added that biblical prophets proved
through miracles that God had spoken to them, Kenekuk announced
that he, too, had performed miracles. "I raised the dead to life," he
explained, relating how he had once breathed new life into a woman
and a child on the brink of death. The Jesuit retorted that Kenekuk had
only helped restore the sick to health; that was no miracle. At first
Kenekuk was offended that a stranger dared contradict him. But the
prophet's anger quickly subsided, for he saw the futility of arguing
theology with a Jesuit. It occurred to Kenekuk that with both
Catholics and Methodists stationed on their lands, the missionaries
would have to compete for the Kickapoos' favor, so he took a neutral
approach. "I realize," he told the priest humbly, "that my religion is
not a good one: if my people wish to embrace yours, I will do as they
say."[29] After about a week with the Kickapoos, Van Quickenborne
grew skeptical of Kenekuk's motives. "God alone knows whether he
spoke sincerely," the Jesuit wrote. He was less suspicious of Pashishi,
who requested "to have a black-robe come and reside among us with a
view to instruct us." With this assurance, Van Quickenborne set out
for Washington to seek federal aid in starting a mission.[30]

After the Jesuit's departure, rivalries between the two Kickapoo bands intensified. Kenekuk disapproved of the Prairie Indians' drinking, gambling, and ill-mannered ways and held Pashishi personally responsible. He threatened to invoke supernatural powers to punish the "sinners" and vowed that if Pashishi refused to repent, he would "blow into a flame that would not be easily smothered" and cause his rival's death.[31] But Pashishi paid little heed to the prophet's threat, and when word of the Seminoles' triumph over United States troops in Florida reached Kansas, the Prairie Indians celebrated with a boisterous dance. After consuming several casks of whiskey, they rejoiced that "the time was near at hand when the white people would be subdued, and red men restored again to their country." As drunken Indians rode through the villages, molesting women and destroying property, Kenekuk rushed to Fort Leavenworth seeking aid from the soldiers.

Federal officials were outraged by the Indians' celebration of an American defeat and later brought charges against Pashishi and his band. The Prairie Kickapoos, however, expressed astonishment that there was "such a fuss about a simple religious ceremony." Asserting that it was the right of all people to dance, an unrepentant Pashishi denied that his followers had caused any serious damage. After scolding the Indians for their behavior, officials agreed to drop the matter. The Kickapoos were, after all, "uncivilized savages"; it should be expected that they would act like children on occasion.[32]

A confident Father Van Quickenborne returned in June 1836, unaware of the bitter feelings that existed between the two bands. With three assistants, the priest began conversion efforts in earnest. But winning Kickapoo souls proved difficult; it was "one thing to come to the Indian mission and another to convert the Indians." Kenekuk, angry because the Jesuits favored Pashishi's band, admonished his followers to shun the blackrobes. But when the Jesuits pressured the Prairie Kickapoos to attend Mass and reform their sinful ways, they too rejected Catholic demands. "We want no prayer," they announced. "Our forefathers got along very well without it and we are not going to feel its loss." Even the outwardly sympathetic Pashishi warned that if a priest ever tried "to change the old customs of my forefathers, I will quiet him and listen to him no more." Despite such obstinacy, Van Quickenborne remained hopeful that "with the help of God and with patience, we can go far."[33]

The Jesuits did not, however, "go far" with regard to converting the

Kickapoos. In 1838 they considered closing the mission, but Pashishi promised that his people would soon change their ways. The Jesuits "had done more good here in a year than others have done in five or six," he proclaimed. "You have cured our children of smallpox, you have befriended us in our needs, and you have been kind even to the wicked. The storm which makes the thunder roar above your heads will not last forever."[34]

Jesuit spirits lifted in the spring of 1838 when the noted Father Pierre Jean De Smet visited the mission. De Smet was impressed when Pashishi acknowledged that Catholicism was the one true religion. If it were not for the "impositions" of Kenekuk, De Smet reasoned, the Kickapoos would make progress.[35] The priest refused to admit that Kenekuk's followers were pious, hard-working, and relatively prosperous.

In contrast, the Prairie Kickapoos continued to suffer the effects of alcohol abuse. Agent Richard Cummins reported that whites who were "void of all conscience" traded whiskey to the Shawnees, Delawares, and Kickapoos. These unscrupulous border settlers plied the Indians with spirits, then tried to steal their horses, guns, and other possessions. Cummins added that several drunken Indians had drowned trying to swim the Missouri, and he urged strict punishment for whiskey dealers, who "condescend to the meanest of acts."[36]

Admitting that the Prairie Band needed to reform, Pashishi regretted that his people failed to get along with Kenekuk's followers. He agreed that "if it was not for the difficulties growing out of drinking and stealing we could live together as brothers, and not be ashamed to look at one another." But the constant bickering proved too much for the Prairie Kickapoos, and by 1839 most had left for Indian Territory, Texas, or Mexico. When Pashishi and twenty families moved several miles away from the prophet's village that year, Kenekuk was left with no further Indian opposition.[37]

In 1839 Agent Cummins counted four hundred nineteen adherents to Kenekuk's religion, about a quarter of whom were Potawatomis. Faithful and obedient to Kenekuk, the Indians worked hard to support themselves. Cummins reported that they "profess the Christian religion, attend closely and rigidly to their church discipline, and very few ever indulge in the use of ardent spirits." Except for mistaking their piety and industry as evidence of Christianity, the agent's glowing account was accurate.[38]

Because most of the Indians remaining on the reservation were faithful to Kenekuk, missionary attempts to win converts proved more difficult than ever, and attendance at the Catholic and Methodist schools was light. By October 1839 Berryman realized that the "detrimental influence of the Prophet" was keeping children out of the classroom. School discipline was impossible to maintain because children "abscond and go home with impunity." Branding Kenekuk a "savage politician" and an "impostor" whose appeal rested on the gullibility of his followers, the frustrated Berryman warned that such men "must be held in check by the counteracting influences of popular virtue, or they will in time barbarize the world."[39]

The Jesuits also resented Kenekuk's influence and indirectly acknowledged his effectiveness by blaming him for their failure to win converts. When the Catholic mission closed its doors for the last time in May 1841, Jesuit Nicolas Point charged that Kenekuk's false preachings had "palsied" Catholic efforts. Point noted in his journal that the Kickapoos were followers of a man "who calls himself 'The Prophet.' "

By force of sheer effrontery and continued hard work, this man, really extraordinary for his kind, has succeeded in assembling some three hundred souls in a temple built for him by the United States Government. He claims to be a special emissary from God. The complete, fantastic story he tells of his birth and mission would be too long to recount in detail here. He descended from Heaven, he says, through a blue opening and, after having soared about through space for a long time, he tumbled down upon our planet. This is but one example of his imposture. The whites, he says, will not be saved because they made all Nature grieve. They cut the grass with their great scythes, thereby injuring the grass so that it wept. They chopped down trees with their great axes, thereby injuring them and making them weep. They ran their great steamboats on the rivers and thereby injured the rivers so that they, too, wept. Rivers, earth, trees and grass all wept. The white man, ingrate that he was, thus made all of Nature mourn. Consequently, he would not be saved. For the Indians the practical conclusion was that, since they inflicted none of these injuries on Nature, they could hope for eternal life, regardless of their stupidity, their sloth, their thievery, their adultery, their murderousness.

And for the most part they were given to these vices. As for Kenekuk, in his capacity of prophet, five wives are not too many for him. No one knows how many men his son has killed. Kenekuk's palace—for he is chief—is as filthy as a stable and his temple, which I actually saw, is just as bad. But the king-prophet has only to speak of his revelations and everyone listens with admiration. The authority for his divine mission is a piece of wood about two inches wide and eight inches long.[40]

Ignoring the Kickapoos' observance of basic Christian morals, Point was outraged that the Indians refused to accept Catholic doctrine. The Kickapoos were a "hideous" people "in every way, especially with respect to religion." The Jesuit regretted that the Catholic mission "had been plunged into the deepest abyss of moral degradation by the scandalous conduct of people who pretend to civilization."[41]

Echoing Point's sentiments, Father De Smet labeled Kenekuk a "false prophet." Blandly ignoring the fact that few if any Prairie people had become Catholics, De Smet praised Pashishi as "a man of good wit and good sense, who needs only a little courage to become a Christian." Because Kenekuk had successfully thwarted them, De Smet was apparently attempting to rationalize the fact that one man, and an illiterate Indian at that, had prevented highly educated priests from converting unschooled "heathens." Chagrined at their failure, he asserted that the prophet was "profoundly ignorant of Christian doctrines" and his followers were more "densely ignorant" of sin, confession, and penance than the "rudest savages," a charge that he must have known was untrue.[42] When the blackrobes left Kickapoo country to reap souls among less obstinate Indians, Kenekuk ignored their parting barbs as the expressions of frustrated men.

Following the closing of the missions in the 1840s, the band prospered without interference from preachers. Under the prophet's guidance, Kickapoo men had worked hard to clear and plow the fields, and despite their use of relatively primitive tools and agricultural methods, their small farms now provided a secure living. Although they owned the lands in common, individual families worked their own small plots. They were subsistence farmers who willingly shared any surpluses with less fortunate kinfolk. Agent Cummins noted in his annual reports, however, that the band as a whole raised a substantial surplus of corn, pumpkins, potatoes, cattle, and pigs, which they sold to white settlers for a considerable profit.[43] These profits were evenly distributed among the band members.

Many whites respected Kenekuk's disciples because they adhered to a Protestant-like work ethic. The Methodist minister Nathaniel Talbott noted that they "raise more corn than any other Indians in this country," and even the Baptist McCoy conceded that the prophet's "influence has made them more industrious." A government-employed teacher found the Kickapoo children intelligent, "their memory quick and retentive, their morals good, their manners pleasant, and they are remarkably active and industrious." A trader called Kenekuk's Potawatomi converts "the best Indians we have: industrious, sober, and most of them religious." Agent Cummins glowingly reported that Kenekuk's band almost equalled whites in their methods of government, farming, and religion. They "evince a determination [and] perseverance; they are at this time truly in the spirit of work, [and] if they continue to progress . . . they will be ahead of any of the Indians in this section of the country."[44]

Their success was all the more remarkable considering the tardiness of federal officials in living up to the financial provisions of the Treaty of Castor Hill. In June 1843 Kenekuk and Pashishi joined forces to petition federal officials to release the promised annuities. Couching their demands in acceptable paternalistic rhetoric, the chiefs pressed officials to fulfill their obligations. "We have always understood from our agent," they announced, "that our great father wanted his red children to lay aside their guns . . . and go to work and live like his white children. [T]his we wanted to do, but how can we work unless we have something to work with?" Shortly thereafter, the funds that would help solidify their hold on the Kansas lands finally arrived. In 1846 Thomas Harvey, superintendent of Indian affairs at St. Louis, reported that the "thrifty" Kickapoos "understand well the value of money" and were prospering.[45]

Kenekuk managed to secure strong intertribal cohesiveness among his followers just in time to meet upcoming crises. Advancing white settlers were again complicating matters in Indian country, and over the past few years the prophet's followers had complained about trespassers on their lands. In 1849, for example, troops had to stop whites from stealing Kickapoo timber. The following year, Kenekuk complained to United States Judge R. W. Wells that the trespassers had built an unauthorized sawmill on the reservation. Since much of their land was prairie, the lost timber caused the Kickapoos considerable hardship.[46]

Compounding this problem was an outbreak of smallpox in 1851, which touched off panic among several Kansas tribes. Although most bands suffered to some extent during the first year of the epidemic, Kenekuk's followers escaped the scourge entirely. Neither the prophet nor his adherents, however, were as fortunate the following year when the dreaded smallpox apparently reached the Vermillion Kickapoos, killing their beloved Kenekuk.

The exact date of the Kickapoo prophet's death in 1852 is unknown, for whites initially ignored his passing. Agent William Richardson reported merely that the band had "lost Keu-e-kuck [*sic*], their principal chief" but gave no date or cause of death. Later accounts based on hearsay are unreliable. One chronicle stated that Kenekuk had predicted that like Jesus Christ, he would rise again in three days. After the chief's death, according to the same report, his adherents, "infested with smallpox, scattered up and down the valleys and ravines to their various villages. Many of them, not able to reach their homes, left their bones to bleach along the trails. Hundreds of Kickapoos died."[47] A catastrophe of this extent would have wiped out most of the band, yet Richardson did not even mention smallpox in his yearly report, which raises doubts as to the accuracy of the second account.

Like many whites who had met Kenekuk, Richardson had mixed feelings about him. He praised the prophet for exerting "a most beneficial influence over a portion of that tribe for some years before his death, in restraining, by all means in his power, the introduction and use of spirits." He could not resist adding, however, that Kenekuk "was notorious for his superstitious quackery—a conjurer of the first water—and regarded by most of his people as possessing supernatural powers."[48]

This view of Kenekuk contained some measure of truth. The Kickapoo prophet had played a vital role in the Indians' determination to survive. Even after his death, they continued to farm intensively and to abstain from drinking, gambling, and warfare, which could have eroded tribal solidarity and made it easier for officials to force them to move. Their agricultural endeavors and religious unity proved a bulwark in their struggle against efforts to dispossess them. The prophet's followers never capitulated to white pressure, for as peaceful farmers they appeared to be acculturating to the dominant society. They skillfully used their cultural flexibility to resist outside threats. To the dismay of missionaries and federal officials, however, they steadfastly rejected Christianity, white education, and individual land allotment.

Following Kenekuk's death, nevertheless, the Vermillion Band Kickapoos entered a period of uncertainty and crisis. The men who assumed leadership of the band—Mecina, Pahkahka, Kapiomah, Nokowhat, Pashagon, and Kewisahhite—possessed neither the charismatic influence nor the dynamic moral leadership of the prophet. The aged Mecina, the former Prairie Kickapoo and a devout convert to Kenekuk's religion, commanded only a small following; Kenekuk's son Pahkahka, or John Kenekuk, an incipient alcoholic, lacked his father's courage, determination, and wisdom. These were the men who led the Kickapoos as they faced the most severe challenge since their removal to Kansas. Fortunately for them, they still held Kenekuk's teachings uppermost in their minds.

In the late summer of 1853, Commissioner of Indian Affairs George Manypenny began negotiating a series of land cession treaties with the Indians of eastern Kansas. At first he encountered stiff opposition from many bands. He complained in November that the Kickapoos, Sacs, Delawares, and Potawatomis "refused peremptorily to sell any portion of their lands; and although the objections were of a trivial character, I was unable to remove them."[49] But with their annuities almost depleted, thieves stealing their timber, and settlers eyeing their fertile fields, the Kickapoos and other bands found themselves in a difficult position. When Manypenny promised them annuities and assurances of permanent title to a portion of their reserve as a permanent home, most bands reluctantly accepted his offer.

Mecina and the other Kickapoo elders informed Agent David Vanderslice in November 1853 that they would go to Washington to negotiate a treaty.[50] Arrangements with other bands were completed, and on April 21 of the following year representatives of the Kickapoos, Iowas, and Missouri Sacs joined Vanderslice aboard the steamboat *Honduras* as it began its journey down the Missouri River from St. Joseph. From St. Louis the Indians traveled by stagecoach and train to Washington. Delegations of Shawnees, Delawares, Miamis, Weas, Piankashaws, Kaskaskias, Peorias, and others also left Kansas for the nation's capital about the same time.

This news delighted white Missourians, who rushed to stake claims to Indian lands just as Congress was approving the Kansas-Nebraska Act. Under the Preemption Law of 1841, it was illegal to take possession of government-controlled lands prior to a public survey. But public land policies did not apply here as in other territories because Kansas was owned by Indians and not technically part of the public domain; the usual methods of obtaining land were therefore not applicable. To land-hungry whites, nevertheless, the Manypenny treaties meant that the land belonged to whoever claimed it first. Indian trader Benjamin Harding observed that as soon as Vanderslice and the tribal delegations departed, several whites crossed the Missouri "and made their claims by laying a foundation for a cabin and writing their names on a tree near by [sic], and now [May 27] there is not a grease spot left unclaimed within my knowledge; and still claim hunters are passing daily." After they had staked their claims, most of the intruders returned to Missouri to await news of the treaties.[51]

The Indian delegations, meanwhile, began arriving in Washington in early May. On May 6, the Delawares sold all of their lands north of the Kansas River, retaining a reduced reservation of about 275,000 acres. Four days later, the Shawnees signed a similar agreement; they were left with 200,000 acres of their original 1,600,000-acre reservation. In addition, the treaty called for dividing much of the reduced Shawnee reservation into individual allotments.[52]

While these treaties were being signed, the Kickapoo, Sac, and Iowa delegates had arrived and settled into a local hotel. Too old to make the journey, the elderly Mecina of the Kickapoos had remained behind in Kansas, which perhaps was fortunate for him. This deeply religious convert to Kenekuk's faith believed that the Great Spirit punished those who signed away tribal lands. He recalled that there had been a "shaking of the earth" when the Kickapoos sold their Illinois homes years before. The forces of nature that greeted the Kickapoo delegation in Washington would have confirmed his fears.

The evening before the treaty ceremonies, a violent storm struck the capital. The *Evening Star* reported that "rain fell in torrents in large drops, pattering upon the roofs like hail, and the gusts of wind that blew at the same time were [a] complete hurricane." Several people were killed when struck by lightning "of no ordinary character." In the House of Representatives, "even the violence of debate was hushed by the eloquence of nature." After the storm, millions of mayflies, "which appeared to fall like rain," descended on the city. The *National Intelli-*

gencer informed readers that shoppers along Pennsylvania Avenue "were very much annoyed by [mayflies], . . . such were the quantities dead on the sidewalks and in the gutters as to produce an offensive smell." Reporters had never witnessed such a sight; the flies "might have been gathered by bushels full."[53]

On May 18 Pahkahka and the other Kickapoo chiefs, accompanied by Vanderslice and interpreter Peter Cadue, trudged through the odor of decaying mayflies to Manypenny's office. There they signed away all but 152,417 acres of their 1,200-square-mile Kansas reservation.[54] When he negotiated the treaties, Commissioner Manypenny believed that the Kickapoos and others could be protected on their reduced reservations. Manypenny was sincerely concerned for the Indians' welfare, and he hoped that individual allotments and other aspects of the civilization program would work quickly to absorb the Indians into the mainstream society. "It is, therefore, in my judgment," he wrote, "clear, beyond doubt or question, that the emigrated tribes in Kansas Territory are permanently there—there to be thoroughly civilized, and to become a constituted portion of the population, or there to be destroyed and exterminated. What a spectacle for the view of the statesman, philanthropist, Christian!"[55]

But Manypenny soon learned that some whites seemed more concerned with seeing the tribes "destroyed and exterminated" than they were with Indian rights. By the time President Franklin Pierce had signed the Kansas-Nebraska bill into law on May 30, 1854, various squatter associations had already organized. "Camps are formed, and tents are dotting all the hills and valleys" of eastern Kansas, one observer reported on June 13. "Thousands are waiting the permit to cross. Large numbers have organized for mutual protection and defense, and have crossed the river, and are locating claims, and staking out farms. Trees are 'blazed' in every direction, and even now much of the choicest land is 'marked.' " An onlooker in St. Joseph informed the *Missouri Republican* later that month that ferryboats were operating from dawn to dark taking settlers across to the new territory. "They come by boats, stages, carriages, wagons, on horse-back and mule-back," he wrote, "and it is no unusual thing to see troops of hardy pioneers passing on foot, with their axes and knapsacks upon their backs, making their way into the forests of Kansas and Nebraska, to hew out a new home."[56]

With so many people rushing to stake claims, it was not surprising that a violent struggle for land ensued that came to be called Bleeding Kansas. Most easterners assumed that the violence in Kansas was the result of agitation between abolitionists and proslavery elements. But the simple quest for land by speculators, railroad agents, and settlers far outweighed the issue of slavery. "Filibustering, banditry, and personal vendettas continued to flourish under the guise of conflict over slavery," wrote one historian, "but underlying these activities were the struggles over the promotion of towns, over the removal of Indians . . . and over the selection of railroad routes."[57]

The fertile lands of eastern Kansas proved an irresistible lure for thousands of settlers little concerned about the slavery question. After touring through Kansas, one observer informed readers of the *New York Times:*

> There are no very steep hills, but the land is rolling enough to appear beautiful, without being incapable of cultivation. Between these elevations wide fields are stretched along, with soil apparently two or three feet deep in depth. The brooks are numerous, and are lined with high trees and shrubbery. Wild fruits and flowers abound along the roadside. The real new England [sic] blackberry, and various roses of peculiar fragrance, thrive side by side. Thick groves, dotted all over the country, add to the splendor of the landscape. I would not, of course, give the impression that the scenery here is lovelier than in any other place. But I have yet to see the spot where all the land can be used for agricultural purposes that surpasses this in beauty.[58]

In the midst of the great Kansas land rush, the Kickapoos and their Potawatomi allies resettled on their diminished reserve along the Grasshopper, or Delaware, River, about twenty-five miles northwest of the new town of Atchison. Despite the conflicts over land and slavery that raged throughout Kansas, the Indians seemed to be doing well. Agent Royal Baldwin reported in September 1855 that they had built "quite comfortable" log cabins and had begun farming. Their lands, he wrote, possessed "extreme fertility; the bottoms are wide and peculiarly adapted to the culture of all the usual grains." A white settler found the Kickapoo villages nestled in "the timber belts, which like threads of dark green through yellow and orange carpets, stretched far" to the south and west. "The beauty of the scene can not be described," the settler noted. "Prairies as far as the eye could reach, rolling in their light green tints, [are] dotted over with bright red wild roses and other wild flowers of every hue and tinge."⁵⁹

Despite this idyllic picture, Mecina and his followers were not content; they detested Pahkahka and the other elders for having sold so much land and refused to settle in the same area. As a result of this separation, Mecina and about thirty others endured severe hardships. Baldwin and interpreter Peter Cadue had to ride through deep snow and "extremely cold" weather in order to reach Mecina's camp in December 1855. "Never as long as I live will the scene . . . be obliterated from my memory," an astonished Baldwin recalled. He found Mecina's people huddled in prayer to the Great Spirit in a "rude wigwam." Most were sick and some had already died of starvation. The Indian agent beseeched his superiors to do something "to relieve the poor destitute creatures."⁶⁰

Fortunately, most of Mecina's followers survived the winter, and by the spring of 1856 they had settled their differences with their kinfolk. Baldwin announced in May that the "disaffected" Kickapoos had rejoined the others. By year's end, Baldwin noted that the hard-working Indians had "been abundantly rewarded by the extremely heavy yields of the various grains and vegetables." He was so enthusiastic about their success at farming that he urged tribal elders to end their communal ways. To become completely "civilized," he told them, they should disband as a tribe, and each family should accept title to its own farm.⁶¹

Most Kickapoos, however, continued to resist land allotment and other civilization efforts. Although they remained peaceful and willing to adopt white customs when they seemed appropriate, the Indians realized that their own ways helped them to remain unified, and unity was vital to their survival in a land virtually overrun by white settlers. On the eve of the Civil War, only a few Kickapoos lived in log cabins or dressed like whites. To the dismay of federal officials, the Indians continued their annual buffalo hunts until the extermination of the southern herd in the late 1870s.

Children began attending government-sponsored schools, even though the adults placed little value on formal education. Extended families worked hard on their small farms—which the Great Spirit had taught them to own in common—but they preferred the time-honored methods of planting crops in the woods and fields near their

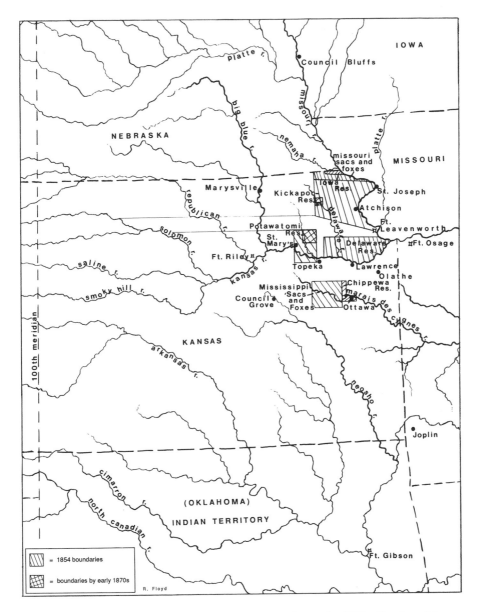

Indian reservations in eastern Kansas, 1854 to the early 1870s. During this period, the Potawatomi, Kickapoo, Missouri Sac and Fox, and Iowa reservations were greatly reduced in size. All other reservations were sold to whites.

homes to the labor-intensive agriculture urged by white officials. One agent complained that their fields were "still in too many instances only tolerable enlargements of the old-time 'Squaw patches.' " Governmental officials and missionaries acknowledged the Indians' industriousness but declared that much still "remains to be done for this benighted tribe of Indians," because they refused to become imitation white farmers of Christian persuasion.[62]

The Kickapoos again faced severe assaults on their Kansas lands during the 1860s. President Abraham Lincoln's commissioner of Indian affairs, William P. Dole, believed that the predominance of white settlement in Kansas hindered the progress of the Indian. "There seems to be no means," Dole announced, "by which he can be secured from falling an easy victim to those vices and temptations which are perhaps the worst feature of our civilization, and to which he seems to have an irresistable [sic] inclination." Even though many southern tribes had joined with the Confederacy and conditions south of Kansas were chaotic, the commissioner advocated concentrating the Kickapoos and others in Indian Territory, where they would presumably be protected by the United States Army. He failed to mention that several thousand Creeks, Cherokees, Chickasaws, Seminoles, and others had already fled from Indian Territory into Kansas during the Civil War; it should have been obvious to anyone that his suggestion for removing the Kansas bands was absurd.[63]

While Dole made plans to "civilize" the Indians, and the Civil War distracted the attention of other federal officials, Kansas politicians and businessmen connived with agents to steal Kickapoo lands. Kansas Sen. Samuel C. Pomeroy, a leading stockholder in the Atchison and Pike's Peak Railroad, worked closely with Indian Agents William Badger and Charles Keith to swindle the Kickapoos out of part of their reservation. Seeking a railroad right-of-way across the Kickapoo reserve, they attempted to persuade tribal elders to accept an allotment treaty. When Chief Nokowhat and others denounced the scheme, agents simply ignored the protests and dealt with Indians willing to accept bribes. In June 1862, Agent Keith obtained the signatures of a few Kickapoo "chiefs," who agreed that their people would cede most of the reservation and accept individual allotments for their people. The so-called chiefs were a drunken old man, a twelve-year-old boy, the boy's mother, and the Kickapoo interpreter.[64]

Because Keith had completed the treaty negotiations in secret, most

Kickapoos were unaware of the underhanded negotiations and demanded that officials rescind the agreement. Despite the obviously
illegal maneuverings, however, the United States Senate ratified the
treaty and President Lincoln signed it into law in May 1863, and much
of the Kickapoo reservation fell into white hands. Chief Nokowhat,
like most other Kickapoos, was outraged. The white men who plotted
to cheat the Indians, however, convinced federal bureaucrats that
Nokowhat and the other dissenters were actually Potawatomis, only
"casually allied with the Kickapoos, . . . and consequently are not
wholly identified in interest with them." When federal officials accepted this falsehood at face value, Nokowhat and sixty followers
headed south in the summer of 1864 to join other Kickapoos already in
Mexico.[65]

During the next several years, a few families accepted individual
title to their Kansas homesteads, while some left to join kinfolk in
Indian Territory or Mexico. The weak-willed Pahkahka, Kenekuk's
son, became an alcoholic and lost all influence among his people. He
and his family accepted an allotment; but like other Kickapoos who
followed this example, he soon regretted his decision. He died sometime during the 1870s when he apparently mistook a quart of lubricat-
ing oil for whiskey and accidentally poisoned himself.[66] Most other
Kickapoos avoided such pitfalls, however, and continued to hold a
small portion of their old reservation in common, refusing to accept
allotment or interference in their affairs. Despite every obstacle, they
were determined to remain in Kansas on their own terms.

Throughout the remaining years of the nineteenth century, the
Kickapoos continued to support themselves and to win the respect of
their white neighbors. Agents continually pressured them to accept
allotments, but most refused. Government Field Inspector Edward
Kenible reported in November 1874 that they remained "disinclined as
a body to take up their allotments in severalty and to labor steadily;
each family somehow managed, nevertheless, to "eke out an existence
by planting from five to ten acres in corn and pumpkins." Kenible
urged his superiors to cut off the Kickapoos' annuities and force them
to accept allotments. He ignored the fact that many of the allotted
Indians had lost their farms and had resettled on the band's greatly
diminished common lands.[67]

Other whites praised the Kickapoos for their progress. Agent
Mahlon H. Newlin reported in 1876 that "their conduct presents many

evidences of improvement and assimilation to the ways of the whites."
Newlin believed that "with their advanced ideas of religion and education added to their industrious habits, I can see no reason why in a few
years they should not become self-sustaining."[68] Field Inspector John
McNeil reported two years later that the Kickapoos possessed finer
farms and had "a much more advanced state of agricultural knowledge" than most other tribes in the West. When McNeil inquired if the
Kickapoos desired to move to Indian Territory, they replied that they
were "resolved to retain their present home." The inspector agreed
that this was a wise decision because most "respectable" whites accepted them as neighbors and their future in Kansas seemed secure.[69]

By the late 1870s, the Kickapoos were among the few Indians left in
Kansas. Unified by Kenekuk's religion and teachings, they had never
forgotten their tribal heritage, and their acceptance of white culture
stopped short of assimilation. Whites never understood their reluc-
tance to abandon the old customs. "While they labor and subsist like
white people," Agent Newlin reported in 1877, "they consider themselves possessed of superior vitality . . . [enabling] them to wear less
clothing and live in less comfortable houses" than their more numerous white neighbors.[70]

The Kickapoos had good reason for clinging to the way of life
Kenekuk had taught them, for their combination of "civilization and
barbarism" in their method of living was the primary reason they
survived. Well aware that others who submitted to efforts to uplift
them from "savagery" to "civilization" had lost their Kansas lands, the
Vermillion people would resist all future efforts to make them Christians and to divide their tribal lands into individual allotments. Their
struggle was never easy, for the 1880s and 1890s would bring renewed
threats to their homes and way of life.

4
THE CHIPPEWAS
AND MUNSEES

The experience of the tiny Chippewa and Munsee bands differed greatly from that of the Vermillion Kickapoos. Whereas the Kickapoos resisted white civilization plans, most Chippewas and Munsees seemed to welcome them. With only about forty members in each band, these Indians should have been especially vulnerable to whites eager to dispossess them. But in the years after 1854, while the Shawnees, Ottawas, and other larger groups succumbed to the wiles of speculators and railroad agents and moved to Indian Territory, the Chippewas and Munsees successfully retained a portion of their holdings. Beginning in 1859, when their bands formed a political alliance, and continuing throughout the rest of the century, they resisted all attempts to evict them from Kansas.[1] Of the thousands of Indians in Kansas when it became a territory in 1854, the sophisticated Chippewas and Munsees were among the few remaining at the turn of the century.

Holding on to their lands was not easy. By the time the Chippewas and Munsees signed their treaty of merger on July 16, 1859, thousands of white settlers had staked claims to nearby lands. As abolitionist "Jayhawkers" fought pro-slavery "Bushwhackers" for political control, Bleeding Kansas gained national attention and the rights of Indians were forgotten. Meanwhile, the Chippewas and Munsees faced both external pressure from squatters and land speculators and internal dissension among tribal members. Because they were two disparate groups, disputes over tribal policy were frequent. Indian agents complained that handling the affairs of these two bands was difficult because each "was jealous of the other and ready to oppose any measure because the other originated or favored it."[2]

Because the two bands were culturally different, intertribal tension was generally evident. The Munsees were part of the politically diverse

Delaware tribe, whose widely scattered bands lived in such places as southern Ontario, Wisconsin, Indian Territory, and Kansas. The Delaware bands spoke one of two closely related Algonquian languages, Unami or Munsee; the majority of Kansas Delawares spoke the former dialect, while their Munsee kinfolk used the latter. In the late 1850s, ethnologist Lewis Henry Morgan found that the Kansas Munsees remained steadfastly independent of the other Delawares; he also noted that the Munsee language was "dialectically different" and "not as harsh and guttural."[3]

Since the mid-eighteenth century, some bands of Munsee-speaking Delawares had endeavored to pattern their lives after the maxims of the Moravian Church. In 1792, hoping to avoid trouble from aggressive American settlers and militia, one band established a separate village along the Thames River in southern Ontario. Known to whites as the "Christian Indians," they worshipped Christ, observed the Sabbath, shunned liquor, and practiced monogamy. They steadfastly refused to participate in traditional Indian dances, religious ceremonies, or other "heathenish" festivals. Those of that band who later settled in Kansas kept up with these traditions. "The society of Christian or Moravian Indians, shows a degree of intelligence and refined demeanor, that speaks well for the labors" of the missionaries, wrote one visitor to Kansas in 1854. "They are well dressed, have clean, comfortable looking homes, and seem to be really good and sincere christians [*sic*]."[4]

Like that of other Delaware bands, the political organization of the Kansas Munsees was rather loosely structured. The function of the chiefs was to act as mediators in disputes and to perform ceremonial functions; chiefs traditionally could not force their will on the people but had to rely on their powers of persuasion when dealing with matters that affected the entire band. When Morgan visited the Kansas Munsees in 1859, the small band was still divided into three matrilineal phratries, or totemic clans—the Wolf, the Turtle, and the Turkey. Each clan had its own chief, who traditionally succeeded to office through the matrilineal line.[5] By the 1850s, however, federal officials were resorting more and more to appointing the tribal leaders, and the role of the traditional chiefs diminished. This practice would have a profound effect on the Munsees and other bands struggling to survive in Kansas.

Before federal officials arranged for their merger with the Chippewas, the Kansas Munsees lived on a twenty-five-hundred-acre reservation near the new town of Leavenworth. Because the other Delaware bands in Kansas had moved to a reduced reservation some distance away, the Munsees found themselves surrounded by white settlers who coveted their lands. Squatters and speculators were a constant source of trouble, and by 1857 fifteen white families had settled illegally on the Munsee reserve. Under considerable pressure from several fronts, the Munsees agreed to sell their lands to speculators in January 1857. But Commissioner Manypenny ruled that the sale violated the Indian Intercourse Act of 1834 and he voided the transaction—only the government was permitted direct purchase of tribal lands.[6]

Such technicalities failed to deter the Kansas attorney general, Andrew Isaacs, who persuaded the Munsees to accept forty-three thousand dollars for their lands a short time after Manypenny had canceled the previous sale. Isaacs argued that the Indians were free to sell because they had been given legal patent to their reserve under the 1854 treaty with the Delawares. Moravian missionary Gottlieb Oehler claimed, however, that Isaacs had gotten the Indians drunk and then bribed the chiefs to sell the band's holdings. But Oehler's protests lacked conviction; he was trying to secure for himself the advance money that Isaacs intended to pay the Munsees for the sale.[7]

Isaacs had powerful friends in Congress, which eventually passed a special bill authorizing the purchase. He also won the support of Oehler by agreeing to pay twenty-three hundred dollars "compensation" for improvements that the Moravians had made to the lands they had occupied on the reserve. On October 13, 1858, "Chief" Job Samuel, never a traditional leader of the Munsees but conveniently appointed chief by the Indian agent, signed away the tribe's lands. "It has been a bold step this," wrote Oehler. "The timid Job is at once made chief, and requests [the] Government to act in their behalf without having had council." The Moravian then blandly asserted that the land cession was "strictly correct" despite most Munsees' opposing it.[8]

By 1859 the Munsee chiefs were listening to the advice of the opportunistic Henry Donohoe, a white man who had married into the band. As was typical of many tribes, important decisions were influenced by individuals familiar with both Indian and white ways. Mixed-bloods such as John Ross of the Cherokees and Joseph Renville of the Sioux, as well as whites such as Simon Girty of the Senecas and Donohoe of the Munsees, better understood the intricacies of racial interaction; these men found many followers among Indians struggling for survival against pressure to give up their lands. Because they spoke English and were sometimes willing to sell tribal possessions, it was convenient for federal policymakers and land speculators to recognize them as official representatives of the Indians. With the exception of Ross and some others, however, many were "paper chiefs" acting on their own—and usually for their own benefit—without the authority of their tribe.[9]

Donohoe was typical. "I am not [an Indian] now, nor ever was by adoption," he confessed to the Moravians, "but I suffered to be called one for reasons of my own, and I think you are not ignorant of those." Although he claimed that he would cease to act as a leader once the Munsees were established on new lands, he enjoyed his role and never voluntarily relinquished it. Although his first allegiance was to himself, he urged the Munsees to remain true to the tenets of the Moravian religion, for he believed that Christianity, citizenship, and individual land allotment would benefit the Indians.[10]

Having lost their land, the Munsees requested and received permission to move onto the small Chippewa reservation on the Marais des Cygnes River, near present-day Ottawa, Kansas. There many unforeseen problems awaited, for the Chippewas, or Ojibwas, still observed the Algonquian religious practices they had brought with them from Michigan in 1839.

Although the acculturated Chippewas had long interacted with the French, the British, and the Americans, they still retained many of their traditional customs. Closely related to the Potawatomis, Ottawas, and other Algonquian-speaking peoples, the Chippewas' ceremonies and customs resembled those of the other tribes. Traditionally hunters, gatherers, fishermen, and traders, the Chippewas had utilized agriculture since the early eighteenth century; farming had become the primary occupation for the Kansas band. Chippewa youths, however, still went on "vision quests," fasting for several days in the hope of meeting their guardian spirit. This spirit usually appeared in the form of an animal, such as a bear or a bird. Each individual received spiritual power from his or her spirit; but some individuals acquired extra powers, allowing them to become religious leaders.[11]

Even though they had modified their traditional customs and adopted many aspects of white civilization, the Kansas Chippewas continually resisted missionary attempts to convert them to Christianity. Indian Agent Francis Tymoney described them as a "quiet, industrious, domestic people, [who] have good farms and cultivate them well." Despite their acculturated ways, they disliked missionaries, who seemed more interested in making profits than in saving souls. "They complain of the ministers of religion," wrote Tymoney, "for not being more attentive to their spiritual wants, and for not disseminating more freely the Divine precepts of the [C]hristian religion among them 'without money and without price.' "[12]

The Chippewas preferred the traditional religious beliefs espoused most emphatically by Chief Eshtonoquot (Francis McCoonse), a man of mixed Indian and white heritage. The spiritual leader of the Kansas Chippewas, Eshtonoquot's actions on behalf of his band initially won praise from white observers. According to Agent Tymoney, Eshtonoquot was "a worthy good man and by nature very intelligent."[13] Lewis Henry Morgan agreed, noting that the Chippewa leader was a "man of intelligence and a good farmer."[14]

Such praise was rare after 1859 because Eshtonoquot found himself at odds with those endeavoring to turn his people into imitation white farmers. The Chippewa chief saw missionaries, federal officials, and other advocates of white civilization as interlopers more interested in expanding personal wealth than in promoting Indian welfare. Like the Kickapoo prophet, he realized that the Kansas lands were valuable and was determined to hold on to them. "By God," he informed Lewis Henry Morgan, "there [is] no comparison to this country; this is a damn big country. We can raise anything. There is no country like it for farming."[15] Eshtonoquot realized, however, that most whites agreed with the sentiment expressed by the *Leavenworth Times* that "honest settlers" should replace the "few worthless redskins [who] are permitted to hold millions of the finest acres in Kansas."[16]

Trusting neither agents nor missionaries, Eshtonoquot warned fellow Chippewas against listening to these advocates of social change. He scorned white customs and religion, quipping that whereas it took the "white man seven years to learn theology, Indians learn [it] in one hour." He urged followers to abide by their traditional beliefs, for anyone choosing the "crookety" path "falls into deep gulf, water carries him away. Bad Indian lost."[17]

Eshtonoquot himself was no stranger to the "crookety" path. Unlike Kenekuk of the Kickapoos, he had a reputation for dishonesty and a weakness for women, whiskey, and gambling. A stout man of imposing presence, he cut a rather striking figure compared with most of his people. One white visitor was impressed by his black coat, moccasins, "wampum sash, calico hunting shirt, fringed gaudy vest, [and] broadcloth leggings ornamented with silver bands and porcupine quills." The chief's silver jewelry "gave a jingle with every step." His rather expensive tastes left him in constant need of ready cash—a scarcity in the West. His impecuniosity involved him in many schemes to make money, and he was not noted for his honesty when profits were to be made. The British Parliament had been amused by his outlandish claims to thousands of acres of Canadian territory during the 1830s. In Michigan his mixed ethnic heritage allowed him to mingle in the white world, and he occasionally passed himself off as a doctor, practicing on white patients for a fee. On one occasion, he reportedly sucked seventeen gallons of fluid out of a white man suffering from dropsy—it took over a year for the patient to recover.[18]

Eshtonoquot apparently spoke French and English in addition to his native tongue, giving him a measure of sophistication that most Indians and even whites lacked. With one of his wives, he had operated a trading post near Detroit; on friendly terms with land speculators, he was willing to sell tribal holdings for a price. After arriving in Kansas with only sixty followers in 1839, he continued to claim that he was the rightful chief of the Michigan Chippewas, and he tried to usurp their annuities. Those who remained in Michigan, not only the majority of his tribe but even his own mother, denounced Eshtonoquot as a thief. As chief of the Kansas Chippewas, he accepted the Munsees as allies in the summer of 1859.

By then Eshtonoquot's son, Edward McCoonse, was eager to assume leadership from his aging father. McCoonse realized that Chippewa custom dictated that his father's property would pass on to others; children inherited their mother's property—the father's possessions went to brothers and uncles.[19] Determined to acquire property and wealth, he worked with his father, forging an agreement with federal officials in July 1859 that called for allotment of forty- to eighty-acre family farms and the sale of the remainder of their eighty-three-hundred-acre reservation. The treaty granted the Chippewas cash payments, farm implements, and all proceeds from the sale of the "surplus" lands. In addition, the Chippewas agreed to provide land to the Munsees in exchange for three thousand dollars. Since there were only about forty Chippewas in the band, many of them children, Eshtonoquot and his son stood to make substantial profits.[20]

Despite the cultural differences between the Chippewas and Munsees, their union was generally problem-free for the next few years. Even a severe drought and the disruption of the Civil War did not stop their small farms from prospering. But in October 1861, Agent Clinton C. Hutchinson wrote that the two bands had not been provided with a school, and the "well-being of the children especially requires that this be done very soon."[21] In the meantime, the agent was busy with plans to make himself rich by building a college for the "well-being" of the neighboring Ottawas.

On August 19, 1862, Hutchinson got his wish for the Chippewas and Munsees when Moravian missionary Joseph Romig, at the invitation of the Munsees, opened a mission and school on the reservation.[22] Romig's new mission included forty acres of prime, fenced land with a small grove of trees and ample water for livestock. A solidly built schoolhouse was furnished with modern supplies, desks, and a blackboard and could also seat one hundred people for church services. Like other members of the relatively small Moravian Church, Romig placed a high priority on education. His spiritual message stressed Christian unity and a close personal relationship with Jesus Christ. He admonished his flock to perform good works, and his services featured congregational singing and other music.

Romig had come to Indian country determined, in his words, to gain "possession of the minds and hearts of the people," and he expected the tribespeople to cast off their ancient habits and customs when exposed to his powers of persuasion. Governmental officials had decided not to expend federal funds on a separate school for so few Indians, but Romig believed that Henry Donohoe could eventually persuade both bands to assist the Moravians financially. The missionary advised church superiors to operate the school at their own expense for now, because it would facilitate his conversion efforts and would give the Moravians control of the lands surrounding the mission.[23]

The Moravian preacher and his wife soon opened elementary and Sunday schools and taught sewing and singing while they "labored to advance Indians in their farming." The enthusiastic couple held high hopes for their new charges, convinced that the Indians appreciated their efforts. Deeply imbued with the ethnocentrism of the day, the Romigs were confident that much could be done to uplift these "half-civilized" yet "not heathen" Indians who seemed eager to learn the ways of the whites. The Romigs were unaware of the immense obstacles to achieving their goals.[24]

One obstacle was Eshtonoquot, who advised his Chippewa followers to reject Christianity. Referring to neighboring Indians such as the Citizen Band Potawatomis, who had adopted the trappings of white civilization and were now rapidly losing their lands, he declared, "we see that those that has [sic] gone on to be citizens, they are not able to take care of themselves." He resented Romig's interference in tribal affairs and accused the Moravian of siding against the Chippewas in territorial disputes. He charged that the missionary's influence had enabled the Munsees to reap most of the financial benefits of the 1859 treaty.[25]

When Eshtonoquot attempted to unite both bands against the missionary and the civilization program, Romig and Indian agents maneuvered to undermine the Chippewa leader's authority. In late 1863 Agent Hutchinson ordered the tribespeople to reject Eshtonoquot's leadership; the agent and Romig agreed to deal only with Indians who were willing to "become citizens, pay taxes, and be subject to the laws of the country." Although most Munsees already subscribed to these principles, many Chippewas were reluctant to reject the advice of their chief. Using threats, cajolery, offers of political favors, and bribery, however, the white men eventually persuaded a number of Chippewas to betray their old leader. Romig justified these actions by reasoning that if the "silly complaints" of the chief were to "prejudice his people against me, he may destroy much of my usefulness here."[26]

Weary of Eshtonoquot's interference in religious affairs, Romig complained that the chief had caused constant turmoil among the Indians, "interfered with the school, and maligned myself, not withstanding my utmost efforts to please him." He lamented that "some of the Chippewa houses are holding dances and most of the young people are attending," and the "noisy music [is] sounding in my ears all night, for it is within hearing and seeing distance." Holding Eshtonoquot responsible for such "sinful" activities, Romig called his rival infirm in body and mind and asserted that the Indians suffered under the rule of this old man. If Eshtonoquot continued to hold sway, Romig feared that he would lose "all hope of doing good or seeing the Indians prosper." He considered it fortunate that "agents have been led to discard [Eshtonoquot] as chief in order to put an end to troubles."[27]

The new government-recognized council proved more to Romig's liking. In November 1863 council members Henry Donohoe and Ignatius Caleb of the Munsees and Lewis Gokey and Edward McCoonse of the Chippewas agreed that abandoning tribal ways and accepting citizenship was the prudent course to follow. McCoonse evidently valued his new leadership role above loyalty to his father, although he may have been convinced that assimilation was the only hope for his people's survival. He joined the other councilmen in denouncing Eshtonoquot, who was, they avowed, "against improvement and encourages degradation and ignorance." On November 30, Donohoe and McCoonse left for Washington to negotiate a treaty that would make their people citizens.[28]

Delighted with this news, Romig now believed a majority of the reservation Indians desired to achieve civilized respectability, and he was certain that his word carried weight with the new leaders. "I had an interesting time with my councilmen," the missionary confidently wrote church elders. They "receive all I say with the simplicity of children and ask questions with familiarity." Romig thought that these "chiefs" would use profits from future land sales to help expand and improve mission buildings. Despite Eshtonoquot's opposition, the bands seemed amenable to selling their property, and Romig encouraged eastern Moravians to act quickly if they wished to acquire Indian lands at a bargain. "If any of the brethren of the Moravian Church wish to emigrate to Kansas I could not recommend any better place," he wrote.[29] It is not clear whether Romig intended from the outset to persuade the Indians to sell their lands or only decided to pursue this course after his arrival. Whichever, he was now determined to induce them to sell out and move to Indian Territory.

With Romig's blessings echoing in their ears, Donohoe and McCoonse arrived in Washington in late January 1864. Representing the Moravian interests, Donohoe sought an agreement that would solidify the church's influence on the reservation and permanently nullify Eshtonoquot's power. His plan included donating forty acres of tribal lands to the Moravian Church. For the scheme to succeed, Donohoe needed the support of McCoonse, who demanded eight hundred dollars for his collaboration. So Donohoe wrote church elders at Bethlehem, Pennsylvania, advising them to pay "some compensation" to the Chippewa delegate. In February McCoonse and Donohoe signed a treaty that, pending Senate ratification, gave the two bands citizenship and assigned land to the church provided that the Moravians continued to educate the tribes' children. The Moravians had paid McCoonse one hundred twenty-eight dollars and although this was considerably less than he had demanded, he accepted it. Unfortunately for McCoonse, thieves stole his money before he left Washington.[30]

Although displaced by the government-appointed council, Eshtonoquot still commanded a following among a few vocal Chippewas who threatened vengeance when they learned what McCoonse and Donohoe had done. Opposed to citizenship, Eshtonoquot and his supporters accused the Washington emissaries of holding secret councils with the missionary and the agent and then sneaking off to the capital without consulting either band. Angered, Eshtonoquot insisted that he was chief and that the agent had no right to intervene in tribal politics; he called on authorities to permit an open council to discuss the treaty.[31]

Eshtonoquot recognized Romig's role in disrupting tribal cohesiveness and accused him of being more interested in enhancing his own wealth than in helping the Indians. The Chippewa leader told all who would listen that he intended to drive the Moravian off the reserve. Throughout 1864 and into 1865, he challenged Romig's every move, ordering the Chippewas to shun Moravian services and to keep their children out of school. He demanded that they reject white civilization and return to traditional ways, threatening to unleash his shamanistic powers against any who refused.

When many Chippewas obeyed their chief, Donohoe and McCoonse angrily complained to the agent that "this old man encourages dancing, evil, and ignorance." Parents were afraid to send children to school because they thought Eshtonoquot was "an old witch" and feared that he would bring death to those who disobeyed him. "He makes them believe that by drawing a picture of a man, woman, or child on a walk or any other place, and placing a heart in the left side and naming the individual to be witched—death or something terrible will follow," Donohoe and McCoonse lamented. They asked federal officials, who had already deposed Eshtonoquot as chief, to issue a "final condemnation . . . that would forever silence this troublesome old Indian."[32]

But it was Donohoe, not Eshtonoquot, who was silenced. Donohoe had forgotten that his influence extended only over the Munsees, and by early 1865 even they were tired of his antics. Both bands were angry that he and McCoonse had spent half of the Indians' yearly annuity on the Washington trip. Realizing that Romig's influence over the Munsees had become more powerful than his own, Donohoe suddenly began quarreling with the preacher, threatening to turn Romig's charges over to the Catholics. But his days as a government-recognized chief were numbered. His problems reached their peak on Easter Sunday, when, according to Romig, Donohoe "beat and kicked his mother-in-law shamefully, for which the agent removed him from the council and the Indians voted him out of the tribe." Moses Killbuck, a Munsee, took his place on the council.[33]

By mid-1865, nevertheless, Eshtonoquot's opponents had gained the ascendancy. In defiance of the chief, and despite his threats of retaliation, most children attended Romig's school at least part of the time.[34] The tribal council ignored Eshtonoquot and asked federal officials to hasten the sale of their "surplus" lands. Because officials thought that reducing Indian holdings to the 40 to 80 acres needed by families and breaking up the reservations was essential to the civilization program, they agreed to the council's request. In June soldiers from Fort Leavenworth began a survey of the reservation. By late fall they had mapped out 1,428 acres to be made available at public auction, and Romig's contention that Eshtonoquot had "no more influence in tribal business than the most ragged Indian on the reserve" seemed accurate. Even so, the missionary feared that the chief would prove a future source of "ferment" and "difficulty." After all, Romig reminded his eastern superiors, this was Kansas and anything was possible out on the "borders of civilization and heathenism."[35]

Because their reservation was apparently being broken up, the Chippewas and Munsees faced an uncertain future in Kansas. Neighboring bands of Citizen Potawatomis, Delawares, and Ottawas had fallen deeply in debt after receiving allotments and had been obliged to sell their farms to meet their obligations; they had no choice but to begin moving to Indian Territory. Yet except for Eshtonoquot and his followers, most Chippewas and Munsees seemed unaware that other Indians were rapidly vanishing from the state. Eshtonoquot repeatedly reminded them that the government's civilization program and allotment schemes were the major forces responsible for the loss of Indian lands, and at every opportunity he denounced the citizenship treaty still pending in the United States Senate. Agent Henry W. Martin reported, nevertheless, that most of the "respectable" Indians favored accepting citizenship and ending their tribal status. He regretted, therefore, that a small minority "zealously opposed" to the treaty could hold up Senate ratification.[36]

Events during the winter months of 1866/67 demonstrated the ability of the two bands to withstand pressure and proved crucial to the defense of their homeland. The agent reported that "one of the severest winters we ever had" killed much livestock and caused suffering and "great privations" among the Chippewas and Munsees. Compounding the difficulties, an 1866 federal ruling declared that the Kansas tribes must either become citizens immediately or leave the state.[37] Since the Senate had yet to ratify their 1864 treaty, the two bands found themselves in a dilemma. Although they were adopting white customs, they would not be citizens until the Senate acted. Romig and the agent, recognizing the opportunity to acquire more land for white interests, pressured the Indians to sell their farms and move to Indian Territory.

Faced with such momentous problems, the two bands might have engaged in their usual disputes and factionalism, but instead they cooperated as never before. On January 11, 1867, the McCoonse-led council informed Romig and Martin that the Indians desired citizenship, but they were determined to retain their Kansas homes. Eight days later, Eshtonoquot joined the council in petitioning against removal. Still opposed to citizenship but not wanting to lose his home, Eshtonoquot rallied to the side of his erstwhile detractors. His people were hardworking, quiet, and peaceful neighbors to the whites, he declared, and they should not have to leave. He denounced the removal advocates, who "never had the good of the tribe at heart."[38] The council's stance was further strengthened by a favorable summer growing season that allowed the Indians to raise an abundant crop. This alleviated suffering and reduced their dependency on governmental aid, enabling them to face future challenges on a better footing. As 1867 drew to a close, the Indians appeared ready to resist all efforts to expel them from the state.[39]

On January 29, 1868, Eshtonoquot died. This misfortune deprived the Indians of their most articulate opponent of removal and jeopardized their struggle to save their homeland. Romig reported with some satisfaction that his adversary, "who was so long a source of trouble to his people and to the church here," had passed away. "He died as he lived," the missionary intoned, "an ignorant heathen and a Catholic." With Eshtonoquot gone, Romig stepped up his campaign to force the bands to move. He was now confident that they would leave Kansas as soon as favorable terms could be arranged with the government.[40]

By late spring of 1868, most of the neighboring bands had agreed to emigrate to Indian Territory. Romig pointed out to superiors that the Delawares had left their reservation, the Ottawas were moving "as fast as they can sell out," and the Sacs and Foxes would leave as soon as Congress ratified their treaty. The missionary wished that some settlement could be worked out before his Indians were left alone. His hopes were apparently realized on June 1, when federal officials signed a new agreement with the Chippewas and Munsees.[41]

The treaty stipulated that individual Indians would receive patents in fee simple, or titles, to their own allotments. Each could sell his holding without consulting the tribe and could move from Kansas whenever he wished. Similar agreements in which other tribes had given up authority over their members had proven disastrous, for they were unable to prevent unscrupulous whites from pressuring individuals into selling their farms. Determined to force their people to move, Chippewa Chiefs Edward McCoonse and Lewis Gokey agreed to ally their band with the Ottawas, then in the process of moving to Indian Territory. Although the two leaders agreed to pay seven thousand dollars for the right to live with the Ottawas in Indian Territory, their true intentions in this matter are unclear. It is clear, however, that McCoonse and Gokey expected to profit from the sale of the band's Kansas holdings.[42]

Certain that his charges would soon be leaving the state, a delighted Romig informed Moravian officials that some of the Munsees had made arrangements to settle among the Cherokees in Indian Territory. But while the Senate again delayed consideration of their latest treaty, the Indians found themselves without effective spokesmen.[43] After Eshtonoquot's death, leadership of the tribes had passed into the hands of less capable councilmen. The positions on removal taken by these members were based mainly on opportunities for personal financial gain.

Deprived of effective leadership and believing they might be forced to move soon, the Indians saw little reason to make repairs on their homes or to plant crops. The confusing state of affairs demoralized some and angered many. A few found solace in alcohol; others resorted to violence. Romig noted with regret "the growing evil of intemperance among our own and other Indians, threatening to destroy their soul and body." When some young men persisted in disturbing the peace and terrorizing law-abiding families, Romig denounced the federal annuity system, declaring that "the sooner all the Indians are removed and compelled by necessity to labor for their daily bread, the better it will be for them temporally and spiritually."[44] His frustration had evidently caused Romig to forget that both Indian bands had labored long and hard to make a living in Kansas. The annuity system had nothing to do with their current situation. He also ignored the fact that annuity payments were not governmental welfare but rather money still owed to the Indians for previous land sales.

When most of the neighboring Sacs and Foxes, with the exception of Mokohoko's small band, emigrated south in November 1869, the tiny group of Chippewas and Munsees stood virtually alone amid a sea of white faces. Along with several hundred Kickapoos, Potawatomis, Iowas, and Sacs and a scattering of others, they were the only former eastern Indians left in Kansas. Pressures on those remaining intensified as citizens, politicians, and the press all clamored to have them expelled.

But by late 1869 most Chippewas and Munsees had made individual commitments to hold on to their homes at all costs. Members of both bands now saw acceptance of citizenship as the key to survival; however, a majority would no longer heed the advice of councilmen, missionaries, or agents—they would decide for themselves whether to move or to stay. Their feelings were stated best by Commissioner of Indian Affairs Ely Parker, himself an acculturated Seneca, when he reported that the two bands were "well advanced in civilization, cultivating small farms, dwelling in good houses, and interested in the education of their children. They have no desire to move, and will, no doubt, soon become citizens."[45]

Despite such official support, the unstable situation of the Chippewas and Munsees extended into the 1870s. Although Romig continued to urge them to sell their farms and move, fewer and fewer listened to his advice. Blaming their "unsettled state of minds relative to their anticipated removal" for their indifference, Romig alleged that "certain enemies of the church" had created an atmosphere of "prejudice" against him. Although most Chippewas had always resented Romig, many Munsees now sided against him as well. Realizing that his influence had waned, the missionary blamed his failure on the Indians' laziness and alcohol abuse, which he claimed had made a shambles of his conversion efforts. "When we look for grapes behold sour grapes," Romig lamented; "some who promised fair and walked well are trapped by the monster intemperance."[46]

Indeed, the changing circumstances that had demanded constant readjustment over the years had demoralized some Indians. A few had "yielded to evil influences and temptations thrown in their way," and missionary reports of the late 1860s made more mention of alcohol abuse than previously. Disease also took its toll. In 1870 Romig noted that "fifty or more" had died since his arrival in the state. Although this was an exaggeration, the combined membership of the two bands had dropped from eighty-four in 1867 to sixty-three just three years later. Some may have moved to Indian Territory, but a physician examining health conditions among Indians in the area noted that the two bands were "diminishing in part from the remains of a syphilitic disease." The doctor warned that unless they were relocated closer to other tribes, they would soon die out. "Constant intermarriage in so narrow a circle," he observed, "tends to a constant physical deterioration."[47]

Against such odds, the Chippewas and Munsees remained in Kansas. After 1870 they outwardly traveled white society's road, and at the time of Romig's departure early in the decade, most professed Christianity.[48] Although Moravians continued to labor among them, the Indians rarely consulted the missionaries on secular matters. Moravian missionary C. R. Kinsey complained in 1881 that it was "impossible to do much under present circumstances," but he hoped that the children might be "kept from falling into the vicious practices" of the majority of adult Indians.[49] The missionaries seemed unable to realize that as the Indians took on the trappings of white society, they would also take on those less desirable characteristics of rural America. The reality of everyday life was far from the moral perfection the missionaries had envisioned for their charges.

The Indians' own ways, however far from perfect, served them well. Members of both bands replaced their traditional garments with trousers and shirts, dresses and petticoats. "The women are as neatly attired as the same number of white women collected in the country," noted one admiring visitor.[50] Although most Chippewas and Munsees had spoken only their native tongue in the 1850s, by the turn of the century most spoke English (their native languages would soon be forgotten). Like their white neighbors, they owned and tended small farms. They could sell their land if they pleased, because the allotment process had removed them from tribal authority; but most steadfastly refused to part with their holdings.[51] Of the thousands of Indians in Kansas subjected to Manypenny's treaties in the 1850s, the Chippewas and Munsees were among the few who remained in the state at the end of the century. Among those bands who voluntarily surrendered their tribal status, they alone managed to stand their ground.

5

THE IOWAS AND
THE MISSOURI SACS

On September 17, 1836, the Iowas and the Missouri Sacs agreed by treaty to exchange their lands in the triangle-shaped region of northwest Missouri for small reservations in Kansas.[1] The two bands, longtime residents of the Little Platte River region, stood in the way of the advancing farming frontier. The 1836 Platte Purchase had given their lands to the state of Missouri and left the Indians with no alternative but to move, since whites considered them unfit to associate with civilized society. "The villages presented each day a scene of drunkeness [sic] and riot," reported Agent Andrew Hughes just prior to the Indians' removal. White settlers, who barely tolerated quiet Indians such as the Chippewas, Munsees, and Vermillion Kickapoos, were horrified by the customs and behavior of the Iowas and Sacs. Indeed, as the least acculturated of all Indian emigrants to Kansas, they would have to modify their ways greatly in order to survive.[2]

Despite their seeming lack of sophistication and an initial refusal to adopt white ways, the Iowas and Sacs would manage to retain a portion of their new lands. Even though their methods differed from those of the Chippewas and Munsees, who sought assimilation into American society, the Iowas and Sacs were just as successful.

Steadfastly traditional in their own way of life until they were surrounded by white farmers in the late 1850s, the Iowas and Sacs were obliged to adjust to changing conditions. They discarded old customs and adopted new ones when necessary, but usually on their own initiative and terms. They considered and sometimes followed the advice of Indian agents and missionaries, but resisted land allotment and other civilization efforts. Although most were eventually forced to accept individually owned family farms, members of both bands rebuffed all efforts to move them to Indian Territory.

The Iowas and Sacs, unlike many frontier bands, displayed little animosity toward whites, preferring only to remain isolated from them. When settlers first invaded their original eastern lands following the Revolutionary War, these Indians began moving west. Although Americans considered the Iowas enemies during the War of 1812, the tribe avoided violence and contributed little to the British cause. The Missouri Sacs remained neutral during that conflict, as well as during the Black Hawk War of 1832. They often boasted of their refusal to assist Black Hawk, who had led the Mississippi Sacs in a disastrous attempt to reclaim their Illinois lands. "Towards the whites [the Missouri Sacs] manifest the warmest friendship at all times," Agent William P. Richardson commented, "and I am fully persuaded they are as sincerely the friends of the white man as any Indians living on our borders."[3]

By the 1820s, the Iowas and the Missouri Sacs had settled in the Little Platte Valley east of the Missouri River. These bands had lived in proximity to each other for many years and, although culturally different, they had formed a loose alliance. The Iowas spoke a Siouan language and were culturally related to the Otoes, Poncas, Kaws, and Osages. Whites found the Iowa social and political structures difficult to decipher.

The tribe was divided into two clan divisions, or phratries; each division consisted of several clans and subclans. The Black Bear clan led the first division, which also included the Wolf, the Eagle and Thunder, the Elk, and the Beaver clans; this division was responsible for planning the winter hunt and other winter and early spring activities. During the winter, the principal chief of the tribe came from the Bear clan. The Buffalo, Pigeon, Snake, and Owl clans made up the second division, which was responsible for agriculture and for planning the spring, summer, and fall events. The Buffalo clan chose the principal summer chief of the tribe. Although leadership positions within the tribe were hereditary, as with most other tribes, important decisions were reached through consensus; a chief's power was not absolute.[4]

Traditionally, the Iowas had lived in villages and planted corn, beans, pumpkins, and other crops; but they also hunted deer and other game. Excellent craftsmen, they made pottery, utensils, weapons, and religious objects out of local materials. From Algonquian neighbors such as the Sacs, they had learned to weave cloth of basswood or cedar fibers.

The Sacs spoke an Algonquian dialect and were culturally related to the Foxes, Kickapoos, and Potawatomis. They lived in villages, constructing their wickiups of branches and bark and covering them with rushes that grew along the rivers. The women tended crops while the men hunted and defended against enemies. Historically, the Sac social organization consisted of several patrilineal clans—for example, the Bear, Sturgeon, Swan, Thunder, and Wolf clans. The principal chief traditionally came from the Sturgeon clan, and lesser chiefs from the other clans; the position of chief was hereditary. The political structure was divided between peace and war organizations. In dealings with federal officials, however, the war chief's influence usually exceeded that of the peace chief.[5]

Many observers considered the Sacs to be less acculturated than the Iowas. Whites familiar with both bands, however, thought that the more aloof Sacs resisted the temptations of frontier society better than the Iowas, who seemed lazy and addicted to whiskey. "The condition of the Iowas is very deplorable," wrote newspaperman Thomas Gladstone. "They lead a life of miserable idleness, wear no dress beyond the blanket, and seem to set no value on efforts made for the amelioration of their condition." Indian Agent David Vanderslice noted that the Sacs were "more provident" than the Iowas and "seldom suffer to the same extent as that tribe." Presbyterian missionary William Hamilton discovered that the Sacs were "a much more independent nation than the Ioways, and I think not so degraded." Hamilton admired the Sacs, even though they practiced their "superstitious rites" and refused "to forsake heathenism."[6]

Most outsiders believed that the Sacs as well as the Iowas were unwilling to change their customs. But by the 1820s both bands had modified their traditional ways, adopting many characteristics of the Plains Indians. Like the Plains tribes, they hunted buffalo on horseback and made tipis of hides for temporary shelters; hunters were able to move quickly to wherever their scouts found herds. Wearing skins adorned with eagle feathers, they performed the Buffalo Dance and other Plains ceremonies in order to make their hunts successful. The Iowa and Sac warriors, like those of the Potawatomis and other immigrants to Kansas, defended their villages from marauding Plains Indians, and young men won prestige by stealing horses and raiding the camps of the Pawnees and other tribal enemies.

When he visited the Iowas and Sacs in the mid-1840s, Swiss artist Rudolph Friederich Kurz noted that their "stalwart forms, the race color, their tents of skins, their dances and games, their family life, all conform to our traditional conception of the Indian." Iowa men fastened eagle feathers to their braided hair; women adorned their heads with "varicolored or else richly embroidered" cloth. Most Sac men shaved all but "a tuft or brush" of hair from the back of the head, but others had long hair decorated with various trinkets. Both bands wore breechcloths, blankets, and beaded moccasins as well as jewelry and bear-claw necklaces.[7]

Many whites called the Indian immigrants "murderous savages" because of their reputation for swift and merciless retaliation against enemies. When Sioux and Pawnee warriors stole their horses or attacked their hunting parties, the Iowas and Sacs joined forces with the Prairie Potawatomis and others to seek revenge. Because they possessed rifles and employed modern military methods, the Iowas, Sacs, Potawatomis, and Kickapoos usually prevailed against the nomadic Plains tribes, who were still armed mainly with bows and arrows. Returning to their villages, the victors performed the traditional scalp dance—a custom that horrified whites. "Since their return [the Iowas] have indulged in the most extravigant [sic] and disgusting manifestation of riot and rejoicing over the scalps of the slain," lamented an observer of one such celebration.[8]

Although the Indians continued to engage in such practices, they had not returned to these "ancient" customs or lapsed into "cultural regression" because of their removal to Kansas. They had never abandoned the Scalp Dance, the Bear and Otter dances, or many of their other traditional ceremonies. Even though the Sacs, Iowas, Potawatomis, and others had long been acculturated, like virtually every other immigrant group in American history, they clung proudly to many of their native traditions. It was true that their warriors gave no quarter to marauding enemies, but neither did whites in similar situations. Agent William Richardson recognized such measures as frontier justice, inevitable in the absence of formal legal recourse. After the Sacs had killed eight Pawnee horse thieves, Richardson pointed out that "white men would have done no less" under the circumstances.[9]

When the Iowas and Sacs emigrated to their new reservations west of the Missouri in June 1837, they were joined by kinfolk of both bands who had moved into the region years earlier to hunt game and to plant crops. Agent Andrew Hughes reported in March 1838 that the earlier settlers had "been scattered in small hunting parties for many years, and having seen their brethren permanently settled they have . . . claimed that they should be fed."[10] Hughes provided for their needs, and

Nesourquoit, a Missouri Sac warrior who worked against Indian agents and missionaries intent on changing the customs of his people. (Courtesy of the Denver Art Museum)

the recently arrived Iowas and Sacs welcomed the reunion with their kinfolk. Among the old settlers was Nesourquoit, a Sac warrior of the Bear clan, who was determined that his people adhere to their customs and religion. Like Eshtonoquot of the Chippewas, Nesourquoit resented white interference in tribal affairs and resisted efforts to usurp Indian lands. His example eventually inspired members of both bands to defy attempts to expel them from Kansas.

Although the Iowa and Sac immigrants warmly accepted their kin-folk back into the fold, they were less enthusiastic in their reception of Christian missionaries. Just prior to the Indians' removal to Kansas, the Reverend Aurey Ballard had urged his fellow Presbyterians to act quickly in building a mission on the new lands. "The Catholics are establishing themselves amongst the Kickapoos," he warned, "and I expect there will be efforts made by the french [*sic*] to get them to visit our Indians." By the autumn of 1838, Presbyterians William Hamilton and Samuel Irvin, certain that God had commanded them to proselytize among the Iowas and Sacs, had answered their denomination's call to minister to "these poor creatures." Hamilton expressed their feelings most emphatically: "Oh! my dear brother, if God permit me to instruct these poor heathen, and point them to Jesus, I shall be satisfied."[11]

But the Indians had little desire to be pointed toward Jesus, for they had practiced their own religions for centuries and had no intention of abandoning them. "Their ceremonies are taught from father to son," the Presbyterians determined, "and they have not been altered in the least, for at least many generations. They neither add nor diminish from these, nor does it appear that they are in the habit of forming new ones."[12]

Irvin and Hamilton reported that although the Sacs "utterly re-fused" to have anything to do with them, the Iowas at least believed that God, or "Grandfather," had created the earth and all things in the world. Convinced that if these Indians were taught English they would understand the Scriptures and become Christians, the white men estab-lished a mission and school on Iowa lands. Comforted by the conviction that they were doing God's work, the preachers were little concerned that most Iowas followed the advice of White Cloud and the war chief, Neumonya, traditionalists firmly opposed to missionary activity. The principal adviser to the chiefs was the more amenable No Heart, who tolerated the Presbyterians and on occasion even attended their services. The missionaries were thrilled in February 1839 when No Heart encouraged many Iowas to announce: "Our children know enough of Indian already [and] we wish them to learn English and become white men."[13]

In most respects, the Presbyterian station was typical of Protestant and Catholic missions in Kansas. Irvin and Hamilton held church services for the Indians, often traveling many miles to scattered locations on the Iowa and Sac reservations. Throughout the 1840s they endeavored to teach Indian children to read and write, and in 1844 they built a manual labor school with tribal education funds provided under the removal treaties.[14]

The missionaries insisted on locating the school on the reservation despite their fears of possible harmful effects on the children, who must continually witness "the degrading and soul sickening conduct of heathen parents and companions." They hoped that if the children became God-fearing, educated citizens, they would serve as models for their pagan elders. "Let religion and education duly balanced and fruitfully cherished be assiduously cultivated among them," Irvin advised, "and soon they will stand up by us and among us [as] the proudest trophies of scientifick [sic] and moral industry."[15]

The Presbyterians were shocked to discover how difficult their task would be when their prospective converts displayed "an innate independency of spirit, which . . . renders them averse to the direction and control of others." Because the Sacs obstinately rejected every overture, the missionaries directed most of their attention to the more amenable Iowas. But even they resisted conversion efforts. The Iowas were "in almost every respect, destitute of any proper mental, moral, or physical culture, and far sunken in vice and superstition," the preachers lamented. Irvin and Hamilton denigrated Iowa customs and watched disapprovingly when "the old father of ceremonies" tattooed the foreheads of young girls. That these tattoos were marks of distinction for an honored few in the highly structured Iowa caste system failed to impress the missionaries. They were determined to destroy tribal culture and were certain that teaching Indians the basic skills of white education while inculcating the virtues of farming and individual land ownership would induce them to become assimilated citizens.[16]

Both bands ignored the teachings of the Gospel, however, and few of the Indians ever attended church services. The Iowas consented to send only orphans of mixed Indian and white parentage to the Presbyterian school; the Sacs refused to allow any of their children to attend. The preachers blamed Nesourquoit for what they regarded as the Sacs' "very great prejudice against the truth." As for the outwardly agreeable Iowas, it seemed to Hamilton "as if the prince of darkness was mustering all his forces to keep this people, not only in their present and degraded condition, but to sink them still lower in vice and filthiness of every kind."[17]

Despite their failure to win converts, the ever-optimistic Presbyterians consoled themselves that the "seeds of divine truth may lie as safely under an Indian blanket or in a smoky wigwam as in the splendid mansion." Although both bands insisted on celebrating the Green Corn Dance and living in "heathen licentiousness," the missionaries had undiminished faith that they would eventually succeed in giving their wards a correct "knowledge of themselves and of the savior."[18]

Throughout the 1840s, however, the Iowas and Sacs rebuffed all attempts to convert them. Indian boys often stopped by the mission to ask for fish hooks and other useful objects but showed no enthusiasm for schooling or the Bible. Although some children attended classes, they were more often interested in the presents Irvin distributed than in learning to read and write. "They are taking offence because I do not give more clothes or greater rewards for learning," he complained.[19]

Irvin found the adults even more difficult. "No regard is paid to the Sabbath day even by those who know better," he informed church officials. While Irvin and Hamilton tried to preach in the villages on Sundays, the inhabitants gambled, drank, and "smoked horses" (traded) with the neighboring Kickapoos and Potawatomis; such activities left little time for church services. On one occasion, some Iowas allowed the missionaries to speak during a feast. "But before [the] meeting was over," wrote Irvin, "not one [Indian] was left of those who were there at the beginning except two who were asleep. This is trying." Their own failure to learn Indian languages, furthermore, forced the missionaries to rely on others to deliver sermons, and the Indians had little respect for those unable to speak their language. "They were disposed to laugh and make sport particularly of Nancy our interpreter," Irvin reported after one service. "They did so bad that she became discouraged and would not or rather could not interpret."[20]

The Presbyterians were constantly frustrated because the Indians clung to tribal customs and religious practices that differed radically from Christianity. When the preachers extolled the virtues of the Bible, the Indians retorted that their medicine bundles, or sacred packs, served them better than the white man's book. "They hold the medicine bag very sacred," Hamilton wrote church officials. "It is always hung up by their lodge." Irvin provided a detailed description of a medicine bundle. "It is a small portable budget [bag or pouch]," he noted, "made up of a number of roots, in which they suppose there is medical virtue, pieces of scalps which have been taken in battle, hieroglyptick [sic] representations of ancestors, [and] their great deeds." These were wrapped together in a "convenient bundle" that leaders of war parties always carried.[21]

After one of Hamilton's sermons, an Iowa questioned the need for the Bible and pointed out that his medicine bundle had always protected him in battle. He offered to "read" or interpret it for a fee, but the missionary refused, saying that "God's gifts were free." On another occasion, an elderly Iowa named Caramonya scolded Hamilton for shooting a weasel, an animal the Indians considered sacred. "To make it good medicine, it must be choked to death," Caramonya explained. If that had been done he could have put the skin in his medicine bundle and gone to war fearing nothing. He added that he had often carried his grandfather's old weasel skin into battle, and although six enemies had shot him, the bullets had failed to penetrate his skin. He was certain that the Bible's powers could not be as effective as that.[22]

The missionaries felt helpless when the Indians rejected their advice and went to war against enemies, as in the spring of 1841 when the Iowas and Sacs joined forces with the Prairie Potawatomis against Sioux and Pawnee marauders. When news that the warriors had killed nine Pawnees reached the reservations on April 21, Irvin was sickened by the "wonderful effect" it had on the Indians. "Their minds were excited, and all labour except feasting and dancing were suspended for near a week," the missionary noted. He was horrified that many of the boys had been taken to the scene of the battle, where they "distinguished themselves by striking the dead bodies of the Pawnees which still lay on the open prairie." One youth proudly displayed a severed Pawnee thumb he had taken as a trophy; most had eaten the flesh of the fallen victims. A tribal elder solemnly informed Irvin that having performed these rites the boys could thereafter go to war without fear.[23]

The Presbyterians were as unsuccessful in teaching Christian ideals as they were in changing tribal attitudes toward war. Concepts such as sin and spiritual retribution were completely alien to tribal thought, but the inquiries Irvin and Hamilton received about hell revealed the Indians' belief that all persons would eventually be reunited with their ancestors in the afterlife. Both the Iowas and Sacs scoffed at the threat that God would send sinners "down to the great fire." One woman informed Irvin that she often fell into fire but had always managed to get out. On another occasion Hamilton, after preaching at length to an attentive audience about fire and brimstone, congratulated himself that the Indians now understood the consequences of sin. But his smile became a frown when an Indian innocently inquired: "Does the devil put the wood on the fire in hell?" His frown deepened when another man wondered whether, if he should climb part of the way to heaven and then fall, "would it not kill him?"[24]

An Iowa named Wawpash informed Irvin that after death Indians made a four-day journey toward the rising sun to reach heaven, which was not far from the headwaters of the Mississippi River. When an incredulous Irvin inquired how infants and the elderly could make such an arduous journey, Wawpash replied that those at the "Big Village" always knew "when persons died and would come and carry them away." They sent horses to carry large or heavy persons to the Big Village. "They have horses plenty and fine grass for them to live upon," Wawpash explained. All "infirmities would be healed in that village," he added. The blind would receive new eyes, for "they had plenty of good eyes there." The good people who went there never died again, but bad ones died three or four times and then turned into birds. When Irvin asked why he did not go there now, the Iowa answered patiently as if explaining to a child: "None go there until after they die."[25]

The Presbyterians scoffed at such beliefs as the superstitions of aborigines, referring to the Indian religious practices as "ancient Idolatrous ceremonies, some of which are childlike and ridiculous." Indians who clung to traditional ways and resisted conversion efforts frustrated the missionaries, who were bewildered at how to counter such stubbornness. "The past is dark, the future *often* appears gloomy," Hamilton admitted. Despite the obstacles, the missionaries trudged on, convinced that time and God were on their side. They ignored threats by White Cloud and Nesourquoit to force them off the reservation, and they were encouraged after a few Iowa children began attending school during the late 1840s.[26]

By then, however, the missionaries could no longer pretend that their efforts to bring about a cultural revolution among the Iowas and Sacs had been anything but a failure. Although No Heart and subsequent chiefs remained on friendly terms with the preachers, the Iowas rejected Christianity. Refusing to live in government-built log cabins, the Iowas, like the Sacs, erected their traditional bark wickiups miles from the mission. When the missionaries ventured out to proselytize, they were often greeted with the refrain, "Our house is empty," and ordered to leave. Only a few orphaned Indian children attended the mission school, and the many years of conversion efforts had reaped a minuscule harvest—one young Iowa girl adopted by Irvin and his wife.[27]

Agent David Vanderslice felt pity for the missionaries, who "devoted the prime of manhood and labored on until old age or death removed them from the stage of action, to Christianize the remnant of a once numerous and powerful people." Vanderslice suggested that governmental employees take complete charge and transform the Indians into yeoman farmers, for only then would they become God-fearing citizens. A visiting Presbyterian minister, Edward McKinney, concluded that although the Iowas had allowed them to preach, it was obvious that Irvin and Hamilton were wasting their time. "The Gospel has not yet obtained any trophies among these people," McKinney mourned, "and to the eye of man there seems to be no prospect of any important change for the better, especially in the case of the adult Indians."[28]

Such assessments were indeed accurate. Stolidly clinging to their traditional religions, the Indians took advantage of the preachers, who not only provided food, clothing, and medicines but also served without reward as doctors and legal advisers to the tribes. Irvin and Hamilton were increasingly distressed by their inability to persuade the Indians to accept Christianity and white civilization. Despite the righteousness of their cause, even they doubted that their endeavors were of any value. The reason for their failure should have been apparent. The more traditional factions dominated both bands throughout the 1840s and early 1850s, and Iowa and Sac leaders, much like the prophet Kenekuk, effectively counteracted efforts to Christianize and assimilate their people. The Indians, noted Hamilton, had fallen "under the influence of those who neither fear God nor regard man."[29]

The war chief, Nesourquoit, was the main spokesman for the approximately six hundred fifty Sacs who refused to have anything to do with the missionaries. Although many Iowas listened to the advice of No Heart and at least tolerated the white men, the traditionalist majority of the six-hundred-member band followed Neumonya, the war chief and tribal spokesman, and the obstinate White Cloud in avoiding the Presbyterians. Even No Heart preferred the customary ways and frequently denied missionary requests for permission to preach in the villages.

Maintaining their customs throughout the 1840s did not mean that the chiefs were "ignorant savages." They realized that whites would eventually settle and dominate the entire continent, and they prepared for the inevitable. Aware that violence against whites would lead to the loss of their lands and the destruction of their people, they admonished their followers to remain at peace. Upon assuming a position of leadership among the Iowas after his father (the elder White Cloud) was killed by Omaha Indians in 1834, White Cloud had advised his people to become peaceful and industrious. Speaking to the Iowa tribal council, he proclaimed:

> My father . . . taught the lessons of peace, and counselled me not to go to war, except in my own defence. I have made up my mind to listen always to that talk. I have never shed blood; have never taken a scalp, and never will, unless compelled by bad men, in my own defence, and for the protection of my people. I believe the Great Spirit is always angry with men who shed innocent blood. I will live in peace.[30]

In late 1843 White Cloud, Neumonya, and twelve other Iowas traveled to Europe under the auspices of a Presbyterian minister named George H. C. Melody. Arriving in London, the Indians were met by the noted American frontier artist George Catlin, their patron and escort on the European tour. The Iowas performed traditional dances and ceremonies before enthusiastic London audiences at Catlin's Indian Gallery at the Egyptian Hall. In Britain they conferred with the rich and famous, including Benjamin Disraeli. Later they crossed the Channel to France, where they had an audience with King Louis-Philippe at the Tuileries Palace. They strolled the Champs Elysées, visited the Louvre, and greeted such noted Parisians as novelists Victor Hugo and George Sand.[31]

As tribal spokesman, Neumonya thanked the Great Spirit for carrying them safely across "the Great Salt Lake" and showing them the wonders of London. He told listeners that the Indian "modes of life are different. . . . Our dances are quite different, and we are glad that we do not give any offence when we dance them." He observed that their

White Cloud, or Young Mahaska, the Iowa leader—an 1837 painting attributed to artist Charles Bird King. (Courtesy of the Denver Art Museum)

Indian garments, "which are made of skins, are not so fine and beautiful . . . , but they keep us warm, and that we think is a great thing." Although impressed by the wealth and splendor of Europe, the Iowas were shocked by the pervasive poverty they encountered in the major cities.[32]

Despite their awe-inspiring European experience, the Indians were rarely intimidated and made it clear that they preferred their own ways and customs. "We are told that you have your dancing-masters," Neumonya told a Dublin gathering, "but the Great Spirit taught us, and we think we should not change our mode." When two Episcopal clergymen preached the advantages of Christianity, Neumonya replied that their own religion had served them well and they would never abandon it. Although Neumonya agreed that Indians had to live with whites in this world, it pleased him that the Great Spirit had set aside a special place in heaven for Indians. He was appalled that whites had killed the Son of the Great Spirit; "red men, we think, have not yet got to be so wicked as to require that." If Indians were supposed to read the Bible, he wondered why "it don't make good people of the pale faces living all around us? They can all read the Good Book and understand all that the black-coats say, and still we find that they are not so honest and so good a people as our own."[33]

This unusual journey gave the Iowas a greater understanding of the differences between their customs and those of the whites. They returned to Kansas in the fall of 1845 with renewed confidence and the determination to build a secure future for themselves. As white settlers swarmed onto their former lands just across the Missouri River, the Indians realized they would need to modify their traditional ways in order to survive, and they placed a greater emphasis on peace, abstinence, and agriculture. "There was much interest manifested by both men and squaws in their farming operations," reported government-employed farmer Preston Richardson, "and, from what I know of them, much more industry than formerly."[34]

The chiefs of both bands agreed that the Indians must avoid alcohol and become industrious family farmers. Nesourquoit endeavored to keep whiskey traders off the Sac reservation and set an example by his own abstinence. Even though his people continued their annual buffalo hunts, they also cultivated corn, pumpkins, beans, and squash and raised cattle and hogs. Like the Iowas, Sac men played a greater role in agricultural pursuits than before. "There are many of this nation who work during the cropping season, assisting their wives and children in securing their crops," Agent Richardson noted. Agent Alfred Vaughn reported that the Iowas "continue to show every disposition to prevent whiskey being brought amongst them; they are all sober and peacible [*sic*] . . . and show every disposition to stay at home and work."[35]

Their efforts to concentrate on working the land, however, were hindered by frequent raids by enemy marauders. The Pawnees were the most troublesome, stealing horses and attacking Iowa and Sac hunting parties on the prairie. The Iowas were angry that the missionaries seemed oblivious to the danger even after numerous assaults on the villages. On one occasion, four Iowa women confronted Irvin as he taught school. "What are you doing here teaching the children letters when the [P]awnees are so near," they demanded to know. They scolded Irvin for being foolish—he should be out recruiting whites to pursue the Pawnees.[36] Despite the logic of such remarks, the Presbyterians continued to counsel the Iowas to abandon revenge raids and to find peaceful solutions to their problems.

Other whites were less complacent than the missionaries, and travelers in Kansas frequently complained of Pawnee thievery. Newspaperman George W. Kendall's expedition, while camped near the Big Blue River, discovered that "some skulking scoundrel" had stolen a gray gelding during the night. "So far we have seen little of the Pawnees," he informed *New Orleans Picayune* readers, "but the sneaking, thieving rascals have not allowed us to pass through their country without levying their customary toll." Trader James R. Mead reported that it was "as natural for Pawnee Indians to steal as it was for them to eat." All of the Plains Indians hated the Pawnees, Mead noted, and the Kansas tribes frequently joined together to fight against what they called those " 'prowling cowards.' "[37]

By the late 1840s most Sacs and Iowas, threatened by Indian agents with punishment and loss of annuities for fighting the Pawnees, became resigned to the fact that they must accept yet another change in their way of life. Peace with other tribes, they reasoned, was the only option. Nesourquoit informed Agent Vaughn in May 1848 that the Sacs had agreed to smoke the peace pipe with the Pawnees; within a few years Sacs and Pawnees were hunting buffalo together on the western prairie. The Iowas also decided to make peace with their foes. When White Cloud led a war party that killed nine Pawnees on May 15, Neumonya and No Heart chastised him for failing to heed their advice to desist, and they agreed with Vaughn's decision to dismiss him from the government-recognized council.[38]

Although White Cloud retained considerable influence over the Iowas, his fighting days were over. By the time of his death in December 1851, the Iowas and Sacs had nearly abandoned their ancient warrior traditions. They still rejected Christianity and formal schooling, but they realized that white settlers would soon demand their removal again, and they were determined not to give them a plausible justification. Thus Iowa and Sac men and boys, who had traditionally proved their mettle through bravery in battle, began seeking other ways to achieve status in the band. Hunting prowess was a mark of distinction; but as buffalo and other animals became scarce, other ways of earning prestige were needed. Traditional Indian games provided one such avenue for the Iowas and Sacs, as well as for the nearby Kickapoos, Potawatomis, and other immigrant bands.

Entire villages participated in lacrosse games as teams of hundreds fought and clubbed with sticks, or crosses, attempting to hurl a deerskin-covered ball into the opponent's goal. Sometimes chaos reigned as players slashed, kicked, and gouged their adversaries in a mad dash toward the goal. Whites were amazed at the skill and stamina displayed by the players as they struggled for hours, even days, on behalf of their clan, band, or tribe.

Strength and agility were requisites in such a fracas; the weak or injured fell by the wayside. On one occasion, the Prairie Potawatomis challenged the Sacs to prove their skill in lacrosse. A white observer, who failed to record the final result, noted that there were one hundred fifty Indians to a side. "A game of Indian ball is one of the most exciting imaginable," the observer noted, "requiring sometimes five or six hours to determine a game. There is nothing like it among white people. The players strip to the skin, reserving nothing but breechcloths, and each has a scoop, made of twigs, with which a ball is caught and thrown."[39]

Indian women played double-ball, a stickball game in which participants tried to swat a piece of buckskin through their opponent's goal. As with lacrosse, timid souls avoided this game. "That's dangerous too, you know," a Potawatomi woman recalled. "Punch your eyes out. They'll hit you . . . I played that game too, but I quit. It's too bad . . . that's what them old ladies play." Although it was a boisterous and rough game, double-ball could have its lighter moments. "One time, I was watchin' 'em down at the dancing ground," an elderly Indian man remembered. "One of them girls missed that ball and grabbed one of them girl's skirts and ripped it off. Oh boy, that woke 'em up, sitting on the sidelines. Oh, that was something then."[40]

Other activities were somewhat less strenuous than lacrosse and double-ball. Horse racing proved one's skill at riding and offered the Iowas, Sacs, and others opportunities for gambling, a passion of many of

The Indian stickball game as played by Kickapoo women, ca. 1940. (Courtesy of the Kansas State Historical Society)

the Indians of Kansas. John Treat Irving once watched two mounted Indians, "as eager as greyhounds in the leash," waiting for the start of a race. When the signal was given, "there was a hard, quick thumping of heels, against the ribs of the horses," wrote Irving. "The next moment they had vanished from their posts." The riders "whooped and screamed" as their mounts "flew over the ground like lightning . . . both horses seemed to be eaten up by fury, at being driven at such a rate." Crossing the finish line, the winning pony "appeared too angry to enjoy his victory."[41] His triumphant rider, however, no doubt happily accepted the accolades of fellow Indians as well as the winnings from his successful wagers.

Some games may have provided little prestige for the participants, but they gave them pleasure and reinforced their identity as Indians. The men and women of most Kansas bands played cards enthusiastically, often betting everything on a single hand. The Potawatomis were fond of John Eight Ten, a game in which players dealt cards they had hidden in a moccasin; they kept score with corn kernels. Women played the Shaking Dish Game, somewhat similar to dice.[42]

Such pastimes often had more significance than was apparent to the casual observer. Certain ceremonies were required before commencing a game of lacrosse, for example. George Catlin, while visiting the Iowas, noted that the lacrosse players first "invoke the aid of supernatural influence to their respective sides; and for this purpose they give a very pretty dance, in which, as in the Scalp Dance, the women take a part, giving neat and curious effect to the scene."[43]

Irvin and Hamilton once found the Sacs "busily engaged" in the "Mockison [sic] game." This was a serious matter to the Sacs. "They displayed much earnestness and great enthusiasm," the missionaries noted, "the game agitating their bodies and extending their bodies to the utmost." The participants were "painted and dressed in a great variety of forms, and made many strange appearances." The preachers were appalled at the intensity shown by the participants in an activity that "to us appears the height of nonsense."

Without realizing it, the two men had pinpointed the underlying significance of such behavior: The Indians were satisfied with their own customs, which reinforced tribal solidarity. "The poor Indians seem wonderfully contented with their old way of living," the missionaries lamented. "Their prejudices [are] strong and hard to overcome."[44] The ability of the Iowas, Sacs, and other Kansas bands to hold on to those customs, however, was about to face its greatest challenge. By early 1853 it was apparent that the immigrant Indians must sell a portion of their lands to alleviate the growing pressures on them to move. In February, the Iowas asked the Presbyterians for assistance in negotiating a new treaty with Commissioner of Indian Affairs George Manypenny.

Like the Vermillion Kickapoos and several other bands, the Iowas and the Sacs delayed making a final decision on the matter. But by the end of the year, they knew that some action had to be taken. Gold-seekers bound for California were helping themselves to reservation timber and other resources, and squatters had built fences on Indian lands. Political debates over slavery, popular sovereignty, the transcontinental railroad, and the formation of Nebraska Territory raged in Washington. Because of this national agitation, the Indians worried that their welfare was of little concern to federal officials. "The 'Nebraska Meetings' and 'conventions' now going on will doubtless increase the annoyance," Agent Vanderslice reported, "and their effect will be to excite the fears of the Indians."[45]

Commissioner Manypenny attempted to allay the fears of the Iowas and Sacs with assurances that governmental officials would never allow all of their tribal lands to be taken. He warned, however, that the two bands must sell part of their holdings and accept individual family farms. When he broached the subject with the Sacs in September 1853, their spokesman, Moless ("Sturgeon"), wondered why the government "was in so great a hurry to get their lands"; the Indian informed the commissioner that the chiefs wanted to negotiate directly with President Franklin Pierce in Washington. Nesourquoit, meanwhile, insisted that his people had no intention of selling their reservation. "Where shall we go? We know the whole country . . . and we know not of any fit for us to live upon." Despite these concerns, on October 7 the Sac chiefs agreed to sell half of their lands to the government in order to retain the rest. The money received would pay their extensive debts to local traders.[46]

In April 1854, five Sac and four Iowa chiefs accompanied Agent Vanderslice and the delegation of Vermillion Kickapoos to Washington for the finalizing of their respective treaties. Moless, Petaokemah ("Hard Fish"), and Nesourquoit led the Sac party, which also included Nokowat and Mokohoko. Leading the Iowas was No Heart, who according to Irvin, was "still the same honest man and friend to the mission and all whites, but he is failing and [they] must now have a leader." The fate of the Iowas, nevertheless, still rested in the hands of this accommodating old man; both White Cloud and Neumonya had died two years earlier. While he agreed that his people must eventually adopt white ways, No Heart was determined that they would remain in Kansas.[47]

Not surprisingly, greedy whites were equally determined to seize as much Indian land as possible, and they hovered near the reservations like buzzards around a dying cow. Barely a day after the chiefs had departed, Samuel Irvin informed his Presbyterian superiors that the Iowas expected to retain thirty to forty sections of land along the Missouri River. He warned Mission Secretary Walter Lowrie that dishonest traders and agents were plotting to swindle the Indians out of their lands. Seeing the need to act quickly or lose a share of the spoils, Irvin advised Lowrie to go to Washington and acquire title to all the Indian land that he could manage. The government-operated farm of the Sacs would be "the most valuable addition to our farm that could be made," he wrote. The Iowa holdings were also valuable. "The land is well worth ten dollars an acre," he pointed out, "and if you could get the right to enter say half a section at govt. price, when the land comes in market it would be very profitable. See what can be done."[48]

The Iowa and Sac chiefs, meanwhile, arrived in Washington in early May. On May 17, No Heart and the Iowas agreed to relinquish more than half their reservation in exchange for annuities and other incentives. The following day the Sac chiefs signed away half of their reservation.[49]

When news of the treaty agreements reached Kansas, most members of both bands believed that their leaders had made the best deal possible under the circumstances; but not all were satisfied with the new treaties. Several provisions offended the more traditional Indians, especially the donation of a considerable amount of land to the Presbyterians. Not surprisingly, the missionaries had received 480 acres of prime Kansas land from the Iowas and another 160 acres from the Sacs.[50] Their prospects for acquiring additional acreage also looked good: Both treaties allowed individual Indians to request patents in fee simple to their own farms; "surplus" lands would then be sold to the general public.

Many Iowas and Sacs realized that the sale and allotment of their lands might disrupt tribal cohesiveness and even cause the Indians to move from their homes. Missionaries and agents, on the other hand, seemed unconcerned about the negative consequences of dispossessing the tribes. Samuel Irvin favored the idea of giving each Indian family title to 160 acres and selling what remained of the reservation—a tribe's "surplus" lands—to whites. The Presbyterian recommended paying Indians cash for the land because they would probably "run through it at once and be brought to rely on their own resources as the best way of inculcating habits of industry and economy."[51]

Agent Vanderslice, who had asserted that the missionaries were wasting their efforts trying to Christianize the Iowas and Sacs, urged that the government be more aggressive in instituting the civilization program, and he saw land allotment as the key. "All attempts to Christianize adult Indians without first [placing] them in homes," he wrote, "where each one may call it his own, where he labors as an agriculturalist or a mechanic, have hitherto failed." With this in mind, Vanderslice began a concerted effort to force the Iowas and Sacs as well as the neighboring Kickapoos to allot their reservations.

The agent knew that considerable profits could be made speculating in Indian lands, and over the next several years he took full advantage of his official position among the tribes for this purpose. In June 1854, he became a charter member of the local Whitehead Squatter Association, whose members were anxious to legally verify their individual claims to lands in northeastern Kansas. Vanderslice got his fellow squatters to pass a motion that exempted him and other federal employees from complying with association bylaws that called for members to stake visible markers to claims on the Iowa, Sac, and Kickapoo reservations; such an action was a violation of federal law. Apparently not overly concerned with legal niceties, association members approved the agent's various land claims on the reservations.[52]

Vanderslice's actions caused the Indians considerable annoyance. In December 1854, the nearby Vermillion Kickapoos complained to the commander at Fort Leavenworth that Vanderslice's attempts to force allotment upon them were aimed primarily at enriching the agent. Several Sacs were also displeased. Although Nesourquoit had signed the treaty along with the other Sac chiefs, he now refused to abide by its terms and ignored repeated orders to move his band onto the diminished Sac reservation. Nesourquoit's followers mistrusted Vanderslice and felt betrayed when the agent slighted them in favor of those willing to do his bidding.[53] The dissidents established a village on the Kickapoo reservation and, like Mecina's small group of Kickapoo followers, temporarily disassociated themselves from those seemingly inclined toward adopting the ways of the whites.

The agent now feared that Nesourquoit would try "to thwart the government in its plans for the welfare of the Indians." When the chief encouraged the Sacs to live together in one large village and resist assimilation, Vanderslice advocated forcing individual families to settle on separate parts of the reservation. "It will doubtless render [me] anything but popular with them," he wrote, "but when they see the benefits in the accumulation of property and comforts in their respective homes, their prejudices will give way." Because Nesourquoit and his followers still refused to move, officials illegally withheld their annuities until the Indians "complied" with the recent treaty.[54]

Although the Iowas conformed and relocated on their diminished reservation, Vanderslice fretted that they also seemed to have made little progress toward civilization. He reported that they had misused their new treaty annuities by purchasing guns and ponies to hunt buffalo. "It is true that they have some fine horses," he wrote, "but instead of purchasing good & substantial work horses, they paid from 100$ to 150$ for such as they believed would run well. . . . The incompetency of these people is so manifest, it is almost imperative on the government to treat them as wards."[55]

Although Vanderslice denigrated tribal customs, he grudgingly admired the Sacs for their independent spirit. But he continued to pressure the intractable Nesourquoit to return to the reservation, ignoring the fact that the chief's people received no annuities and lived by their own resourcefulness. To admit that Indians could care for themselves might undermine the agent's authority and lessen opportunities to exploit them.

After resisting for two years, Nesourquoit's people finally gave in to governmental pressures and moved to the reservation in November 1856. They soon regretted their decision. Nesourquoit resented Vanderslice's favoring of chiefs more willing to accommodate the agent and traders. He was also dissatisfied with the location of his new village and angry that the stipends promised him under provisions of the treaty were not being paid.[56]

Early the following year, Nesourquoit sent Joseph Tesson to Washington to complain about the government's failure to abide by the 1854 treaty. A rather notorious character of Winnebago and white descent with ties to dishonest traders, Tesson delivered Nesourquoit's grievances to the commissioner of Indian affairs in March 1857, then returned to Kansas. When federal officials failed to respond, Nesourquoit took matters into his own hands. Without consulting Vanderslice or members of the government-sponsored tribal council, Nesourquoit, Mokohoko, and Tacockah accompanied Tesson and trusted interpreter "Mexican George" Gomez on another trip to Washington in December 1857.[57]

Their unauthorized visit initially caused a minor stir at the Interior Department, but arrangements were made for the Sacs to speak with President James Buchanan on December 31. The meeting in the East Room of the White House proved to be largely ceremonial, for delegates of the Poncas, Pawnees, and Potawatomis, as well as congressmen, foreign ministers, and cabinet officers, were also in attendance. Following a brief speech by the president, the Indians were each permitted only a few words with the chief executive. They later posed for the camera in front of the South Portico, the earliest known photographs of Indians taken at the White House.[58]

A few weeks later Acting Commissioner of Indian Affairs Charles Mix agreed to a more formal conference with the Missouri Sacs. A governmental clerk described their entrance into Mix's office on January 20, 1858: "The chiefs wore red blankets, which in the case of [Nesourquoit] and [Tacockah] were thrown loosely over the left shoulder, leaving the right shoulder and arms bare, and [exposing] clusters of

"Mexican George" Gomez, the interpreter for the Missouri Sacs. (Courtesy of the Kansas State Historical Society)

The earliest known photograph of Indians taken at the White House, December 31, 1857. Among those in attendance were the Missouri Sacs Nesourquoit, Tacockah, and Mokohoko and their interpreter, "Mexican George" Gomez. (Courtesy of the Wichita State University Library)

brass rings which ornamented the same." Nesourquoit wore a bear-claw necklace and in his hair a carved figure of a fish. Even more impressive was Mokohoko ("Jumping Fish"), "an uncommonly fine-featured young man and very stalwart in figure." The Indians looked like "children of nature, 'fresh from the hand of god,'" and their excessive ornamentation showed that they had made little progress in the arts and refinements of civilized life."[59]

The Indians were more sophisticated than the bureaucrats may have thought. Complaining that Sac women and children went hungry while governmental chiefs, traders, and the agent stole their lands and annuities, Nesourquoit refused to be mollified by Mix's patronizing manner. Grasping the commissioner's hand and staring intently into his eyes, the chief demanded that the government live up to its treaty commitments. "We have been treated as wards, as children by the Government, in fact too much so," Nesourquoit fumed. "Not only have we been treated as children and wards, but like negroes."[60]

Mokohoko, whose membership in the Sturgeon clan and leadership abilities would eventually make him a leading chief, reiterated Nesourquoit's words. Obviously excited and perhaps a bit nervous, Mokohoko spoke his mind:

Father, you have listened to what our chief has said. What he told you in a very few words about the poverty of our women and children is true. I am glad, as has already been spoken, that the Great Spirit hears all we say and sees all we do. As we thought that the government had not fulfilled all its stipulations with us in former treaties, we formerly sent a friend here [Tesson] to make every thing straight. But as he did not get all the satisfaction or information required, we have come here on the business, accompanied by our friend, and hope to be more successful this time. We want you to make every thing in the treaties straight, so that we may get something for our women and children, who are poor and in want of your aid.

Father, we felt aggrieved when we saw money which was ours by treaty stipulations go into other hands; and I again repeat what was said by our chief, that you would yourself, if in our situation, complain if money which belonged to you was taken and given to another. We view precisely in that way the taking from us of a portion of our annuities and giving it to others who are not entitled; but now that we are received here, we hope that the government will do us justice in our present business and make everything straight.

This man [pointing to Nesourquoit] has been our chief for years past, and we consider him the principal chief of the tribe; and, feeling grieved at the manner we have been treated at home, and at the manner in which our treaties have been carried out, he has accompanied us here to lay our complaints before you.[61]

Mokohoko concluded by pointing out that their agent had been a disruptive influence in tribal affairs and demanded that Mix dismiss Vanderslice from the federal service. "If he must be an Indian agent," Mokohoko continued, "let him not be for us, but for some other tribe. We do not want him any longer, and he may do for somebody else." The independently minded Mokohoko, who had signed the 1854 treaty along with Nesourquoit, also had had second thoughts about his decision, and he would dedicate the rest of his life to defending the customs and lands of his people from men like Vanderslice.

A week later the delegation again met with Mix, who scolded them for their unauthorized visit to Washington and implied that their complaints were frivolous. When Nesourquoit refused to be more specific in his complaints against the government, Mix grew angry. The chief had fallen under the spell "of bad white men." The commissioner bluntly informed Nesourquoit that "his actions . . . would seem to indicate that he is nothing more than a boy, a little child." Abruptly cutting the conference short, Mix ordered the Sacs to return to their reservation immediately.[62]

The visit to Washington proved a humbling experience for Nesourquoit, convincing him that he must abide by the treaty. Along with the Iowas, he and many Sacs agreed to settle and farm the land; several even began to consider the advantages of holding title to their own farms. When the chief discovered that Joseph Tesson was in league with unscrupulous traders, he severed all ties with him. "My eyes are opened and my ears are unstop[p]ed," Nesourquoit told Vanderslice. "I can now see and hear. While I was blind and deaf I was foolish, and thought he [Tesson] meant us good, but now I can see that what he wanted was to get our property, our money, and our land."[63]

Nesourquoit's eventual decision to cooperate with the agent's civilization program and to accept the government's five-hundred-dollar annual salary as a treaty chief angered many of the more traditional Sacs.[64] By 1860 Mokohoko and about a hundred followers had abandoned their homes to join the Sacs and Foxes of the Mississippi on their lands along the Marais des Cygnes River ninety miles to the south. Their departure left the Missouri Sacs with just over a hundred members; over the past two decades nearly four hundred kinfolk had either succumbed to disease or abandoned the reservation. The Iowa population had also declined; in 1860 only about half of the original six hundred who first settled in Kansas remained.[65]

On the eve of the Civil War, the Missouri Sacs and Iowas began a concerted effort to adapt to their radically altered situation. They were determined to keep their lands and make a living despite all obstacles, and they began taking on the trappings of white society. There was no alternative if they were to retain their lands; as Vanderslice pointed out, their reservations were surrounded by white settlements.[66] Because the Indians owned the finest farmland and timber in the region, whites were eager to dispossess them.

Recognizing their tenuous position, both bands endeavored to win the acceptance of their white neighbors. Both had become resigned to the fact that abandoning their old ways was unavoidable. They could no longer depend on hunting, so they concentrated on agriculture. Farming in Kansas was, however, unpredictable, and after a long drought resulted in a poor autumn harvest in 1860, tribal elders were forced to throw themselves upon the mercy of the federal government.[67] "We can no longer resort to the region of game, being cut off by vast districts intervening and populated by the whites," they told officials in December, "and the range of the Deer, Elk and Buffalo now in the far off plains, mountain slopes & valleys is not accessable [*sic*] to us, because the tribes which inhabit these regions are not only large and powerful, but are hostile to us border tribes." In exchange for larger annuities, the chiefs were willing to surrender more land and even accept individual allotments.[68]

By early 1861, Sac Chiefs Petaokemah, Nesourquoit, and Moless had decided to sell their entire reservation and use the proceeds to buy a portion of the Iowas' holdings. With land prices reportedly as high as twenty-five dollars an acre along the Kansas-Nebraska border, the Indians evidently expected to make substantial profits and pay their debts to local merchants. In March 1861, therefore, the Sacs as well as No Heart, Naggarash, Mahhee, and the other Iowa chiefs assembled at the agency headquarters and signed a new treaty. As an extra incentive for parting with their homes, each Sac chief received legal title to 160 acres of their old lands.[69]

This treaty, more than any other, signaled an end to the old ways for the Sacs and Iowas and, while the country was at war for the next four years, both labored to prove themselves worthy and loyal neighbors to the whites. Although their lands had not yet been officially allotted, families spread out over their 16,000-acre reservation and claimed small plots for their individual farms. In May 1862, Lewis Henry Morgan found that the Iowas had "made great strides in farming, fencing, and raising stock, which if it continues will tend to increase their numbers."

Reports by Indian agents during the war years confirmed Morgan's assessment of the Iowas as well as the Sacs. Both bands supported the Union cause and several young men enlisted in the army. Doing battle with southern secessionists allowed warriors to earn prestige in a way acceptable to their white neighbors. Those who stayed behind remained quiet and avoided antagonizing the local farmers. The Iowas even passed their own laws against alcoholism, and the agent paid Iowa police for flogging violators. Sac Chief Nesourquoit reportedly never drank whiskey and encouraged others to follow his example.[70] After the war, the two bands continued to build their new lives as accepted members of the community. They plowed their small fields and built log cabins; they dressed and acted like typical rural people struggling to make a living as farmers. Like most immigrants involved in the long process of acculturation, however, their old ways persisted for many years.

A local newspaperman, L. J. White, attended an Indian wedding in 1883 and found the Iowas and Sacs attired in traditional dress. "The most fashionable costume," he reported, "was moccasins, leggings with fringes . . . , a breech cloth, loose shirt trimmed with silver breast-plates, and bead garters, silver bracelets, armlets, head bands, bear claw collars, and all the beads they could carry, belts, and ribbons tied in their hair." White was amazed that such a sight was still possible. The Indians lived in a world of their own, he wrote, "every day full of something to occupy your attention, and the rest of the world goes on without even a ripple of interest, and you hardly know where the time goes."[71]

The newspaperman failed to recognize that despite their ceremonial dress, the two bands had changed dramatically over the past half century. Like the Vermillion Kickapoos, the Chippewas, and the Munsees, the Iowas and Sacs had discovered their own practical formula for keeping their homes. They maintained some of their traditions but abandoned those offensive to whites. Their peaceful and unobtrusive ways proved the key to success. "We split off from our people during the Black Hawk War on account of their taking up the tomahawk against the whites," the Sacs had pointed out in 1863, "and have always been a friend to the pale faces, and always been loyal to our Flag, and listened to our Great Father in every thing he says to us."[72]

Although these peaceful Indians eventually surrendered most of their lands, they retained enough to make a living. By the time they accepted individual land allotment in 1887, many of the more traditional tribe members had abandoned the reservations and moved to Oklahoma. But even those who stayed remembered their Sac or Iowa heritage well into the twentieth century. Although some Indians may criticize the Iowa and Sac descendants of those early pioneers for becoming, outwardly at least, imitation white people and abandoning most of their ancient traditions, they maintained their reservations along the Kansas-Nebraska border. Other Indians may have fought to the death in defense of their lands, but most failed and their people suffered as a result. By wisely adapting to conditions beyond their control, the Iowas and the Missouri Sacs avoided a similar fate.

6

"VAGABOND TRESPASSERS": MOKOHOKO'S BAND OF SAC INDIANS

Although the Missouri Sacs, like the Iowas, have remained relatively unknown, their kinfolk, the Sacs and Foxes of the Mississippi, have been the focus of considerable attention.[1] American literature and folklore have centered on the exploits of Black Hawk, who led the Mississippi Sacs in a bloody struggle to reclaim their western Illinois lands. Although the Black Hawk War of 1832 proved disastrous for the Indian participants, Black Hawk himself has been proclaimed a courageous hero by many scholars.

Historian Donald Fixico has recently maintained, however, that Keokuk, Black Hawk's rival for leadership of the Mississippi bands, was the real hero of the Sacs. Advocating peaceful coexistence with whites, Keokuk remained neutral during the 1832 war and afterward saved his people from complete annihilation. He agreed with federal officials that the Indians should abide by their 1804 removal treaty and settle in Iowa. Before his death in 1848, Keokuk consented to another treaty, ceding the Iowa lands for a reservation along the Marais des Cygnes River in eastern Kansas. "Although personal gain motivated Keokuk," writes Fixico, "he probably did more good things for the Sac and Fox than Black Hawk did."[2]

Black Hawk was indeed courageous, but his leadership resulted in the death of many people. Keokuk advocated peaceful relations with whites, but he always seemed eager to exploit his friendships with them. In fact, Keokuk often connived with Indian agents and traders to make quick profits, and he willingly accepted bribes in exchange for tribal lands and resources, hardly a mark of integrity. It is clear that although some of their actions may have been praiseworthy, neither Black Hawk nor Keokuk was truly heroic.

There was one Sac leader, however, who always seemed to place the welfare of his people above his own personal interests. He was Mokohoko, the "fine featured" and "stalwart" man who had once spoken on behalf of the Missouri Sacs before the commissioner of Indian affairs.[3] Although his actions may not have been heroic in the classical sense of the term, Mokohoko was indeed a champion of the Indian cause. A member of the Sturgeon clan, which had traditionally provided the foremost chief of the Sacs, Mokohoko possessed sound leadership abilities. In the early 1860s, he left his home near the Kansas-Nebraska border and assumed a leading role among the Mississippi Sacs and Foxes, living ninety miles to the south in present-day Osage and Franklin counties.

When Keokuk's son, Moses Keokuk, moved the Mississippi bands to Indian Territory in 1869, Mokohoko and over one hundred followers refused to surrender their lands, declaring that leaving Kansas "would be like putting our heads in the mouth[s] of great Bears to be eaten off."[4] Without financial assistance from the federal government, they defied removal attempts, maintaining themselves on small tracts of marginal land while peacefully and unobtrusively working as seasonal farm laborers. Their unwavering determination to hold on to at least a portion of their Kansas holdings rested on Mokohoko's sound leadership.

Although Mokohoko had never been the dominant chief of the Missouri bands, he was intelligent and had endeavored to emulate the methods and actions of tribal elders. He had been a longtime protégé of Nesourquoit, the same Missouri Sac whom federal officials and missionaries had denounced as an "aspiring demagogue."[5] He had twice accompanied Nesourquoit and other Missouri Sac delegates to Washington, gaining valuable insight into the workings of the federal bureaucracy. But unlike his mentor, who eventually caved in to governmental demands, Mokohoko was not mollified by official assurances that his band's rights would be respected. Indeed, his mistrust of whites and their intentions was confirmed during the late 1850s as Indian agents and missionaries pressed forward with the civilization program, and traders continued to cheat the Sacs and Iowas on the Great Nemaha reservations.

With white settlements surrounding their lands, Mokohoko realized that the Missouri Sacs faced an uncertain future. Because the Mississippi Sac bands seemed more stable and secure than his own bands, he decided that the time had come to rejoin those kinfolk to the south. By July 1860 Mokohoko and several followers had merged with Makasawpe's band, whose traditionalist members most likely realized that their aged chief's days were numbered. They would need a capable man to lead them in the difficult years ahead.[6]

Despite his proven leadership abilities and his stature as a member of the Sturgeon clan, Mokohoko would need to win a following at his new location. Ironically, Nesourquoit's decision to sell a considerable portion of the remaining Missouri Sacs' lands contributed to Mokohoko's rise as a chief. On March 6, 1861, Nesourquoit and three others signed a treaty that not only brought the Missouri Sacs much needed annuities but also granted each chief 160 acres of valuable land. Because the chiefs already received a five-hundred-dollar annual salary, it appeared that they had become more interested in their own welfare than in that of their followers.[7] With nowhere else to turn, a number of discontented Indians went south and joined forces with Mokohoko. By the time Makasawpe died shortly thereafter, more than one hundred had moved, and Mokohoko's ascendancy as a chief had been assured.[8]

His rapid rise as leader was not welcomed by everyone on the Marais des Cygnes reservation. As elsewhere in Kansas, Indian agents and missionaries were endeavoring to supplant traditional ways with their own, urging the Sacs and Foxes, the neighboring Chippewas and Munsees, and other bands to accept Christianity, farming, and formal schooling. Most whites naturally praised Indians willing to cooperate and denounced traditionalists such as Mokohoko's followers, who clung to their old ways. Those Sacs "would never have any Missionary among them," recalled settler Cyrus Case, "so their children . . . got no schooling. They were detirmined [sic] to stick to their wild tribal customs." Case admitted, however, that the Sacs "had good moral virtues, and when they sat at my table adopted our ways."[9]

In October 1863 Agent Henry Martin complained that Mokohoko "bids defiance" to education and mission work and "refuses even to live in the house built for him, and pitches his bark wickyup right under the very eves [sic] of the houses." Indeed, most Sacs and Foxes rejected white ways and refused to live in the stone or frame houses. "The Indians didn't want the houses," government-employed stonemason Henry Judd recalled. "They would build fires in the middle of the floor. They would live in their wickyups, stable their ponies in the house and cover the walls with their Indian drawings."[10]

Even though more than half of the approximately seven hundred Sacs and Foxes now considered Mokohoko a leading spokesman, Martin dismissed him from the government-recognized tribal council. The agent assigned to Moses Keokuk (also known as Keokuk) the important function of distributing the semi-annual tribal annuity payments.[11] Predictably, the junior Keokuk made the most of this opportunity to enhance his prestige and to ensure his own profits. Like his father, he readily adapted to the federal bureaucracy. Unlike Mokohoko, he had no hereditary claim to the title of chief; his power lay in his ability to win the recognition of federal officials as a leader to the Indians. Keokuk realized that this government-granted political power was a means to wealth, and by obtaining and selling tribal land allotments in Kansas he made considerable profits.

Mokohoko, on the other hand, generally placed his followers' well-being above his own. By observing the actions of Nesourquoit on the Great Nemaha reserve, he had learned his lessons well; unlike Nesourquoit, however, neither threats nor monetary considerations could induce him to yield to governmental demands. His efforts to protect his people's interests became an unending crusade against federal officials and Indian rivals such as Moses Keokuk.[12]

Complaining bitterly about his dismissal from the tribal council, Mokohoko directed his energies over the next couple of years toward resisting the federal civilization program. He actively lobbied officials to remove Martin as agent to the tribes. When Moses Keokuk journeyed to Washington to defend the agent in the spring of 1866, Mokohoko could hardly conceal his anger. On April 12 he and fifty-one other leading Sac and Fox men sent a harshly worded letter to the commissioner, asking that Keokuk's defense of Martin be ignored and demanding the immediate dismissal of the agent. "Our people feel that in this matter they have been outraged and wronged," the Indians proclaimed. "They know that their Agent is not placed over them for the benefit of any one clique or faction, but for the benefit and welfare of the whole nation." Martin had not been unbiased but had "singled out a chosen few and made *them* the recipients of all the honors and emoluments which it has been in his power to bestow—and no matter what asserting may be made to the contrary, *they do desire* the appointment of an Agent who will deal fairly and impartially with all of our people."[13]

Receiving no immediate reply to their complaints, Mokohoko

stormed off to Washington in May to confront federal policymakers. The nation's capital city held little awe for the experienced Sac chief; his previous visits had given him a sophistication that most other traditional Indians lacked. After consulting a lawyer, he informed Indian Office officials that Agent Martin had removed him from the tribal council because he "would not be mixed up in his schemes to steal the Indians' money." Mokohoko accused the agent, the traders, and Keokuk of conspiring to "wrong us very much."[14]

Fearing that an investigation of the matter would be undertaken, Martin had already rushed to defend himself in Washington. On May 18 he told superiors that Mokohoko had no authority to represent the Indians. "He was at one time a chief," Martin admitted, "and was removed because of his contumacious and most unreasonable and stubborn opposition" to assimilation. "He is opposed to schools, to all religious influences, to holding lands in severalty, to agriculture, to living in houses, to wearing civilized apparel, to all kinds of manual labor, and in short to everything that can be supposed in any manner to tend towards civilization." The agent demanded that Mokohoko be ordered back to Kansas without delay, before the "spirit of insubordination and discontent" spreads to others on the reservation.[15]

Martin knew that he had the support of Moses Keokuk and the other governmental chiefs back in Kansas. But he also realized that those Indians represented a distinct minority of the tribe. Negotiations had been under way for a treaty that would move the Sacs and Foxes to Indian Territory, and Mokohoko's actions threatened to upset those plans. Keokuk and the agent stood to make huge profits from the land sales, and they were unwilling to let the traditionalist factions get in their way. But a July 1866 petition signed by Mokohoko and one hundred forty-five other men complaining about Martin's highly questionable conduct proved hard to counteract—a thorough investigation would have to be made.[16]

Special Agent W. R. Irwin and other officials arrived on the reservation in the fall of 1866 to conduct the inquiry. When Irwin called the Indians together for a council on October 6, Mokohoko informed him that the Indians resented Martin's efforts to steal their lands and change their ways. The Sac leader then vented his anger against Keokuk, who dressed like a white man, sent his children to school, and lived in a government-built house.[17] "It looks a white man's house," he said in disgust. Because of its carpets and fancy furniture, he added, one could not even "spit towards the wall or on the floor."[18]

Although his testimony caused Martin and Keokuk some concern, Mokohoko realized that the investigation would probably end without punitive action against his adversaries. After consulting his followers, he agreed to drop all charges and accepted the offer of recognition as chief with full authority and the payment of expenses for his trip to Washington. The outcome of the incident strengthened Mokohoko's belief that whites had a low opinion of Indians who resisted assimilation; governmental officials rarely ruled in their favor.[19]

His suspicions were confirmed in February 1867 when Martin and others connived with Moses Keokuk to sell the Indians' homeland. Mokohoko was on his winter hunt beyond the Arkansas River and was not consulted about the treaty that would move the Sacs and Foxes to Indian Territory. Special Commissioners Vital Jarrot and Hiram W. Farnsworth informed superiors in Washington that Mokohoko suffered "a bad ulcer on his thigh" and was unable to attend the proceedings. But they both had "not the least doubt that the treaty just made will be satisfactory to all the tribe, Mokohoko included."[20]

They were either naive or less than honest, but even as late as July 1867 the new agent, Albert Wiley, predicted that Mokohoko and his "peaceable, docil [sic], and inoffencive [sic]" followers would comply with the government's wishes.[21] Wiley admitted, however, that Mokohoko, whose followers comprised over half of the Indians, insisted that officials listen to his demands. Increasingly impatient, Mokohoko warned Wiley that there might be trouble, for even "a snake will squirm when tramped upon."[22]

Mokohoko realized, of course, that violence was not a feasible option for small numbers of Indians completely surrounded by white settlements. Until Keokuk's faction moved to Indian Territory, therefore, Mokohoko desperately sought other ways to invalidate the treaty and save the Sac and Fox lands. Like Kenekuk, the Kickapoo prophet, he hoped to maintain the sympathy of the local white community by encouraging his followers to treat even the most offensive settlers kindly. Refusing to acknowledge the legality of the removal treaty, Mokohoko, over the next two years, boycotted council meetings, avoided the agent, and refused to send delegates to select new homes in Indian Territory.

But when his efforts to overturn the treaty seemed hopeless, he finally consented to meet with Central Superintendent of Indian Affairs Enoch Hoag and other officials. Local settler Jabez Adams, Jr., later recounted the details of that meeting of August 19, 1869:

The council was held in an enclosed greensward—embellished by fine shade trees. Besides the Chiefs and Braves whose business it was to be there, it seemed that every indian living on the Reserve was there. Indians formed an inner circle around the officials; whites the outer circle. The ground was covered with people for many rods.

My first surprise that day was the intelligent features of many of the noted indians. In this brief account only two chiefs, Keokuk and Mokohoko, will be mentioned. In symmetry and physique they were perfect. Keokuk fair, almost like a white man; Mokohoko, dark. Their physiognomies beamed with intellectuality and showed strong marks of philanthropy. They were neatly dressed and made a fine appearance before the vast audience. . . .

Keokuk and Mokohoko were the principal orators, and responded promptly when called. With the Sac & Fox Tribe they were the Clay and Webster. For, like them they were noted for their eloquence, and esteemed for their untiring efforts for Right.[23]

Adams was somewhat mistaken about the motives of Keokuk, whose untiring efforts were aimed at negotiating a more favorable land deal for himself in Indian Territory. Keokuk put on quite a show of denouncing the treaty—which he had already signed—before white officials and the Indians. He finally conceded that the Sacs and Foxes would move, but he resented "the Treachery of the Paleface" in forcing Indians out of Kansas.[24]

Following Keokuk's speech, Mokohoko pointed out that he had not been party to the treaty; thus his people would remain in "peaceable possession" of their present homes. With an ironic wit honed by many past encounters with white officials, he continued:

Now my dear people, our noble Keokuk has been persuaded to put his hand to a "Paleface" paper; and they say it gives away our Kansas homes. O, tell me not such sad words! We cannot give up

Mokohoko, leader of the traditionalist Sacs. (Courtesy of the Kansas State Historical Society)

Moses Keokuk. *(Courtesy of the Kansas State Historical Society)*

this happy home we have loved so long. I'll never, never, NEVER put my hand to the paper that says we must leave here!

My own people who follow me shall live here in peace with these good paleface people so long as the moon and stars shine by night and the sun illumes the day.[25]

But Mokohoko lacked the power to stop the federal bureaucracy, which declared the treaty valid. On November 25, 1869, therefore, while whites waited eagerly to claim reservation land, the Sac and Fox emigration from Kansas began. Most of the Fox Indians, weary of feuds between the leaders of the Sac bands and distrustful of Keokuk, decided to join kinfolk who had resettled in Iowa many years before. There they would remain, resisting all attempts to remove them.

Mokohoko had similar plans to defy the authorities, and when several hundred Indians and twenty-nine ox-drawn wagons started the journey south, most of his followers had already left for their annual winter hunt on the western plains. Federal officials expected—or at least hoped—that the Sacs would leave for Indian Territory soon. But Mokohoko refused to abandon Kansas and demanded to speak with the president, who he thought would look sympathetically upon their cause. "Mokohoko declines to go at present," Superintendent Hoag reported that December. "Most of his band are hunting buffalo, and it is thought they will go direct from the plains to their new reservation, south. Mokohoko claims that he is not a party to the late treaty, and expresses a desire to visit his 'great father' in Washington. I am informed that he is operating with the Prairie band of Pottawatomies, and would suggest that an interview with the Commissioner [in Washington] might result in good."[26]

Throughout the following year, the chief remained steadfast in his determination to stay in Kansas, repeatedly disobeying agents' orders to leave and insisting on visiting the president. Attracted by Mokohoko's courageous stand, many Sacs who had already moved to Indian Territory returned to Kansas. Even the loss of federal annuities that this entailed did not prevent their return.[27] Because they had moved onto marginal lands in scattered locations near the Marais des Cygnes, white settlers put little pressure on the peaceful Indians to leave. A valuable asset to farmers in need of cheap labor, the Indians were considered a harmless curiosity bedecked in their ceremonial bear-claw necklaces, colorful robes, beaded moccasins, and jewelry.

In February 1871, Commissioner of Indian Affairs Ely S. Parker granted Mokohoko permission to present his case in Washington. The chief left the following month accompanied by Chippewa leader Edward McCoonse, a trusted friend who was actually allied with white interests. But all attempts by McCoonse and others in the capital to persuade or cajole Mokohoko into leaving Kansas failed. Federal officials asked only that Mokohoko take his followers to Indian Territory "within a reasonable time."[28]

Fortunately for the Sac chief and his followers, federal officials were reluctant to evict them forcibly because President Ulysses S. Grant's Indian Peace Policy was currently in vogue. This program, also known as Grant's Quaker Policy, was a cooperative effort on the part of the federal government and various churches to bring fundamental change to the administration of Indian affairs. Humanitarians who had once fought to abolish slavery now admonished federal policymakers to right the wrongs done to the nation's Indians, and President Grant answered their plea. Grant's plan originally called for appointing Quakers, or Friends, to the Northern and Central superintendencies—parts of Nebraska, Kansas, and Indian Territory—and military officers to the nation's other agencies. Members of Congress, urged on by reformers, rejected this proposal, and as a result representatives of several other religious groups filled the remaining agency assignments.[29]

Shortly after taking office, Grant had appointed Ely Parker, a Tonawanda Seneca and his former aide-de-camp, as commissioner of Indian affairs; under the direction of Parker and subsequent commissioners, Protestant and Catholic church officials nominated Christian superintendents, agents, and teachers to take charge of the reservation system and to hasten the assimilation of the nation's Indians.[30] To facilitate the entire process, the president agreed to the formation of an independent Board of Indian Commissioners, made up of leading Christian reformers who would moniter federal expenditures for Indian affairs and watch over other aspects of Indian policy. Grant and other policymakers hoped that this board, along with the preachers, priests, and other "honest Christians" working on the reservations, would ensure fair treatment for the tribespeople and eliminate the rampant corruption in the Indian service.[31]

Considering the relatively small size of their memberships, both branches of Quakers—Hicksite and Orthodox—played a leading role in the attempt to provide better treatment for the Indians. The Orthodox Quakers took charge of the Central Superintendency, which was headquartered in Lawrence, Kansas, and included Kansas and Indian Territory. These Friends earnestly believed that all humans had the potential to realize God's "universal divine light" and that patience and mildness on the part of Quaker agents would prove successful in civilizing the Indians. In 1869 Enoch Hoag, a self-educated Iowa farmer and former abolitionist, became the first Quaker superintendent at Lawrence.[32] The kindly Hoag, who continually tried to coax Mokohoko's people into leaving the state, was generally unwilling to take decisive action against the stubborn Sacs. Such indecisiveness, as well as the inability to understand tribal customs, contributed to the ultimate failure of efforts by Quakers and other religious denominations to revitalize the Indian service.

The Sacs often took advantage of the Quakers' warmheartedness. When he returned from Washington in the spring of 1871, Mokohoko continually ignored Hoag's orders to emigrate, insisting that the vague instructions issued in the capital allowed his people to remain in Kansas. Indian Office officials had already cut off the Sacs' annuity payments in an effort to force the recalcitrants to leave. Refusing to bow to financial pressure, the Indians survived by their own resourcefulness. They still ventured west to the hunting grounds each winter; but as the buffalo herds diminished during the 1870s, the Sacs had to rely more on smaller game such as deer, rabbits, raccoons, and prairie chickens. Women planted corn in small clearings and gathered nuts and berries along wooded river banks. The people raised dogs for the meat, a delicacy served at the frequent feasts and ceremonies that helped to reinforce tribal cohesiveness. To supplement their hunting, gathering, and planting, the Sacs hired themselves out to settlers in Osage County. The women and children washed clothes, churned butter, tended livestock, and performed other domestic chores; the men split rails, mended fences, made hay, and helped with the harvests.

Local settlers, who had initially demanded that the band be removed, found Mokohoko's Indians to be trustworthy and hardworking. Settler Max Morton recalled that they were always "perfectly honest, no good in threshing, but good workers in cutting and husking corn." When Charlie Cottrell bought a farm near Melvern, Kansas, in the early 1870s, he discovered that his one hundred Indian neighbors were quite an asset. "Of course they could draw no annuities as long as they remained away from their tribe," he remembered, "so they worked for the 'whitey' man, in corn hoeing or corn cutting or husking, they did well, we had them, they were good workers." A local storekeeper reported that the Sacs worked hard and "earned very much more than if they had been with their tribe. I have met bands of 20 or more corn cutters and huskers going to and from work."[33]

The Sacs were always friendly toward whites, who appreciated their kindness, although they sometimes misunderstood their ways. Charlie Cottrell's son Bayard became close friends with an Indian boy named Sioke. "Bayard was shown many tricks of Indian hunting and fishing," his father related. "He was always welcome to their camp. One Sunday morning he went down to their camp, and they insisted that he stay for their dinner. They went so far as to kill a fat puppy for soup. After giving many excuses, he managed to get away."[34]

The Indians were eager to please. The elder Cottrell noted that they "attended all Fourth of July or other big white folks' celebrations, dressed in picturesque garb, partly white and partly Indian folks style." Local resident Elmer Calkins recalled that no celebration "was held near or far by old settlers but there was a good attendance from Indians generally well dressed in a semi-civilized manner."[35]

Although Mokohoko's people often pleaded poverty and asked governmental officials for food and clothing, the income from part-time employment provided for most of their relatively modest needs. They never got federal assistance, but they owned an abundance of ponies, in earlier times a sign of wealth and prestige, and whites who dealt with these "sober and honest" Indians found that "they always had money to spend." Merchant Charlie Cochran recalled that he often saw them at Lemuel Warner's store in Melvern. "I used to trade with them some," Cochran wrote, "and I used to see the old Sac & Fox squaws of Mo ko ho ko's Band trading there [Warner's] a lot; they liked Warner and his wife. They always kept their word with him. The bucks worked out and allowed the squaws to buy living with some of the earnings."[36]

In May 1873 the tribal council members asked permission to return to Washington and restate their case to remain in Kansas. Following the example of the Chippewas and Munsees, the Sacs offered to relinquish their tribal status—to stay in Kansas, they would become citizens, dependent on themselves for survival. It "would be to our permanent good," they declared, "to sever our relations to the tribe and become the adopted children of the United States."[37]

That summer Mokohoko again prodded reluctant officials to allow him to visit the federal capital "to say our sayings, [and] lay our grievances before the department by words of our own mouths and receive an answer . . . as to whether we have any rights for a home here." He was sure that the president would be sympathetic, for had not the "great father" once promised that they "should have this land for [their] home as long as the water run"? Although Mokohoko assured officials that he would accept the president's decision in the matter, neither he nor his followers had any intention of leaving Kansas voluntarily.[38]

Superintendent Hoag believed that Mokohoko's powerful influence was the major obstacle to the Indians' removal, and late in 1873 he granted the chief's request to visit Washington. But Mokohoko was sick and unable to make the journey; he died in January 1874. Fearing that news of his death would accelerate their removal, his followers did their best to conceal it. They never revealed the location of his grave, but they likely honored his request for burial in a timber bottom along the Marais des Cygnes River. "When my life is out," he had instructed them, "wrap me in my blanket, . . . circle around my grave and let my friends and brothers say the last words for Mokohoko."[39]

It was Mokohoko's own last words, not those of his mourners, that had a lasting impact on the Sacs of Kansas. He had admonished them from his deathbed never to abandon their lands and to inform the president about their mistreatment. Sympathetic to Mokohoko's traditionalist views, the Indians were inclined to heed his advice. In November 1874, therefore, council members again won permission to present their case in the capital. Pledging to emigrate peacefully if that should be the president's decision, tribal spokesmen Pawshepawho and Mayapit arrived in Washington early the following year. Keokuk's removal treaty, they declared, "was consummated against our will. We at that time protested and we still protest against said treaty." They asked officials "to let us retain our land and homes in Kansas."[40]

On February 1, 1875, Commissioner of Indian Affairs Edward P. Smith emphatically denied their request. "The question is settled," Smith told them, "if you remain in Kansas you remain without any country. . . . [Y]ou cannot do anything for yourselves so long as you wander about Kansas without any homes." The commissioner tried to appeal to their cupidity by pointing out that both chiefs would receive a five-hundred-dollar yearly salary if they agreed to take their people to Indian Territory. "If I had an offer to go down into the Indian Territory and have a farm, cattle, and $500 a year, and be a King," he intoned, "over against staying in Kansas and being kicked about by everybody and having nothing, and not being a King, I think I should go."[41]

Three days later, the chiefs met with President Grant, who claimed that he lacked the power to allow the tribe to stay in Kansas and warned that they must abide by the treaty.[42] Although Pawshepawho and Mayapit returned to their people without achieving their goal, they resolutely resisted all efforts to remove their tribe. The Sacs would rather be "vagabond trespassers" in Kansas, as officials called them, than "kings" in an alien land.

In November 1875, Superintendent Hoag reluctantly ordered Agent Levi Woodard, a fellow Quaker, to evict the Sacs from Kansas. When Hoag visited them to ask for their cooperation, they bluntly replied: "We don't harbor anything bad. The most we have in our minds is the welfare of our children—we are not going to the Territory. That is all we have to say."[43] But on November 20 Woodard arrived with a detachment of United States infantry to remove them.

The removal proved almost as difficult for the whites as it was for the Indians. Gathering and transporting the tribespeople, whose camps were scattered several miles along the Marais des Cygnes, was a perplexing logistical problem for Woodard and the soldiers. Making matters worse, most of the men had already left for the winter hunt; they had no intention of moving to Indian Territory. Hostility from the forty-five remaining Sacs would have complicated matters even more, but they offered no resistance and willingly helped load the wagons. After the women and children climbed aboard, the chiefs requested that they be allowed to remain behind briefly in order to conduct religious rites.[44] Their houses rested on sacred ground and could not be abandoned without the proper rituals.

After an eighteen-day journey, the Sacs arrived in Indian Territory, where Agent John Pickering attempted to mollify the newcomers. Pickering noted that they seemed "sullen and indifferent, but manifest a feeling of kindness toward their relatives here, and are being better reconciled to their situation." His assessment was far from accurate, however. Agent Woodard reported in March 1876 that Mokohoko's people still refused "to affiliate in any way that will indicate their recognition of [Keokuk's] treaty." By the end of the month, as rumors abounded that they intended to return to Kansas as soon as there was sufficient grass to feed their ponies, George Nicholson, chief clerk of the Central Superintendency, informed Woodard that every effort must be exerted to keep them on the reservation. "If they should leave they will be compelled to return, by force if necessary," wrote Nicholson. "Thou art requested to inform this office of their departure, should they do so, in order that steps may be taken to return them."[45] But these instructions were never acted upon; force was a necessity alien to Nicholson as well as most of his Quaker colleagues.

Some federal policymakers were willing to employ harsh measures to force their will on Indians. But Washington bureaucrats were shocked when a bill for twenty-five hundred dollars arrived for the removal of Mokohoko's band from Kansas. The Indians could have moved themselves much more quickly and economically, as they proved in mid-April 1876 when they packed their belongings and returned to their old homes. There they remained for several more years because officials refused to allocate funds for another costly relocation attempt.[46]

Back in Kansas, the Sacs continued as before, hunting small game and raising corn in isolated plots not wanted by whites. They worked for neighboring Chippewa and white farmers, who, appreciating their services, spoke out on their behalf. Edward McCoonse of the Chippewas beseeched Secretary of the Interior Carl Schurz "to do something for these poor wandering Indians" determined to stay in Kansas "'til they die." McCoonse suggested that the government purchase two sections of land from his band and donate it to the Sacs. Not noted for his philanthropy, the Chippewa was very likely trying to dispose of inferior acreage for a profit.

Local white citizens petitioned Congress in 1879 on behalf of the "industrious and honest" Indians, who "would do well here if they had a section of land." They argued that it was "unjust to force away people from their homes against their will and consent." But their intentions were also questionable—a few offered land for sale and others urged federal officials to pay the band's arrears in annuities, a potential windfall for local merchants.[47] Regardless of the motives behind these recommendations, Mokohoko's people would have been able to remain in the state if federal bureaucrats had approved them. Washington officials, however, were still determined upon removal and ignored all pleas to allow the band to remain. Whether logical or not, decisions had to be carried out regardless of circumstances, and years earlier it had been decided that they must move.

In the East, meanwhile, a heated debate raged between well-meaning humanitarians and the Interior Department over the nation's treatment of Indians. The policy of assigning Quakers and other religious denominations to the Indian service had been largely abandoned by the late 1870s, and officials were groping for a new direction in Indian affairs. The Indian Peace Policy had failed to stem corruption in the Indian service; two of Grant's commissioners of Indian affairs—Ely Parker and Edward P. Smith—had resigned after being accused of questionable dealings. Throughout the 1870s, Indian agents, various federal officials, and governmental contractors had routinely cheated the Indians. The reformer Carl Schurz, who became secretary of the Interior in 1877, discovered the difficulties involved in eliminating corruption when his own commissioner of Indian affairs, Ezra Hayt, was charged with irregularities and had to resign.[48]

Schurz also found himself embroiled in disputes with eastern humanitarians over what direction a new Indian policy should take. The humanitarians focused particular attention on the celebrated *Standing Bear v. Crook* case of 1879. In an effort to retain their Nebraska homes, Ponca Chief Standing Bear and thirty of his followers had offered to sever their relations with the main body of the tribe, which had been transferred to Indian Territory. The Poncas' lawyer had asserted that under the Fourteenth Amendment Indians who surrendered tribal affiliations were free of governmental authority and enjoyed the same rights as white citizens. Acknowledging that he had never been called on to hear a case that appealed so powerfully to his sympathy, United States District Judge Elmer Dundy agreed with the lawyers; he ruled that individual Poncas had an inalienable right to "life, liberty and the pursuit of happiness" and that federal officials could not force them to return to the reservation.[49]

The Ponca trial became a cause célèbre in the East during the early 1880s as philanthropists Helen Hunt Jackson, Wendell Phillips, Herbert Welsh, Sen. Henry L. Dawes, and others stepped up their criticisms of federal Indian policy. The so-called Friends of the Indian, who championed individual land allotment, formal education, Christianity, and citizenship for American Indians, expected Secretary Schurz and federal officials to make broad application of Dundy's ruling. But Washington bureaucrats, although sympathetic to the plight of the tribespeople, refused to permit any other Indians to leave their reservations and lead "wandering vagabond lives" in the nation's territories or states.[50]

The Ponca decision should have given individual Indians the right to choose between affiliation with their tribes or American citizenship; it failed to do so, however. By the mid-1880s, most humanitarian groups were directing their energies toward devising a general allotment act, and they paid little attention to governmental actions against other Indians who attempted to sever relations with their tribes and abandon their reservations.

In September 1886, federal officials finally announced that the Ponca decision did not apply to Mokohoko's people, who must be expelled from Kansas. In a statement that blatantly contradicted the facts, Commissioner of Indian Affairs John D. C. Atkins announced that the Sacs had "no rights" where they were and must be removed for their own benefit, for they were "of the very lowest grade of humanity. [G]rossly ignorant and steeped in superstition . . . they are simply a roving band of ignorant vagabond trespassers, naked and starving, without any means of support whatever, and in fact are in a most deplorable and pitiable condition."[51]

This assessment of Mokohoko's Sacs, as Atkins probably realized, had no basis in reality. Although the Indians adhered to their traditional customs and religion, it would take a narrow-minded man to call them superstitious. They depended on their own resourcefulness to earn their living, not on governmental largess, which was denied them, and they were rather prosperous considering their modest needs. For seventeen years after Keokuk's removal treaty had taken effect, they had defied the authorities. It was Mokohoko's leadership that gave them the strength and courage to persevere. In contrast to Black Hawk's dramatic and seemingly heroic actions, Mokohoko's peaceful stratagems appear cautious and colorless; yet because of them his people remained entrenched for years on lands they did not legally own. Their passive resistance came from inner strength and courage, qualities less conspicuous than heroism on the battlefield but, in this case, more productive of results.

Now, to justify their unwarranted removal from Kansas, Atkins and other officials used the lame excuse that the Indians were "utterly ignorant and devoid of reason" and had been "mere dependents for existence upon the bounty of the Government."[52] Of course, that "bounty" had been cut off seventeen years earlier. Ignoring this fact and insisting that they were a "nuisance to the white settlers," Secretary of the Interior Lucius Q. C. Lamar ordered Inspector E. D. Bannister to remove them. Lamar advised the inspector "to make the Indians feel that they are consenting, though it may be reluctantly, to return to the reservation [and] not that they are being driven there by military force." Bannister, who apparently lacked confidence in his ability to manipulate Indians, ignored the suggestion and requested the Army's assistance.[53]

Although the Sacs were neither "devoid of reason" nor dependent on governmental largess, Lt. John Haines with twelve United States cavalrymen arrived on October 15, 1886, to escort them south. When the removal began about a week later, the Indians again offered little resistance. On the first day of their grim pilgrimage, a few attempted to flee, but the soldiers quickly tracked them down. Many settlers and even the troops were sympathetic to the "crying and weeping" Indians who were forced to abandon their Kansas homes.[54]

Lieutenant Haines reported that although the Indians were "sulky" and "somewhat stubborn" during the two-week journey, they gave him "no trouble whatsoever, being orderly and well behaved in every way." The somewhat perplexed army officer also noted that "these Indians are hardly the 'Ignoran[t] vagabond trespassers, naked and starving without any means of support' as reported" by civilian officials. "The extent of their trespassing," he wrote, "was living on a narrow strip of land on the river-bank about twenty yards wide, and using a private road to reach this land." When they stopped at the various towns on their trek south, furthermore, they paid for their own provisions, refusing to accept any money from Inspector Bannister.

Unlike most governmental officials who decided Indian policy from behind desks in Washington, Haines evidently had much firsthand experience. He knew the difference between poor, naked tribespeople and prosperous " 'blanket' Indians" such as Mokohoko's band. From many local settlers he learned that the Indians were not considered a nuisance, had "never been known to steal, and have been honest and straightforward in all their dealings, and with few exceptions the people in this neighborhood were sorry to see them go."[55]

Arriving in Indian Territory on November 5, Pawshepawho and the

Pawshepawho, successor of Mokohoko. (Courtesy of the Kansas State Historical Society)

other chiefs advised their followers not to accept annuity money from the authorities. When they refused to cooperate with the inspector and the agent attempting to settle them on their new lands, Capt. Edward M. "Jack" Hayes arrested Pawshepawho and a few of his "most stubborn" supporters. "Persuasions, arguments, appeals to their interests,

[and] threats had no effect on them," Hayes informed superiors, "and, as a last resort, it was decided to try severe treatment." Although the army officer reported that "the Indians were in a bad frame of mind" and capable of violence, after four days in the army guardhouse they relented and agreed to settle peacefully on their new lands.[56]

Like Mokohoko before them, the chiefs understood the futility of violence and sought other solutions to their problems. They again demanded the right to argue their case in Washington; but, although Pawshepawho and six others visited the capital in February 1887, their pleas were in vain.[57] They returned in March, defeated but still determined to maintain their traditional ways in Indian Territory. Although the land was soon to be distributed in individual family allotments, they insisted upon tribal ownership and erected fences to separate themselves from Keokuk's people. For years they remained aloof from outsiders and clung to their traditional ways.[58]

Even though their strategies resembled those of the Vermillion Kickapoos and others who managed to remain in Kansas, Mokohoko's people were forced to move to Indian Territory. Like Kenekuk of the Kickapoos, Mokohoko had advised his people to work hard and to remain at peace with their white neighbors. They had readily accepted a new economic outlook when survival made it necessary to work for white farmers, but they clung to their traditional ways in most other respects. In Mokohoko they had a leader who eloquently and forcefully voiced their traditionalist views, and his legacy of intractability in the face of financial, social, and physical pressures sustained them even after his death. Officials assumed that without his leadership, the Indians would voluntarily move to Indian Territory, but the Sacs remained adamant. Their strategy of passive resistance should have succeeded—their cause was just and their methods appropriate.

Although Mokohoko's people failed to retain their Kansas homes, they did manage to maintain a separate and distinct way of life. If they had been made citizens and given farmland in Kansas, it seems likely they could have continued to support themselves without governmental assistance, as they had for more than a decade and a half. But unimaginative bureaucrats robbed them of their chance.

7

THE PRAIRIE POTAWATOMIS
AND THE STRUGGLE
AGAINST LAND ALLOTMENT

The Prairie Band Potawatomis were as determined as the unfortunate Sacs to defend their lands, but where Mokohoko's people ultimately failed, the Potawatomis avoided expulsion from Kansas. Their spokesman during the crucial years of the late nineteenth century was a Prairie Potawatomi named Wahquahboshkuk, or Roiley-water.[1] In the 1880s and 1890s Wahquahboshkuk and the Prairie Band worked closely with several of their Citizen Band kinfolk as well as some Mexican Potawatomis (those who had left Kansas during the Civil War and settled in Mexico for several years before returning in the mid-1870s) and the Kickapoos to defend the interests of all Indians in Kansas. Wahquahboshkuk attracted a large following among tribal forces opposed to missionaries, formal education, and the government's land allotment program.

During the 1880s and 1890s, Wahquahboshkuk's followers proved to be a constant source of irritation to Indian agents and other federal employees. "This faction represents superstition, ignorance, and sloth, as arrayed against religion, education, and industry," Agent H. C. Linn reported in 1881. Ten years later, army Lt. John C. Gresham was advising superiors that these Indians were "very vicious and have had [a] large influence in obstructing or delaying the execution of the plans of the Government."[2]

Federal officials focused special attention on Wahquahboshkuk.[3] "He is a fanatic of the worst Indian type," Agent J. A. Scott wrote in 1893, "and would be dangerous if he possessed courage and more intelligence." But Wahquahboshkuk and his followers were indeed intelligent, and the loss of annuities, threats, and even prison failed to intimidate them into abandoning efforts to protect their lands and tradi-

Wahquahboshkuk, or Roiley Water, of the Prairie Potawatomis on one of his trips to Washington, D.C. Photo by Delancey Gill of the Bureau of American Ethnology, June 1898. (Courtesy of the Smithsonian Institution, National Anthropological Archives)

tions. According to Scott, Wahquahboshkuk was "determined to resist the laws and regulations established for the government of Indians, and in this purpose he has constantly been aided by members of the tribe who . . . take pleasure in antagonizing the government in their effort to improve the condition of the Indian."[4]

The agent should have realized that the self-reliant Prairie Potawatomis, like many other bands, had successfully managed their own affairs for generations. They could have done with less "effort" on the government's part "to improve" their condition. Retreating before the advancing tide of white settlement, the Prairie Band had moved several times before settling along the Kansas River in 1847. Determined to retreat no farther but aware that white domination of the entire continent was inevitable, they steeled themselves for the next assault. It would hit them hard and they would suffer further setbacks, but in the end their resolution withstood the challenge. Despite the machinations of men like Agent Scott, the Prairie Potawatomis would remain in Kansas.

Originally from northern Illinois and southern Wisconsin, most of the Prairie bands had settled in Iowa during the 1830s.[5] In 1846 they agreed by treaty to move from Iowa to a new reservation intersected by the Kansas River in present Shawnee, Wabaunsee, Jackson, and Pottawatomie counties.[6] "It is a beautiful portion of Kansas," observers agreed, "comprising much of the best soil, the finest timber, and purest water."[7] By the same treaty, those Potawatomis who had lived for several years along the Marais des Cygnes River in Kansas consented to relocate on the same reserve. Known as the Woods and Mission bands, and later lumped together and identified as the Citizen Band Potawatomis, many of these Indians cooperated with missionaries and Indian agents.

Governmental bureaucrats, more concerned with efficient administration than with the needs of Indians, had made it official policy to concentrate all members of a tribe on the same reservation. They expected the different Potawatomi bands to live together harmoniously.[8] Agent Richard Cummins reported in September 1848 that "this large tribe, formerly divided into several distinct bands—each antagonistical to the other—each claiming interests denied by the others—the dire cause of jealousies and alienation—are ... happily brought to assemble around [the] council fire, and to speak with one tongue."[9] The happiness, however, was mostly in the mind of the agent. This forced reunion disrupted tribal political structures and almost resulted in the loss of the Potawatomis' Kansas lands.

Although the Prairie Potawatomis eventually refused to abandon their Kansas reservation, such attachment to a particular location was relatively unusual for them. Historically, the individual bands had moved occasionally, for this served to lessen intratribal tensions and enabled the Indians to avoid potentially disastrous encounters with more powerful tribes.[10] They thought they had found safety in Kansas, but by the mid-nineteenth century white settlement had reached the

Missouri River, near the eastern border of Potawatomi lands. Instead of safety, they found themselves caught in a vise between the whites and the Plains tribes controlling the territory to the west. Resettlement in Indian Territory was always a possibility, but the Prairie Potawatomis rejected that alternative. Although their options were limited, they did not stay in Kansas simply because they had no choice; a combination of factors caused them to cling to their new homelands.

One factor proved to be the cultural diversity of the Indians who eventually identified with the Prairie Band. Years before the Prairie Band settled in Kansas, Potawatomis from Indiana and Illinois under the leadership of Nozhakum had settled near Kenekuk's Vermillion Kickapoos along the Missouri River, a few miles from Fort Leavenworth. By 1840 a number of Prairie Potawatomis from Iowa had joined them and built log cabins and harvested abundant crops of corn, potatoes, and beans along the Missouri River.[11] "We have removed from Council Bluffs," the émigrés from Iowa explained in 1844, "on account of the desolate [sic] habits of our chiefs and head men, in not listing to the wishes of our Great Father the President . . . to cultivate the soil, and raise stock for their own use."[12] From among these two groups came the Potawatomis who would settle in Mexico many years later.

Accepting Kenekuk's leadership, many of these Potawatomis attended religious services and adhered to the prophet's strict moral code. Although the Indians were content, some federal officials were displeased with this arrangement and demanded that the Potawatomis return to their own people. The superintendent of Indian affairs at St. Louis, Thomas Harvey, noted that although the Potawatomis were well behaved and few drank whiskey, they refused to allow their children to attend school. Harvey blamed Kenekuk, alleging that the prophet exerted a "harmful influence" over them. "They have among them one who is called the Prophet," he added, "who teaches some absurd notions: I understand his doctrines are rather moral but his practices are not in accordance with his theory."[13]

Federal officials cut off the annuities of these Potawatomis in 1847 after the Indians refused to move to their tribe's new reservation on the Kansas River. For no obvious reason save bureaucratic expediency, officials wanted all members of the same tribe on one reservation. Undaunted, the two hundred fifty Potawatomis declared that they were followers of Kenekuk and wished to be affiliated officially with the Kickapoos. Nozhakum pointed out in December 1849 that they had "formed strong attachments" to Kenekuk's people and "cannot now part." While agents insisted that they move to the Kansas River reserve, trader Samuel Mason urged that they be allowed to stay, for they were "among the best Indians we have, industrious, sober and most of them religious, and they . . . can't live with the Indians on the Kansas [who] are lazy and drunken."[14]

On February 8, 1851, the Vermillion Kickapoos also requested that the Potawatomis be allowed to remain. Kickapoo leaders Kenekuk and Mecina pointed out that the two bands had lived together for several years and had intermarried to a considerable extent. Potawatomi spokesmen Nozhakum and Keotuck added that their people had "imbibed the religious tenets of the Kickapoo Prophet . . . which they hold sacred, [and] their manners and habits have undergone an almost entire change since their residence among the Kickapoos." On May 9, Superintendent of Indian Affairs David D. Mitchell arranged a "national compact" between the two bands. Nozhakum's people agreed to pay the Kickapoos eight thousand dollars for the privilege of living on their lands and sharing in their future annuities.[15]

Unfortunately for Nozhakum's band, Kickapoo annuities expired in 1852, the same year the prophet Kenekuk died. Two years later, when the Kickapoos signed a new treaty that revived the annual payments, the Potawatomis were not included even though Nozhakum had become the spiritual leader of the prophet's religion. Many of the Potawatomis suffered as a consequence. On February 27, 1857, Agent Royal Baldwin found the majority of these "hungry and destitute" people ready to move. Keotuck informed the agent that they were willing to relocate "near where the Reserve of the Kickapoos and Potawatomis join. We wish that our Great Father would listen to us, as we are in a very poor situation and only have him to look up to for assistance."[16]

Over the next few years, most of these Potawatomis packed their belongings and moved to the nearby Kansas River reserve. But even though they lived apart from Kenekuk's people, they continued to follow the prophet's sound advice. Kenekuk had preached that selling Indian land was a violation of the Great Spirit's commands; the earth was sacred and "mere men were forbidden to sell it." It was fortunate that they and most other Potawatomis took these words to heart, for their Mission Band kinfolk were willing to accept individual land allotments and to sell their share of the tribe's reservation.[17]

Throughout the 1850s, tribal factionalism flared on the Potawatomi reserve as the various bands struggled for dominance.[18] Many members of the Mission Band were of mixed Indian and white parentage; their ancestors had intermarried with Frenchmen in Indiana and Illinois. These mixed-bloods were never accepted as members of the traditional clans in the patrilineal Potawatomi society, and they found that most avenues to prestige or political power within the tribe were closed to them. They were familiar with the customs and beliefs of their white ancestors as well as with Indian ways, and many believed that they could improve their status by cooperating with the governmental civilization program.

Although most Potawatomis adhered to their traditional religions, a number of the Mission Band were Catholic and heeded the advice of Jesuit missionaries. The priests, who had lived among those Potawatomis on their Marais des Cygnes lands, accompanied them to the new reservation and established St. Mary's Mission. The blackrobes were soon meddling in tribal affairs, naturally siding with their Indian converts on matters of tribal policy. Staunch advocates of the government's civilization program, the priests labored to eradicate all vestiges of tribal religion and to rid Indians of "all that formerly served for the worship of the devil."[19]

The priests were confident of success. Father Maurice Gaillard reported in 1855 that the typical Catholic Potawatomi resembled the white man "in his dwelling, his manner of life, his application to work, [and] his social and domestic habits." Father John Duerinck noticed that the Catholic children no longer showed "that uncouth behavior, that haughty temper, that fondness for their Indian ways that used to mortify us to the quick."[20]

Praising the priests' work, Agent George W. Clarke informed his superiors in Washington that the Catholics were providing a great service to the Potawatomis. Clarke admired the "neat cottages and little fields of the 'Mission Indians,' and the air of comfort and good order apparent throughout the neighborhood." The agent happily noted that the Indians had asked to end their communal ways and become individual landowners.[21]

Newspaper editor J. Evarts Green, after traveling through the area in

Group of Potawatomi boys at St. Mary's Mission, 1867. (Courtesy of the Smithsonian Institution, National Anthropological Archives)

the mid-1850s, described the mission in glowing terms. "One Sunday morning I was riding through the Pottawatomie reservation," he related:

It was rolling prairie. There were no signs of human life. As I rose to the top of a little prairie ridge, and was able to look into the valley below, I was surprised to see a village spread out before me, such as you may see about Quebec or Montreal. It looked as if it might have been there about a hundred years. I was perfectly amazed. There were a few little cottages, built after the French manner, and a church with its tinned [tined] spire; and, as I sat on my horse, looking down, the bell in the steeple of this church tingled, the door opened, and a priest came out, clothed in cassock and with a shovel hat on his head. Behind him was a procession of about one hundred Indian children, marching two and two, that perfect gravity and demureness in their dusky faces that is so fascinating in these Indian children. They were all neatly clad in white aprons; and they moved with perfect decorum and sobriety as they turned into the door of the largest building, which I supposed was a school. . . . I had seen for myself that at this Jesuit Mission of St. Mary's *something* was doing for these Indians. They had learned something and were at school.[22]

While the Mission Band won praise and admiration for their efforts toward assimilation, the Prairie Band earned the scorn of many white observers. The Prairie Potawatomis steadfastly rejected the priests' advice to assimilate as well as their conversion efforts. These Indians preferred their traditional religious beliefs, which emphasized the sacred clan bundles. These bundles contained special powers that protected the clan and the village, and each came with special rituals that had been prescribed by the Great Spirit.[23]

The Prairie Indians saw little need for Catholic ritual. They kept their children out of the Catholic school and implied that they preferred the less domineering Baptists, who also operated a school on Potawatomi lands.[24] Not surprisingly, such obstinacy infuriated the Jesuits. "There is in this country a certain class of men called *medicine-men*, or jugglers," Father Duerinck railed. "Very ignorant, they are distinguished only by the pride of their character." Offended that any "ignorant aborigine" dared to rebuff him, Duerinck blamed the devil for turning the Prairie Band against the Catholics. Nor did Protestant missionaries escape the priest's wrath. He was horrified that the Baptists taught boys and girls together in the same classroom; "needless to say . . . this cannot be without detriment to morality." The priest rejoiced when Methodist attempts "to sow cockle" among the Indians failed.[25]

Persuaded that Indians were basically motivated by the same desires and feelings as whites, Duerinck advocated breaking up what he called "communism" among the Potawatomis. The government should, the priest suggested, "give them [individual] title to the land and you will see them vie with each other in their improvements." He insisted that they abandon their "lazy" and "worthless" ways of "hunting, rambling, and marauding" for hard farm work. But, he added, "if they be too lazy to work let them die; they must die once at all events, and they might as well die just now as at any other time." The Jesuit's plan made exceptions for orphans, widows, and the sick.[26]

Governmental officials agreed with the idea of individual allotments and sale of the surplus lands. The former superintendent of Indian affairs at St. Louis, David Mitchell, had suggested in 1849 that "one section of land be given to each head of family" and the government purchase the remaining lands for the "pioneers of the country." Agent David Vanderslice observed a few years later that his Sac, Iowa, and Kickapoo charges possessed "a country much more extensive than they need and can well dispose of a part" for money to educate their children. Agent Royal Baldwin urged the Indians of Kansas to end their communal ways, insisting that to become completely "civilized" each must own his own farm. Agent Clarke recommended harsh punishment for members of the Prairie Potawatomi who refused to work the fields. Because Clarke's wards continually tried "to distract and stifle" the civilization program, he also declared that the government should "exercise a dictatorial rule over the tribe."[27]

Unfortunately for the Prairie Band, Indian agents and the Jesuits joined efforts to break down tribal cohesiveness and to make imitation white farmers out of the Indians. In September 1857, Agent William Murphy damned the Prairie Potawatomis because they "despise the principles of civilization, look upon work as a disgrace, and when they hear those Indians who cultivate the soil speak of sectionalizing [allotment] they immediately denounce them, and charge them with endeavoring to swindle them out of their land." Two months later, Murphy asserted that a large majority were now "extremely anxious" to accept allotments and become citizens; only "the poor 'Prairie band' of Potawatomis appear to be confirmed in their ignorant obstinacy." Until leaving office on the eve of the Civil War, Murphy actively sided with the faction that came to be known as the Citizen Band. Working closely with Kansas land speculators intent on swindling the tribe, he found the credulous Mission Indians easy to manipulate.[28]

In the fall of 1861, as North and South mobilized for the Civil War, negotiations for a new Potawatomi treaty began. During the preliminary discussions, newly appointed Agent William Ross announced that to remain in Kansas all Indians must accept allotments and become United States citizens. Most Prairie Potawatomis boycotted the councils and did not hear Ross; at the same time, he did not hear their protests against allotment. Meanwhile, an Indian named Shagwee, an erstwhile opponent of the Prairie Band, denounced both citizenship and allotment.[29] Fearing that all Indians would be evicted from their lands if they did not actively defend themselves, Shagwee pointed out that the 1846 treaty had guaranteed that Kansas "should be my last and permanent home." If they accepted individual farms now, their lands would quickly fall into white hands. "Like so many leeches they would suck my blood until I should be dead of exhaustion." Shagwee concluded that his people were "not advanced enough in civilization to become citizens."[30]

When Ross again insisted that the opposing factions settle their differences in a peaceful, civilized manner and accept allotments, Shagwee reacted angrily:

> You have the brass of advising us to peace and union, while at home you take up arms against each other, and fight to the knife. The South is arrayed against the North, the son fights against his father; brother against brother. Your country is turned into one vast battlefield; and those rich plains which once produced so abundant crops, are laid waste, and reddened with the blood of American citizens. Sir, restore peace and union among yourselves, before you come and preach to us.[31]

Despite his vehemence, Shagwee joined many other Potawatomis in signing the new treaty on November 15, 1861. It is not clear whether he accepted allotment for personal gain or because he feared losing everything if he refused to sign. Fortunately for the Prairie Band, it was allowed to continue holding its lands in common. Only those "who have adopted the customs of the whites and desire to have separate tracts assigned to them" would receive titles to their own lands.[32]

When the United States Senate ratified the treaty on April 15, 1862, the Prairie Indians retained only about 77,000 of their original 560,000 acres in Kansas. The other factions, now lumped together and called the Citizen Band, accepted individual allotments to 152,128 acres, while the Leavenworth, Pawnee, and Western Railroad Company won the right to the remaining "surplus" lands. Various factions within this railroad company would spend several years vying for control of the best available Potawatomi lands. In the scramble for land, Indian rights were largely ignored.[33]

Meanwhile, Agent Charles Keith and several businessmen had arranged a similar land cession treaty on the nearby Kickapoo reservation. In the summer of 1864, after federal officials ignored protests by Kickapoo elders that the treaty was negotiated illegally, Chief

Nokowhat led sixty of his followers to Mexico. Many Potawatomis went with Nokowhat's Kickapoos. Indian refugees fleeing Confederate forces in the South had crowded into Kansas and caused considerable disruption on the reservations. Weary of the constant strife and factionalism, Captain John, or Shaquah, and his small traditionalist band of Potawatomis decided to accompany Nokowhat's people as far as the Red River. Although they intended to return to Kansas after spending the winter hunting, Captain John and his people remained away for several years.[34]

The émigrés to Mexico also included some of Nozhakum's people, among them "the great brave" Chequmkego, or Clap of Thunder Shaking the Earth. Although Chequmkego had signed the Potawatomi allotment treaty, many of Nozhakum's other followers had boycotted the proceedings. With their deep attachment to the land, they disagreed strongly with the allotment treaty and abandoned Kansas in protest. Perhaps in Mexico they could hold their land in common as the Great Spirit had commanded. If that proved impossible, they could always return to Kansas as long as like-minded kinfolk there continued to hold out against allotment.[35]

In Kansas, meanwhile, the Citizen Band found itself in a difficult position. The 1861 treaty provided for the government to withhold titles to Potawatomi allotments until the individual Indians were declared competent to handle their own affairs. By mid-decade, however, because of the growing impatience of whites, land patents and citizenship were being conferred without regard to competency, and Kansas speculators easily swindled many Indians out of their farms. On February 15, 1865, Special Allotting Commissioner Edward Wolcott observed that "a very considerable number of those who have obtained certificates of naturalization are totally unfit to become citizens, or to be [entrusted] with the management of property or money." If they obtained deeds to their own farms, Wolcott warned, most Potawatomis would be unable to "protect themselves against sharpies."[36]

The apparent success in "civilizing" the Mission Potawatomis made the resistance of other Kansas bands intolerable to agents and missionaries. Unfortunately, most of those who submitted to the admonitions of the whites lost their Kansas homes and were forced to move. Some officials even recognized the problems associated with the civilization program. "The Quapaws, Senecas, and Senecas and Shawnees, are fast passing away [from Kansas]," Agent Peter P. Elder wrote in

August 1865. "Whiskey, want of vegetable living, scrofula, exposure to the malarias incident to timber and water localities. More than all others, attempted civilization." Those bands that lived in "their natural way" and were "not so much connected with the whites," he continued, had not suffered as much.[37] As individuals outside the authority and protection of their band, most Indians were unable to defend themselves from those eager to acquire their lands.

Agent Luther Palmer pointed out a year later that "no sooner does [an Indian] become possessed of money, or property that he can dispose of, than he proceeds at once to make it available . . . for present enjoyment, never seeming to reflect that his means may become exhausted until his last dollar is gone." The agent predicted that these Indians would become paupers dependent on the government or fellow band members for support.[38]

Washington policymakers paid little attention to such warnings, however, and many Potawatomis and others who accepted citizenship and allotment quickly lost their lands. The Kansas state legislature compounded the problem by ruling that allotted Indians were subject to the same taxes as white citizens. As a result, over the following years many more lost their farms because of delinquent taxes.

By 1867, pressure on the entire tribe to sell its lands and move to Indian Territory had intensified. On February 27, Citizen Band representatives Shagwee, Mazhee, and Mianco, along with B. H. Bertrand and Joseph N. Bourassa, two mixed-bloods recognized by governmental officials as Potawatomi leaders, met with Commissioner of Indian Affairs Lewis G. Bogy in Washington and signed a new treaty. It specified that a Potawatomi reservation would be established in Indian Territory for all Citizen Band members who wished to settle there, but those who had accepted allotments could remain in Kansas. Not surprisingly, the welfare of the Indians played a secondary role in these negotiations. The families of the mixed-bloods received several thousand dollars for the part played by Bertrand and Bourassa in negotiating the deal.[39] The treaty also granted the Atchison, Topeka, and Santa Fe Railroad the right to purchase the tribe's "surplus" lands at one dollar per acre as soon as the treaty was ratified, and railroad officials were eager to take possession.[40]

The United States Senate ratified the treaty in July 1868, and during the following year a Citizen Band delegation selected a new reservation in Indian Territory. Meanwhile, the dispossession of the allotted Indians in Kansas continued. The situation deteriorated so rapidly that Superintendent Hoag reported in 1871 that the allotment policy was "ruinous" and should be ended. According to Hoag, citizen Indians were unable "to withstand the corrupting influences which are thrown around them by designing and dishonest men, who cling to them like leeches, until they have possessed themselves of all their property, and then abandon them to the charge of public and private charity."[41]

Except for sharing in the proceeds from the land sale, the Prairie Potawatomis were not overtly affected by the 1868 treaty; the "exclusive rights" to their common lands were still guaranteed. Many of the Potawatomis in Mexico, however, had been recognized as Citizen Band members who were entitled to allotments, and the treaty inadvertently provided a loophole for dispossessing them. Article 8 specified that deceased allottees were considered United States citizens, and under certain conditions Kansas state courts had authority to settle and dispose of the estates of deceased citizens.[42]

This article gave the state the opportunity to dispose of Indian lands under the cloak of legality. Nothing having been heard from the Mexican Potawatomis since the Civil War, tribal "leaders" Joseph Bourassa, George L. Young, and Eli Nadeau—classic examples of the opportunistic men who had dominated the affairs of the Citizen Band for years—seized this chance for personal gain. On February 10, 1871, these members of the Citizen Band business committee submitted a list of thirty-eight "deceased" Indians—now eligible for citizenship—whose "heirs" were entitled to receive their fee simple deeds to allotments. The thirty-eight were still alive in Mexico, but that was easy to overlook in the scramble for profits. Assisted by local attorney Benjamin F. Payne, notorious in Kansas for his unsavory reputation, Young and Nadeau persuaded the Kansas courts to appoint them executors of the estates. In June they collected over thirty thousand dollars when the allotted lands were sold at auction, but they had no intention of surrendering the money to valid Indian claimants.[43]

Complicating the already confused situation, Oliver Polk, John W. Polk, and Richard Bertrand, longtime traders on the Potawatomi reservation, went to Mexico in search of the missing Indians. They found the Potawatomis and allegedly persuaded them to sell their Kansas lands. When the three men returned to Kansas, they sold the supposed titles to other speculators, who then resold them to white settlers. The result was even greater confusion, as the new purchasers and those who had previously "inherited" the land fought over the titles in the courts.[44] Perhaps none of this would have mattered to the absentee Potawatomis if they had remained in Mexico, but that was not to be permitted.

Texas citizens and military officials had complained that for many years bands of Mexican Kickapoos, Comanches, and Apaches had plundered across the Rio Grande into Texas. The Indian raiders had carried off the livestock, property, and children of hapless Texas settlers and bartered their stolen goods to the Comanches or to Mexican citizens in northern Coahuila.[45] Indian Agent John D. Miles of the Kansas Kickapoo reservation discovered, on arriving in Santa Rosa in May 1871, that Indian labor and trade were vital to the local economy, and Mexican citizens resented American efforts to remove the tribes. Miles was one of the many Quakers appointed to office as part of Grant's Indian Peace Policy, which was intended as a turn away from violent confrontations with the tribes. When he tried to persuade the Kickapoos and Potawatomis to return peacefully to the United States, however, they refused. The agent would soon realize that peaceful methods were not always as effective as force, and he would often sacrifice his Quaker principles to necessity during his career in the federal service.[46]

The effectiveness of force against Indians was clearly demonstrated on May 18, 1873, when Col. Ranald Mackenzie and his United States cavalrymen crossed into Mexico and surrounded the unsuspecting Kickapoos and Potawatomis. Because most of the Indian men had left the previous day to hunt, the soldiers' task was relatively simple.[47] The troops killed many Indians and chased panic-stricken women and children across irrigation ditches and through corn and pumpkin fields. Taking the women and children into custody, Mackenzie spirited them across the Rio Grande to be held until the men agreed to move to Indian Territory. Among the hostages were several Potawatomis; it mattered little that they were peaceful and that there was never any proof of their participation in raids on American citizens.[48]

Just three days before Mackenzie's troops violated Mexican sovereignty to storm the Indian camps, American Commissioners Henry M. Atkinson and Thomas G. Williams had arrived in Saltillo to negotiate the peaceful removal of the tribes. Neither was aware of Mackenzie's plans, and after the May 18 attack, it was several days before they were able to convince local Mexican officials of their peaceful intentions. The Mexicans finally helped them establish contact with one small band of frightened Indians, whose spokesman agreed to cooperate. In June, Atkinson and Williams wired the commissioner of Indian affairs that Chequmkego, "head chief of [the] Kickapoos and Pottawattomies," had accompanied them to Texas to check on the captive women and children.[49]

Long before the attack on their villages, the peaceful Mexican Potawatomis had sent word to the Indian agent in Kansas that they were definitely alive and wanted to return to their reservation.[50] Having expected a peaceful visit from American officials, Mackenzie's raid left these Indians bewildered and frightened. They did not understand why soldiers had abducted their women and children.[51] Not surprisingly, Atkinson and Williams found it difficult to answer "the often repeated question as to how it was that at the very time we . . . were in Mexico to treat with them, that the United States soldiers should have gone into Mexico to attack, kill, and capture their people." But the commissioners convinced the Indians of their sincerity, and at a July 14 council in Remolino, Mexico, all of the Potawatomis and many Kickapoos agreed to return to the United States.[52]

Late the following month, Chequmkego assured Atkinson and Williams that their return journey would be peaceful.[53] The sympathetic commissioners agreed to allow the Indians to travel unescorted through Comanche country, for the Potawatomis and Kickapoos insisted that it was safer than passing near Texas settlements where vengeful whites might attack them. On August 28, 1873, four hundred Indians started north; their route took them across the Llano Estacado in West Texas and into Indian Territory, where Chequmkego and most others remained. Unfortunately, the elderly Captain John died on the journey north. But his family and several other Potawatomis continued on to Kansas, which they had not seen for ten years.[54] Arriving in Kansas, they immediately asked to be admitted as members of the Prairie Band. Although they later won a monetary settlement on their lost lands, the Mexican Potawatomis would remain forever suspicious of the federal bureaucracy.[55]

The Mexican Potawatomis found many things changed on the Kansas reservation, for most of the old Mission or Citizen Band members were gone. By the early 1870s, most had lost their farms and had either moved to the new reservation in Indian Territory or were squatting on

Prairie Potawatomi lands. Agent Joel H. Morris reported that the allottees regretted their decision to accept citizenship. The Indians in their
"sober moments," wrote Morris, "say that they were intoxicated with
the idea of becoming citizens of the United States and exercising their
right of franchise. They have squandered their land and money in
gambling, drinking whiskey, and other evil habits, and are now thrown
upon their own resources as poor as the poorest."[56]

In the summer of 1873, Citizen Band spokesman Joseph Bourassa
declared that the government's allotment program was a total failure.
He pleaded with Superintendent Hoag to provide funds to remove the
destitute Indians, who had "spent all their head money, sold most of
their lands, and now they are selling their last and only ponies for a
mere song, they even sell the last coat they have on their backs for
liquor." Bourassa, who had signed the allotment treaties and had taken
part in the Mexican Potawatomi swindle, played on Hoag's Quaker
sympathies. "Let us imagine for a short time, we are living in the days
of William Penn, the truest friend the poor Red man ever had, then we
would all feel like aiding in the good cause," he wrote. "If my people
can only get their father the Superintendent to help them a little they
would soon settle in [Indian Territory], which is the best thing they
could do."[57]

Although the Citizen Band had fallen on hard times, the Prairie
Potawatomis were relatively prosperous; they had wisely refused allotment and had peacefully retained their lands in common. Their
seventy-seven-thousand-odd acres in Jackson County possessed fertile
soil, streams, and sufficient timber for the four hundred fifty Prairie
Indians living on the reserve. Despite their being denigrated as savages
by many outsiders, their willingness to accommodate themselves to
new conditions was indicated by the many children who now attended
a boarding school established by the Quakers. Although some families
still preferred the traditional bark wickiups, most Prairie Potawatomis
lived in log houses. Like the Vermillion Kickapoos, moreover, many
Potawatomi men now engaged in farm labor—a major break with custom. Their small gardens of corn, beans, potatoes, and squash,
supplemented by game and their treaty annuities, adequately filled the
needs of most Prairie Potawatomi families.[58]

Their prosperity caused Agent Mahlon Newlin to admit that they
had made the correct choice by not taking title to separate farms.[59]
"After a careful consideration of the situation of the Indians of this

agency," Newlin wrote his superiors in September 1874, "as compared with the sectionalized class of Pottawatomies, I cannot but conclude that the Prairie band subserved their best interest by remaining as wards of the Government."[60]

The situation was similar on the Kickapoo reservation. According to Naomi Hadley, clerk of the Friends Committee on Indian Affairs at Lawrence, the Kickapoos had made significant progress. Hadley reported in 1876 that these "Indians are prosperous, are improving in farming methods and stock raising, and are building houses."[61] Soon afterward, the allotted Kickapoos announced that they no longer wanted American citizenship and petitioned to rejoin their tribe on the common reserve. Many had already lost their farms, and Kansas businessmen and politicians were pressuring the rest to sell.[62] These Indians realized that with the exception of the tiny Chippewa and Munsee bands, all other allotted tribes had lost their lands and been forced to leave Kansas. The allotment experiment, first proposed and enacted by Commissioner George Manypenny years before, had proven disastrous. Most Potawatomis and Kickapoos were aware of this fact, and they stood guard against those who advocated allotting all Indian reservations. Allotment had resulted in dispossessing most Kansas bands, and it was likely that it would do the same for all other Indians.

The Indians' problems with the federal bureaucracy would only intensify, for the 1880s were years of great crisis for Indians throughout the United States. Despite convincing evidence that earlier allotment experiments had resulted in the exploitation and dispossession of most Kansas bands, the self-styled Friends of the Indian urged Congress to enact a similar policy nationwide. "The reservation must go!" became the cry of eastern reformers determined to transform Indians into self-reliant citizens in their own image.

By the early 1880s, the Boston Indian Citizenship Association, the Women's National Indian Association, the Indian Rights Association, and various other groups were pleading the Indians' cause. Genuinely concerned for the welfare of the tribes, reformers denounced the lack of governmental action following the famous *Standing Bear v. Crook* case; Mokohoko's Sacs and others had not been given the same chance to renounce their tribal status and become citizens. Helen Hunt Jackson's 1881 book, *A Century of Dishonor*, depicting the history of governmental abuse of the tribes, aroused much sympathy and helped unify the reform crusade.[63] In October 1883 the various groups joined together for the first of many meetings at a resort hotel on Lake Mohonk, New York. The annual Lake Mohonk Conference subsequently became the most influential promoter of that old panacea for uplifting and civilizing the Indian—Christianity, formal education, and land allotment.[64]

Most reformers agreed that the reservation policy needed to be abandoned. Charles C. Painter of the Indian Rights Association argued that unlike Topsy of Harriet Beecher Stowe's *Uncle Tom's Cabin*, federal policy was a machine that had "never 'growed up.' " Instead, it "had been nailed and glued together, piece by piece, by divers workmen, acting without concert or plan, during the past two hundred and sixty years, . . . with no intelligent comprehension of an ultimate purpose, and necessarily without any wise adaptation of means to such purpose." Massachusetts Sen. Henry L. Dawes insisted that "the only solution of the problem is in making of the Indian a self-supporting citizen." When that happened, Dawes continued, the governmental machine could forever disappear "like an April cloud before the sunrise." He agreed with Commissioner Hayt's contention that policymakers should promote citizenship and individual ownership of property for all Indians. "The system of title in common has . . . been pernicious" to Indians, Hayt wrote, "in that it has prevented individual advancement and represses that spirit of rivalry and the desire to accumulate property . . . which is the source of success and advancement in all white communities."[65]

Such rhetoric won almost universal acceptance in the East. Few listened to Sen. Henry Moore Teller of Colorado, the secretary of the Interior from 1881 to 1885, or George Manypenny, the former commissioner of Indian affairs, who both denounced the allotment proposals. "Now, divide up this land and you will in a few years deprive the Indians of a resting-place on the face of this continent," Teller predicted. Any allotment legislation proposed to Congress "ought to be entitled 'A bill to despoil the Indians of their lands and to make them vagabonds on the face of the earth,' because, in my view, that is the result of this kind of legislation."[66]

Manypenny charged that allotment was sponsored by a motley collection of "railroad monopolists, land-grabbers, [and] cattle kings or cowboys, who all have their covetous eyes set upon" Indian lands. Referring to the allotment treaties he had negotiated with the Delawares, Shawnees, Miamis, Kickapoos, and others in the 1850s, Manypenny pointed out that the agreements had served to dispossess the tribes of "their noble lands in Kansas."[67] He had been convinced at the time that allotment would produce favorable results but freely admitted that he had been wrong. Manypenny's treaties, made in good faith and ignorance, had only tragic consequences for the Indians:

> I had provided for the abrogation of the reservations, the dissolution of the tribal relation, and for lands in severalty and citizenship; thus making the road clear for the rapacity of the white man. I had broken down every barrier. I had committed a grievous mistake, and entailed on the Indians a legacy of cruel wrong and injury. Had I known then, as I now know, what would result from those treaties, I would be compelled to admit that I had committed a high crime.[68]

The powerful arguments of Teller and Manypenny were rejected by the well-meaning reformers and bureaucrats. Blinded by their fervent belief in the melting pot myth and untroubled by the slightest possibility they might be wrong, the humanitarians plunged headlong into the crusade with an almost religious conviction that allotment was correct and incontestable. Herbert Welsh of the Indian Rights Association asserted that the Indian now lived "isolated from our own civilization, by language, by traditions, by the pauper-ration system, and, geographically, by means of his reservation, which completely separates him from the manifold influences both for good and evil which are considered in the term civilization." Welsh advocated the destruction of the reservations, the primary protectors of Indian isolation.[69] Not surprisingly, Welsh and other reformers also brushed aside the protests of Indians, who overwhelmingly opposed allotment, as unworthy of their consideration, and they stubbornly refused to believe the compelling evidence that their course was wrong.

After Congress had debated the matter for years, the idea of ending tribal authority and giving each Indian family its own farm was finally accepted as a necessary step toward assimilation. On February 8, 1887, President Grover Cleveland signed into law the General Allotment (Dawes) Act. It specified that each Indian family was to receive 160 acres; single adults and orphans were entitled to eighty acres. The federal government would hold the patent to each allotment for twenty-five years or until the individual Indian was deemed competent to handle his or her own affairs. The Dawes Act also made each Indian accepting an allotment a citizen of the United States subject to the laws of the state or territory where the individual resided.[70]

Senator Dawes, the sponsor of the allotment legislation, and other eastern humanitarians viewed Indians as children who had no idea of what was best for them. "The only way is to lead him [the Indian] out into the sunshine," Dawes proclaimed, "and tell him what the sunshine is for, and what the rain comes for, and when to put his seed in the ground." Allotment, he maintained, would magically transform and civilize the Indian. "The idea is to make something of him, to make a man of him," Dawes wrote. The Indian "is to be led out from the darkness into the light; he is to be shown how to walk, how to help himself. He is to be taught self-reliance, or he will never be a man."[71] Even eastern reformers like Herbert Welsh, who actually visited reservations in the West, were blinded by the fervor for allotment. In the West, Welsh and his associates most often encountered only those Indians who had attended formal schools, frequented the missions, and favored assimilation; they rarely met with traditionalists who kept alive the "old and savage customs."[72]

On the Kansas Potawatomi reservation, meanwhile, the disaster of earlier allotment experiments remained obvious. In November 1885, United States Indian Inspector Robert Gardner had reported that Indians holding their lands in common were relatively prosperous. He noted, however, that there were "residing within this reserve about 250 Citizen Pottawattomis, who are a disaffected and disturbing element." These Indians had no lands or visible means of support and should be forced to move.[73]

The Indians remaining in Kansas were well acquainted with the damage that allotment had caused, and they protested against efforts to implement it. On April 8, 1887, exactly two months after the president signed the Dawes Act, Inspector Gardner explained the law's provisions to Prairie Band leaders. But he got nowhere in his efforts to convince them of the advantages of allotment. "They refuse most emphatically to have their lands allotted to them in severalty," Gardner wrote. He advised the Indians "to act sensibly" and accept allotments soon; if they failed to decide in four years, he warned, officials would make selections for them arbitrarily.[74] Gardner had already admitted that the Indians who held their lands in common were relatively prosperous, whereas the Citizen Band members had lost their allotted lands and were destitute. The agent seemed oblivious to the contradictions in his reasoning.

In the fall of 1887, Agent Charles H. Grover's report to Washington explained what should have been obvious. The Indian was not stupid; he knew "what the sunshine is for, and what the rain comes for, and when to put his seed in the ground" as well as any white person. Indians denounced allotment for what it was—"a cunningly devised scheme to dispossess them of their lands." The Prairie Potawatomis and the Kickapoos, Grover wrote, were "strenuously opposed to taking their land in severalty, deterred by a full knowledge of the misfortunes" that had befallen members of either band who had earlier accepted titles to their farms. Because of the "great frauds" and "grievous wrongs" that resulted from past allotments, Grover was unaware of "a single member of either tribe who favors the policy."[75]

What the Indians needed was an advocate who could explain and defend their opposition to allotment. The Potawatomis had never really had an all-powerful chief and their tribal council usually expressed the consensus of the entire village—they had always been an egalitarian people.[76] But there had been individuals who had taken it upon themselves to advocate the Potawatomi cause. One such individual was Wahquahboshkuk—the most outspoken Indian critic of allotment in Kansas during the 1880s and 1890s. Born sometime in the early 1840s, Roily-water earned the status of warrior among his fellow Potawatomis and eventually assumed the role as a "chief" of the Fish clan; he was never considered a chief by federal officials.[77]

Assisted by a number of Potawatomis from the Citizen and Mexican bands and the nearby Kickapoos, all of whom had firsthand experience with the failure of allotment, Wahquahboshkuk gained considerable support from all Indians in Kansas opposed to governmental efforts to undermine tribal autonomy. "The Indians are not satisfied with the manner in which our affairs are conducted," he informed the acting commissioner of Indian affairs in June 1886. "We do not think we are honestly dealt with and we ask the department to closely scrutinize into our affairs and see that justice is done us."[78] When preparations were made to evict the indigent citizen Potawatomis from Kansas in 1888, Wahquahboshkuk rushed to their defense and helped stave off removal for a few years. He knew that tribal solidarity was important, and these victims of the civilization program could help in the struggle against allotment.[79]

In August 1889, newly appointed Agent John Blair provided additional evidence against the Dawes Act. Observing that each Indian family already occupied and farmed separate tracts of land, the astute agent questioned the need for individual land patents. He also pointed to the results of earlier allotting of Indian land as further reason to abandon the policy. The citizen Potawatomis and Kickapoos were "totally without resources," Blair noted, "and having contracted wretched habits of life through a condition of abject poverty and dependence extending back through a long period of years, they are exhibited by the Indians holding lands in common as an illustration of the certain fate of all Indians who take lands in severalty, whatever the conditions might be."[80]

Blair's assessment reflected the attitude of Wahquahboshkuk and the other Indians. The agent's superiors, however, were not pleased with his outspoken criticism of a policy they held sacred, and they ordered Blair to carry out his duties and leave Indian policy to "experts." These experts persuaded President Benjamin Harrison to issue an executive order on September 1, 1890, requiring all Potawatomis and Kickapoos to accept title to their own farms. Compulsion was necessary because the Indians, for reasons most federal officials could not fathom, refused to cooperate. Special Allotment Agent Henry J. Aten had complained that the Indians were "inclined to procrastinate, and do not want to break their tribal relations, as they prefer obeying their chiefs to the authorized agents of the government." Irked at being rebuffed, Inspector Gardner grimly noted that the time had come for Indians to "feel the strong arm of the Government and its powers."[81] Before carrying out allotment, officials ordered the eviction of those citizen Potawatomis and Kickapoos who had no legal claim to reservation lands. Although federal representatives recognized these Potawatomis and Kickapoos as citizens, the officials did not hesitate to violate the Indians' constitutional rights by deporting them to Oklahoma.

On July 15, 1891, however, Agent Aten warned his superiors that trouble might ensue if removal was attempted, for the citizen Potawatomis and Kickapoos, supported by Wahquahboshkuk, vehemently opposed the action. "Wah-quoh-bosh-kuk has stated publicly, and otherwise assured the Citizens, that he will protect them and prevent their removal, and has otherwise shown a very dangerous tendency towards violence."[82] When Agent Blair reluctantly attempted to begin the removal, Wahquahboshkuk and several other Indians stood in his path.

The Indians threatened to kill him or anyone else who dared to attempt the removal of their comrades.[83]

Believing that discretion was the better part of valor, Blair abruptly resigned his post, leaving the agency vacant until J. A. Scott assumed authority over the Kansas tribes in August. Afraid to confront the angry Indians alone, Scott called for a detachment of the Seventh Cavalry to assist in the removal. The Seventh Cavalry, Custer's old outfit, had recently been responsible for the massacre at Wounded Knee on the Sioux reservation in South Dakota. When the troops under Lt. John Gresham arrived at the reservation on August 17, 1891, they promptly arrested Wahquahboshkuk and an Indian named Uwactote and confined them at Fort Riley. Lieutenant Gresham advised superiors that the two prisoners represented the "worst elements" of the Prairie Band. "Without question in the minds of all here," he wrote, "it is indispensable to the interests of the Government and the welfare of the Indians that these men be placed under military control for a long period, certainly several years."[84]

A week later, the soldiers herded over one hundred citizen Indians from the Potawatomi reservation. Agent Scott uttered a sigh of relief as the dejected Indians peacefully left their Kansas homes for Oklahoma. "I believe there would have been little difficulty in the removal of the Citizens," Scott wrote, "had they not been encouraged by a small faction of the Prairie Band calling themselves braves, to remain under the promises that they would protect them."[85]

Although confined in the guardhouse at Fort Riley, Wahquahboshkuk refused to be intimidated and continued to agitate against allotment. By September, his followers had hired Topeka attorney J. C. Tillotson, who began habeas corpus proceedings on behalf of the two prisoners. Scott insisted, however, that the Potawatomi leader was a dangerous influence and should not be released. Indeed, the agent asserted, the tribal council had requested that the prisoner remain in custody. Scott failed to mention that the government-recognized council simply echoed the wishes of the agent and did not reflect the feelings of other Indians. He was forced to admit, however, that most Potawatomis looked forward to the return of the outspoken critic of governmental policy.[86]

Officials who thought the Prairie Band leader would be humbled by imprisonment were disabused of that fantasy in March 1892 when Wahquahboshkuk and his comrade were released and returned to the reservation. In April, Scott was shocked to learn that Wahquahboshkuk and Uwactote had filed suit in the United States district court, asking twenty-two thousand dollars in damages for false arrest by the agent and Lieutenant Gresham. Even more distressing was the fact that many Indians now believed federal officials had relented and allotment would be abandoned. Inspector Benjamin Miller reported that most Potawatomis had refused to cooperate and were "using all their influence to prevent the completion of the work." The Indians believed, he said, that if they present a solid front against the program, officials "will finally yield and they will be allowed to hold their lands in common as at present."[87] The Indians' hopes soared even higher when Wahquahboshkuk left for Washington confident that federal officials would heed their cry against the theft of their lands.[88]

This was one of several trips to Washington that Wahquahboshkuk made during the 1890s. Although he found federal policymakers unsympathetic, after each visit he assured followers that officials were merciful and that it was only a matter of time before the allotment policy would be repealed.[89] Encouraged by his unfounded optimism, the Potawatomis as well as the Kickapoos continued to resist, and the resurgence of intertribal religious ceremonies and dances reflected their determination to defeat the government's plan.[90] These ceremonies disturbed Agent Scott, who reported in October 1892 that he had dismissed Chief Kewahkouk as a member of the Kickapoo tribal council for disobeying orders not to attend a dance on the Potawatomi reserve. More to the point, Scott admitted that Kewahkouk's "opposition to allotment and to education also rendered this course necessary."[91]

Scott was unable to take similar action against Wahquahboshkuk, for officials had never recognized him as a chief. That he commanded a considerable following on both the Potawatomi and Kickapoo reservations despite this fact greatly irritated the agent. "He is not now, neither has he ever been a member of the Council of the Prairie Band, but as an alleged head warrior of the Band, has been a constant source of trouble in the transaction of business," Scott railed. He added that this "evil and malicious" Indian should be expelled from the reservation. The agent was further incensed in November 1892 when Wahquahboshkuk cautioned Indians not to accept their annuities, for it "would commit the annuitants to allotments." Scott charged that the Potawatomis and Kickapoos who followed this advice ranked

A Potawatomi and Kickapoo delegation in Washington, D.C., June 1898. Standing left to right: Peter Curley and Wahquahboshkuk; sitting: Kewahkouk (Kickapoo) and James Thompson. (Courtesy of the Smithsonian Institution, National Anthropological Archives)

among the "most trifling" Indians in Kansas. They were under the spell of Wahquahboshkuk, who under ordinary circumstances would have only a small following, but under existing circumstances, "all opposing allotments will naturally side with him; while this will be less than one half the tribe, it gives him a dangerous influence."[92]

Whether or not Scott intentionally underestimated the number of Indians opposing the assimilation policy is not clear, but it seems doubtful that he could have been so badly misinformed. With the exception of a few mixed-bloods whom agents had cajoled into accepting allotments, the vast majority of the approximately five hundred twenty-five Potawatomis and two hundred forty Kickapoos sided with the opposition. The traditional Indians led the fight and collected enough money to finance legal counsel and to send their leaders to Washington. By the spring of 1893, they had collected twenty-five hundred dollars to send Wahquahboshkuk, James Thompson (Nibakwa), and two others back to the capital. Scott was distressed that such a large sum could have been "drawn from the oldest, poorest, and most needy Indians"; these "dupes" actually believed their leaders could accomplish their goals.[93]

Unsuccessful in his efforts to persuade Washington policymakers to reverse the allotment act, Wahquahboshkuk attempted to have Scott removed as agent to the Kansas tribes. While in Washington on February 3, 1894, the Indian leader informed Secretary of the Interior Hoke Smith that Scott and his chief clerk, George James, were dishonest and that the tribespeople wanted them dismissed. "They do not treat the common Indians well," Wahquahboshkuk insisted. "Ever since Scott has been with us he has been disturbing our peace. He does not pay any attention to us full-blooded Indians, and says that he will help the whites and half-breeds on the reservation."[94] Wahquahboshkuk could have added that James was a white man who had lived at the agency for many years and rarely passed up opportunities for personal gain. Indeed, in 1891 James had been the only "Potawatomi" who openly accepted an allotment. Lewis F. Pearson, who would succeed Scott as agent, once called James "the most notorious 'Squaw-Man' who has ever resided within the limits of this Agency, comprising five tribes."[95]

Special Agent Aten, meanwhile, doggedly continued his efforts to break up the reservations. Through intimidation and threats he coerced several more of the acculturated Potawatomis and Kickapoos to accept title to their own farms. By August 1894, the situation on the

Potawatomi reservation had grown tense as the governmental agents and those under their influence faced outraged Indians. Many members of the banished Citizen Band had returned from Oklahoma and were also agitating against allotments. On August 3, Scott reported that the troublemakers "have been very aggressive and are openly declaring that . . . allottees will be driven from the Reservation" and that the fences surrounding their farms would be destroyed. He requested federal protection for the cooperative Indians and urged the immediate and forceful completion of allotment for all Potawatomis.[96]

On August 31, Commissioner of Indian Affairs Daniel M. Browning complied, instructing Aten to warn the Potawatomis and Kickapoos to select lands within thirty days or assignments would arbitrarily be made for them. The Dawes Act authorized such forced allotments, if necessary, four years after a presidential directive had been issued to sectionalize a particular reservation. President Harrison had issued such an order for the Kansas bands on September 1, 1890; no action had been taken, and four years had now passed. The full weight of the law was about to fall on the Potawatomis and Kickapoos, and they could not avoid it. The federal bureaucracy had become a paternalistic juggernaut not to be denied. By the end of the year, allotments had been made for all Kansas Indians, including the dejected Wahquah-boshkuk.[97]

For the next few years, the Indians still held to the hope that the policy could somehow be reversed. Wahquahboshkuk continued protesting against allotment and warned his followers to maintain solidarity. In February 1896, he and other Potawatomi leaders complained that the "halfbreeds" and "quarterbreeds" had gotten "too high tune for us and want to rule over us poor Indians." These Potawatomis claimed that George James and others had bullied many into accepting allotments and were constantly stealing the Prairie Band's money.[98]

Agents continually complained that the outspoken Wahquah-boshkuk and "his small band of faithful followers" were hindering the civilization program. "This element still clings to their inherent idea of a 'romantic barbarism,' " Agent Pearson reported in September 1896, "and it will require years of time and patient care and the exercise of much tact and kindly consideration to bring them to a full realization of the error of their ways." The agency clerk, Frederick Luther, acknowledged that the Indians at least had "the merit of consistency, in that they steadily repudiate the idea that in reality there has been an allotment, and positively refusing to accept the suggestion of even such an action as at all binding upon them." The notorious George James, who secured for himself the job as Potawatomi agent in 1897, denounced Wahquahboshkuk and his "gang of 'Kickers.' " James alleged that these Indians had "no regard for the truth and are vicious, and would be dangerous if they were not cowardly." He reported, moreover, that the anti-allotment forces were growing, for several more citizen Potawatomis in Oklahoma had lost their lands and were now returning to Kansas.[99] Many of these citizens as well as the Mexican Potawatomis became members of the Prairie Band, bringing with them a renewed determination to hold their band's lands in common as the Great Spirit had commanded.

Unfortunately for the Indians, allotment was indeed binding. Despite the efforts of Wahquahboshkuk and others, the policy was enacted. Wahquahboshkuk's stand had been courageous. When a lesser man might have faltered, he had gone to prison for a cause he held dear. His actions to stave off allotment were based on his own observations, and he readily accepted the help of those who had firsthand experience in dealing with allotment—the citizen Potawatomis and Kickapoos and the Mexican Potawatomis who joined forces with him. Wahquahboshkuk knew that the allotment policy had proven disastrous for others caught in its grip. His methods of passive resistance, public agitation, visits to Washington, and refusal to recognize counterproductive governmental policies had worked for others in the past. He could not know that they would fail this time.[100]

The allotment policy, regarded as a miraculous device to bring Indians into the modern world, brought only disaster wherever it had been employed. As early as January 1900, Potawatomi Agent William R. Honnell admitted that the Kansas bands had "not been benefited either morally or physically by the allotment to them of lands." Similar reports emanated from other Indian reservations for the next thirty-five years as millions of acres of tribal lands fell into white hands. President Theodore Roosevelt's 1901 observation that the Dawes Act would serve as "a mighty pulverizing machine to break up the tribal mass" would prove tragically prophetic.[101] For the Prairie Potawatomis and other Indians remaining in Kansas, the future appeared to be anything but bright.

8

THE TRIUMPH
OF INDIAN KANSAS

One Fourth of July two young photographers, C. C. Isely and his brother, were uninvited spectators at the Green Corn Dance on the Kickapoo reservation near the towns of Horton and Hiawatha in northeast Kansas. The two white men intended to photograph the ceremony, but when they entered the dancing grounds with tripod and camera, an angry Kickapoo rushed toward them. He was a handsome Indian, the Iselys later said, with his black hair in braids hanging down his back and his multicolored coat bedecked with jewelry.

"I understand that you men want to take some pictures of our ceremony. If you try to do so, I warn you that you will get into trouble." His manner was curt, but his English was perfect.

Surprised, the white men explained that they simply wanted to honor the Kickapoos by recording their festival for posterity. But the Indian adamantly rejected their request. "When I want pictures," he exclaimed, "I will get them in Hiawatha."[1]

The ceremony proceeded without further interruption from the Iselys, who considered the Stars and Stripes waving nearby an indication that Indians had the constitutional right to practice religion without interference. The brothers watched in wonderment as Indian men, young and old, danced in a wide circle, many with sleigh bells fastened to their leggings. In the center of the dance ground stood a huge drum that eight men beat simultaneously; they and all the other men sang in a pitch and volume that alternately rose and fell. At least two Potawatomis joined in and danced vigorously. "The performance was fantastic," C. C. Isely recalled, "weird beyond telling, yet entrancingly interesting."[2]

This dance occurred on the eve of the twentieth century, in 1897, but Indian culture was still vigorous in Kansas. The remaining Kickapoos and Potawatomis, as well as the Iowas, Missouri Sacs, Chippewas, and

Munsees, had overcome tremendous obstacles in their quest to survive. For many, a renewed religious spirit was an important factor in the struggle to hold on to their lands and traditions. Most Kickapoos and Potawatomis, the largest of the Kansas bands, clung to their Indian faiths; during the 1880s and 1890s, furthermore, both bands experienced a revitalization of their traditional religions. Some Iowas and Sacs, on the other hand, had begun to profess Christianity. Their Christianity differed, however, from that taught by the missionaries because they had kept various traditional Indian elements.[3] The Chippewa experience was similar to that of the Iowas and Sacs, although by the turn of the century most Chippewas had joined the Munsees in following a more conventional form of Christianity. While their methods differed, each band had achieved its goal of remaining in Kansas.

Unlike the others, the Chippewas and Munsees had virtually assimilated into the dominant American culture; the 1890 United States census reported that these two bands had "almost ceased to be Indians" in the ordinary sense of the term. Their quest for equality with whites, however, had not always been problem free. Chippewa leaders Edward McCoonse and Lewis Gokey died in 1888 and 1889, respectively, leaving their small band in less capable but slightly more honest hands. McCoonse's sons, Robert and William, continued the family tradition of corruption; these descendants of Francis McCoonse (Eshtonoquot) missed few opportunities to acquire the lands and procure the annuities of less sophisticated neighbors. During the years after their father's death the brothers were charged by agents as being "the most troublesome and altogether unreliable members of the tribe, and . . . a constant source of trouble and annoyance" to their people and to the government. Robert was considered especially troublesome. In December 1894, Agent L. F. Pearson reported that Robert McCoonse, "a character not above reproach," was wanted by the authorities in Indian Territory. The Chippewa had returned to Kansas to claim the annuities of one of his "adopted" daughters. This had aroused the anger of the Moravian missionary, who also claimed to have adopted the girl and was collecting her annuities.[4]

Despite his penchant for accumulating property and wealth by shady means, Robert McCoonse, like his opportunistic grandfather Eshtonoquot, was ever ready to defend the rights of all Chippewas and even Munsees. In 1897 the United States Congress passed a bill that

The Chippewa and Munsee Indians at the final payment, November 8, 1900. The bearded man in the center is the Moravian missionary Joseph Romig. (Courtesy of the Kansas State Historical Society)

provided for terminating the government's relations with the two small bands; it also created a commission to settle all tribal land matters, including the issuance of land patents or titles to each family and the sale of the remaining acreage. Two years later, Robert McCoonse and Agent William Honnell accompanied the federal commissioner to appraise the lands, and the three men managed to settle matters to the satisfaction of almost all of the eighty-seven Chippewas and Munsees. The government would buy the surplus lands for $42,700.[5]

The ceremonies that accompanied the Chippewa and Munsee final settlement and payment on November 8, 1900, illustrated to white spectators the degree of acculturation that the two bands had undergone since the mid-nineteenth century. The Moravian Joseph Romig had returned as their missionary after a thirty-year absence, and he assisted Agent Honnell and other officials in handing each Indian a legal patent to his or her land and a check for $491. The elderly Romig, recalling the raucous 1860s, was pleased that "not a single case of rioting or drunkeness [*sic*] occurred at the time or afterwards." The Indians spent their money wisely. Indeed, a year later they pooled their cash and paid $23,000 to buy their own surplus lands back from the government. They were ready to enter mainstream American society, and they understood that their tribal relationships had come to an end. With a certain prescience, Romig wrote in April 1903 that it was "probable" that these Indians "will before many years be known only in history."[6] The Chippewas and Munsees had become assimilated citizens. The irony was not lost on those hardy individuals—they had retained their lands, but they were no longer Indians.

The Iowas and Missouri Sacs had also become so highly acculturated by the late nineteenth century that many agents predicted a similar fate for them. The 1890 census counted one hundred sixty-five Iowas and eighty-seven Sacs on their small reservations straddling the Kansas-Nebraska border. The census report described them as a "civilized" and "fairly educated" people who "seem to be prosperous and happy." The Iowas were particularly "advanced; they dressed in "citizens' clothes" and acted very much like white people, "many of them so near white that the Indian blood is quite difficult to discover." Although an 1883 executive order granted them a reservation in Indian Territory and many had moved there, these "progressive" Indians stayed and reluctantly accepted allotments to their farms in the early 1890s.[7]

Both bands nevertheless continued to revere their tribal heritages, and they often relied on traditional religions in the face of adversity. Agent John Blair reported that the Sacs practiced their traditional faith, but white visitors often mistook Sac religious ceremonies for Christian rites. The Indians had good reason to pattern their ceremonies after Christian models, for they realized that whites would then be more likely to accept them as neighbors rather than demand their removal. Sometimes, however, they threw propriety to the wind. When officials arrived in 1890 to pressure the Iowas into accepting allotments, they were greeted by "a grotesque dance to the music of a bass drum accompanied by sleigh-bells." The white men were shocked that Indian "heathens" still "invoked aid" from the Great Spirit when conducting tribal business.[8] Although the Iowas as well as the Sacs relented and accepted allotment, they adamantly refused to move to

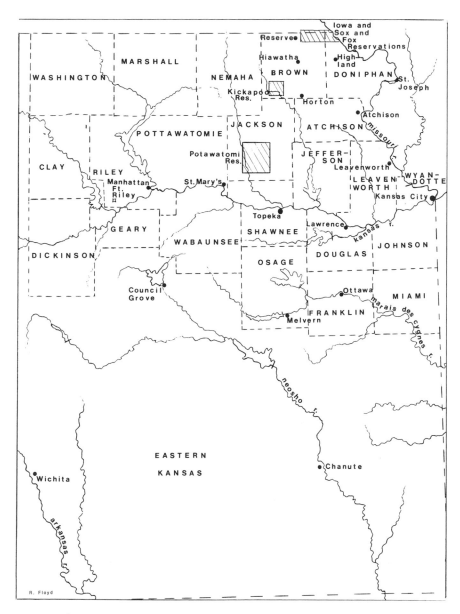

Present-day eastern Kansas, showing the Potawatomi, Kickapoo, Missouri Sac and Fox, and Iowa reservations.

Oklahoma. They may have been acculturated, but their land meant much to them and they still cherished their old customs.

By the early years of the twentieth century, most Iowas and Missouri Sacs spoke English and many could read and write. Participation in traditional ceremonies declined as the Indians blended in with the local farming community. In the summer of 1922, anthropologist Alanson Skinner declared that both tribes had "definitely abandoned their customs in favor of ours." He added that some Iowas were Christians, but others were "peyote devotees." How Skinner could have considered members of the pan-Indian peyote faith as being completely assimilated is difficult to ascertain—the use of peyote in religious ceremonies is exclusively an Indian custom. Indeed, the Iowas and Sacs continued to call themselves Indians; although acculturated, they had maintained an identity separate from their white neighbors. That their small reservations still exist gives ample testimony to this fact.[9]

The Iowas and Missouri Sacs had been wise in refusing to leave Kansas, for in the 1890s their kinfolk who had been removed to Oklahoma were plagued by white squatters who encroached on their lands and stole their possessions. Allotment also took its toll. Many Indians lost their Oklahoma farms, but Mokohoko's Sacs, now led by Chief Pawshepawho, endeavored to defend themselves against the forces of assimilation. In September 1892, their agent, Samuel Patrick, wrote to his superiors that the one hundred Indians had shunned tribal councils, refused to send children to school, and were generally "stubborn and rebellious." Although they had been forced to accept allotments, they still lived in a village and farmed their contiguous lands "without regard to individual ownership." Patrick lamented that they had evaded "the true meaning and intent of the allotment law" and clung to traditional ways. "Yet I must say," he added, "that this band is above the average for sobriety, honesty, industry, and thrift, notwithstanding their determination not to follow the ways of the white man."[10]

Mokohoko's band fared relatively well for the next few years. Indian agents reported that their lands were the most fertile of the entire Sac and Fox reservation. On March 10, 1899, however, disaster struck as smallpox broke out and forty-three Sacs soon died; this was a devastating blow to a people who had long struggled against great odds to live as they thought the Great Spirit intended. Despite the tragedy, the survivors picked up the pieces and continued to live as before. Agent W. C. Kohlenberg reported that they still acted as though allotments had never been made. Even more striking was the persistent rumor that the Indians intended to raise money, purchase land in Kansas, and reestablish their "old-time reservation."[11]

The Sacs never returned to Kansas to live but remained in Oklahoma and maintained their traditional ways well into the twentieth century. Even today, many still remain aloof not only from whites but from more acculturated kinfolk; they continue to pay tribute to Mokohoko for his courageous stand against the forces that sought the destruction of their tribe. These people are still proud to call themselves Indians who never willingly submitted to the demands of the whites.

The greatest challenge that faced the Kansas tribes in the late nineteenth century had been defending their lands. Although Mokohoko's strategy of passive resistance ultimately failed to overcome governmental policy, the Kickapoos and Potawatomis retained their Kansas homes by following tactics similar to those of the luckless Sacs. They were fortunate that their paper chiefs, unlike Moses Keokuk of the Sacs, had not signed away all of their lands. Traditional Kickapoo and Potawatomi leaders dominated tribal affairs, despite interference from paternalistic Indian agents and the government-recognized chiefs. The revival of Indian religious ceremonies in the 1880s and 1890s, moreover, reinforced tribal solidarity during the crucial battle against the forces of allotment.

The Kickapoos and Potawatomis had undergone revitalization movements in the past; the prophet Kenekuk's teachings during the 1830s and 1840s in favor of group solidarity and against selling tribal lands were still followed in the late nineteenth century. Although several of Kenekuk's adherents accepted allotments in the late 1860s, they soon regretted their decision and asked to rejoin kinfolk holding lands in common. Members of the prophet's faith successfully followed a dual strategy of winning acceptance from whites and maintaining a uniquely Indian way of life. Agent Blair reported in 1890 that they "practiced a more advanced religion" than other Indians. Their spiritual leader was Nozhakum, the son of the elder Nozhakum who had brought many of his Potawatomis into Kenekuk's fold years before. The younger Nozhakum, wrote Blair, impressed both Indians and whites "by his directness, fervor, and sense of deep responsibility evidenced by his manner and conduct in both public and private life."[12]

Although whites considered the highly acculturated members of Kenekuk's faith good neighbors who eventually would merge into mainstream American life, that religion actually served to reinforce Indian ways. Services were held in the Kickapoo or Potawatomi languages until the 1920s and 1930s when English began to appear. The prayer sticks would always prevail over the Bible. Adherents to the faith gave their children traditional names and disciplined them with the whip in the manner prescribed by Kenekuk. Their spiritual leaders, furthermore, passed on the knowledge of the prophet's teachings and rituals to their successors. "I preach the same principals [sic] that old man [Kenekuk] did," wrote John Masquequa in 1906, "and conduct the same form of services." These services are still being held in Kansas by the Kickapoo and Potawatomi descendants of Kenekuk's followers, who never relinquished their homes or their unique customs.[13]

Most Potawatomis and Kickapoos, however, shunned the Kenekuk church in favor of faiths that more closely resembled traditional Indian religions. One such belief was the Drum Religion, or Dream Dance, introduced by Potawatomis from Wisconsin in the early 1880s. This religion was a mixture of Christianity and traditional belief and centered on the Great Drum, which possessed supernatural powers. This drum, adherents believed, could solve the Indians' problems by bringing them renewed power.[14] Reporting in 1884 that the creed consisted "principally of dancing and exulting," Agent H. C. Linn advised his superiors that the new faith was not a matter for official concern. "In those dances," he noted, "the moral tendency is very good, as the teaching is in accordance with the Ten Commandments." Like Kenekuk's followers, moreover, the dancers abstained from alcohol and gambling during their ceremonies. "Under its teaching, drunkenness and gambling have been reduced 75 per cent," Agent I. W. Patrick wrote a year later, "and a departure from virtue on the part of its members meets with the severest condemnation." Agency physician Wilson Stuve, who attended several dances on the Potawatomi reservation, echoed these assessments. In 1888 Stuve testified that he had never seen "anything of an immoral character at the dances; on the contrary, the dances are exclusively of a religious character."[15]

The Drum Religion spread rapidly among Indians desperate for solutions to the complex array of problems facing them. This religion lifted morale, strengthened the old clan networks, fostered intertribal solidarity, and enabled the Indians to present a united front against allotment.[16] Most Potawatomis and Kickapoos realized that allotment would likely result in their destruction as tribes and the loss of their farms, and they prepared to defend themselves. The dances gave meaning to their world, a world turned upside down by bureaucrats and reformers who refused to consider the overwhelming evidence that allotment was destructive to the Indians.[17]

The ceremonies so effectively roused Indian spirits that whites began to worry, and following Wahquahboshkuk's release from prison in 1892, the agents' attitudes toward the Drum Dance abruptly turned hostile. On October 7, 1892, Agent J. A. Scott reported that the Indians had been dancing for two weeks, and he warned that an uprising similar to the Wounded Knee tragedy in South Dakota two years earlier was brewing in Kansas. Scott asserted that the Potawatomi and Kickapoo dance was similar to the Sioux Ghost Dance—which he had never witnessed—and that violence was imminent. He lamented that the Indians had rejected Christianity for a religion that "conceives a God for the Indians alone," and he alleged that their ceremonies encouraged drinking and gambling. To avoid trouble, the agent ordered the Indians to confine themselves to their own reservations.[18]

The dances continued, nevertheless, despite interference from Scott and subsequent agents. Although allotment was forced upon the Indians and much of their reservation lands eventually fell into white hands, their religions have survived and even prospered. Their ceremonies reinforced their resolve to remain in Kansas and enabled them to maintain a sense of pride in being Indians. They did not, however, wish to antagonize whites; on the contrary, they usually kept their ceremonies private to avoid white scorn or interference. The Drum Religion, Kenekuk's church, and the traditional bundle ceremony as well as the peyote religion introduced in 1910 are uniquely Indian faiths and still attract large followings on the Kansas Potawatomi and Kickapoo reservations.[19]

In many ways, the religious practices and moral outlook of the Potawatomis, Kickapoos, and other Kansas bands paralleled the teachings of conservative Christianity and made the Indians more acceptable neighbors to whites. But even those who professed Christianity retained a distinctive Indian character in their religious observances that set them apart from other Kansans. The Iowas, for example, had rejected the staid Presbyterians Irvin and Hamilton but embraced the teachings of the charismatic "Holiness" Church in the late 1890s. This faith was introduced by a certain Sister Mollie, a white woman who preached against drunkenness and vice. Agent George James reported in 1897 that this woman had successfully "encouraged and promoted the practice of honesty and virtue" among the Iowas.[20]

Whatever religion the Indians professed, they took their beliefs seriously and remained skeptical of strangers who endeavored to change them. The Potawatomis showed little concern when Russian immigrant Ike Gillberg arrived in July 1919 to preach among them. Methodist missionary Milton M. Thorne, however, was greatly alarmed that Communists were scheming to take over the reservation. Thorne advised federal authorities that Gillberg used the teachings of "spiritualism or some other ism" to "cloak" his real purpose of "spreading I.W.W. or Bolsheviki propaganda, or some other kind of 'ganda among the Indians." Thorne was relieved when Agent A. R. Snyder informed him that the Indians considered Gillberg to be "a joke." But Snyder thought that Gillberg might inculcate the Indians with the "Lenine [sic] doctrine." The agent suggested that Thorne keep his "ear close to the ground," and if the Russian "be foolish enough to hand out any [Communist] propaganda, kindly advise me immediately in the matter and there will be no trouble in making 'quick work' of him."[21]

Missionary efforts among the Kansas Indians, usually of a more conventional nature than Gillberg's, have continued to the present day. Catholics, Methodists, Presbyterians, Baptists, and others have won many converts, even among the Potawatomis and Kickapoos. Tribal religions, however, remain viable, and, as is customary with Indians, individuals may be members of two or three different sects at the same time. One can profess Catholicism, for example, and also take part in the Dream Dance or the peyote ceremonies. Although Catholic authorities might object, the Indians see nothing wrong with this.

Throughout the twentieth century, the Indians of Kansas have continued to fight for the right to worship freely and to secure an adequate living in Kansas. The struggle to determine their own destiny while retaining their identity as Indians, however, has not been easy. In the 1920s, federal officials forced Kickapoo, Potawatomi, Iowa, and Sac children to leave their homes and attend nearby Haskell Institute or

Potawatomi dancers in Topeka, 1925. (Courtesy of the Kansas State Histor-ical Society)

Genoa Boarding School in Nebraska. Assimilating Indians remained the stated goal of federal officials such as Commissioner Charles H. Burke, who in 1925 announced that schools had "enabled the Indians to make greater progress than any other pagan race in a like period of which there is any written record." That "progress" involved Indian children reading and writing English, dressing like whites, going to church, and learning farming or a domestic trade. At Haskell Institute, a few young women found the opportunity to specialize in nursing, clerical work, or teaching. Most of what the students learned, however, had little practical application when they went back to the reservation. In return for this education, moreover, the children endured such hardships as overcrowding, malnutrition, frequent epidemics, and harsh discipline.[22]

Besides formal schooling, other factors disrupted life on the reservations and pushed Indians closer to the white world. During the 1930s, the Indians of Kansas faced severe hardship as the Great Depression forced many to leave their homes. Although they remained on the official tribal census rolls, almost half of the reservation Indians moved to nearby cities such as Topeka, St. Joseph, and Kansas City in search of work; some even moved as far away as Oregon and Washington. The Indian Reorganization (Wheeler-Howard) Act of 1934, championed by Franklin Roosevelt's commissioner of Indian affairs, John Collier, provided some relief. It overturned the Dawes Act, ending the practice of land allotment and restoring the remaining surplus lands to tribal ownership; it also allowed for the restructuring of tribal governments.[23]

Although the act helped the Kansas Indians, with the exception of the Prairie Potawatomis, to reorganize their tribal councils, and federal loans enabled all the bands to buy supplies, equipment, and land, some of the old problems remained unsolved. By the time Commissioner Collier left office in 1945, poverty had become a way of life on the Kansas reservations. "The Indians do not have anything to farm with," a Potawatomi woman explained. "The people haven't even got a horse. They are just there, and they are just living and some have to go to Topeka to earn their livelihood."[24] The New Deal had made little impact on the Kansas bands, and many more Indians left the reservations in search of work.

During the years following World War II yet another governmental program to "emancipate" the Indians emerged, posing as severe a threat to Indian survival as the Dawes Act. "Set the American Indians Free!" was the slogan of the new plan—a plan called "termination."[25] Championed most emphatically by Dillon S. Myer and Glenn L. Emmons, commissioners of Indian affairs under the Truman and Eisenhower administrations, respectively, the advocates of termination asserted that Indians possessed the same capabilities as other Americans and that federal supervision violated their basic rights as individuals. Accordingly, the long-standing relationship between American Indians and the federal government must now be severed.

The power of the Bureau of Indian Affairs "has been too far-reaching and has gone on too long," Nebraska Sen. Hugh Butler wrote in September 1953. Butler, the chairman of the Senate Committee of Interior and Insular Affairs (the House of Representatives had an equivalent committee), was determined to press for termination. The policies of the Bureau of Indian Affairs under the New Deal, he noted, had only "delayed the adjustment" of Indians to American life. "I feel strongly that any Indian who is competent to handle his own affairs should have the right to do so. Along with such rights would naturally go responsibilities of private citizenship." According to Butler, the old paternalistic governmental policies were obsolete: "I think you will find a great many Indians deeply resent the policies which have kept them in the status of 'wards of the government.' "[26] He failed to mention that the "responsibilities of private citizenship," which included paying taxes, had already cost great numbers of Indians their lands and way of life.

Such opinions as Butler's predominated in a conservative America mesmerized by the fear of Soviet aggression and domination—Indian tribes are, after all, "socialistic" entities—and during the 1950s, Congress attempted to end federal protection and jurisdiction over several tribes, including the Kickapoos, Potawatomis, Sacs, and Iowas of Kansas. Like the Dawes Act, however, the termination policy proved catastrophic for those unfortunate enough to be caught in its grip. The Menominees of Wisconsin and the Klamaths of Oregon, two tribes affected by termination, lost their lands, possessions, and self-respect when federal protection was withdrawn and the Indians, as individual citizens, attempted to manage their own affairs.[27]

The termination policy was a direct assault on tribal solidarity, and it angered most American Indians, who cried out in protest against its implementation. In Kansas, the Potawatomi, Kickapoo, Sac, and Iowa tribal councils each passed resolutions opposing the plan. These Indians realized that if federal oversight was withdrawn, the state would tax their lands; in the late nineteenth century, many Kickapoos, Citizen Potawatomis, and others had lost their allotments for failing to pay taxes. As Ralph Simon of the Kickapoo council explained: "I have been brought up to depend on Uncle Sam to take care of my taxes and hold my land, and it is the way I was raised up." Simon had not taught his own children to be taxpaying citizens. "In other words, the whites raise their families to be conservative and to know their obligations, where, on the other hand, we weren't brought up that way."[28]

The Indians of Kansas were irate that such a bill could even be proposed, considering the long train of abuses their people had suffered under past governmental policies. Fortunately, they had gained valuable experience in defending themselves against the federal bureaucracy, and they took immediate action to counter the termination proposal. In the summer of 1953, the Prairie Potawatomis hired attorney O. R. McGuire of Washington, D.C., to defend their band's interests. In

November, hoping to rally public sympathy to their side, band members alerted local newspapers that Uncle Sam was "up to his old tricks in Indian affairs—he still wants to break his treaties with the Indians, which he swore when he made them would be good forever and ever, and take the Indians' land away from them."[29] A short time later, an overwhelming majority of the Potawatomis voted in favor of sending delegates to Washington to speak against termination. Their lawyer, McGuire, helped plan the defense strategy; but the Indians themselves would carry the responsibility of defeating the termination proposal.[30] Unlike the fight against allotment, this battle would not be lost.

Early the following year, just before the tribal delegates were to leave by train for Washington, two hundred Potawatomi men, women, and children gathered at the home of tribal chairwoman Minnie Evans for a traditional feast.[31] Joe Western, a reporter for the *Topeka State Journal*, looked on as many of the Potawatomis jammed into the Evans living room for the start of the festivities. The Indians first passed around an old calumet, or peace pipe, which their ancestors had brought to Kansas in the 1840s; everyone then took a drink of water—the symbol of life. The reporter noted that James Wahbnosah, one of those chosen to go to Washington, "led the ceremonial rites, asking continued blessings through fire (to cook the food and for warmth) from the spirits of the universe and from the Creator. The eating came next, and after that, Frank Masha, 73, one of the oldest members of the tribe, rose to ask the spirits of the universe to fulfill the wishes of the tribe."[32]

Four days later, February 18, 1954, Minnie Evans, John Wahwassuck, and James Wahbnosah of the Potawatomis, and Vestana Cadue and Ralph Simon of the Kickapoos spoke against termination before a joint hearing of House and Senate subcommittees on Indian affairs in Washington. Despite the tension-filled atmosphere, not to mention the usual patronizing and ethnocentric rhetoric of the congressmen, the Indians spoke with a united voice in opposition to the termination plan. Indeed, the delegates were as steadfast in defense of their people's rights that day as Kenekuk, Mokohoko, and Wahquahboshkuk had been in earlier times, as they argued in favor of continuing the federal supervision of the Kansas bands.

Like the eloquent Kenekuk over a century earlier, Vestana Cadue, the Kickapoo tribal chairwoman, scolded federal officials, instructing them of their duty to abide by the old treaty obligations and demanding that they withdraw the termination measure. "We feel that this

Kickapoo women in Horton, Kansas, ca. 1916–1917. (Courtesy of the Kansas State Historical Society)

bill should not become law," she asserted, "because in doing so we are thrown upon the public not as assets but as liabilities." She pointed out that very few Kickapoos would be able to keep their lands if taxes were assessed. "We want our lands to remain for our children and our children's children as was promised our forefathers when they were forced to move from place to place always with the assurance that they would be protected and their treaty rights respected."[33]

Minnie Evans was the most outspoken of the delegates that day. She realized that her Potawatomis and others could not afford to lose what little remained of their original reservations. Determined to defeat the termination proposal, she refused to back down in the face of tough questioning from the chairman of the Senate subcommittee, Arthur T. Watkins of Utah. Her stand against termination took courage, for she knew that past opponents of governmental policy had been sent to jail. She reminded Senator Watkins and the other congressmen that during the 1890s, agents had violated the Potawatomi treaty and had gone "to work and forced allotments and when these two old men

[Wahquahboshkuk and Uwactote] defended that treaty, [the authorities] placed them in Fort Riley."[34] Federal officials had already threatened to confine her in a women's penitentiary for denouncing the allotment program and for advocating a complete return to the common ownership of the Potawatomi reservation.[35]

During her testimony, nevertheless, Evans forcefully reiterated her stand against allotment, termination, and all other plans that appeared designed to rob Indians of their lands. "Well, our main trip here," she announced, "is to hang on to the treaty laws, what the United States made with our tribe, and they [officials] made those rules and agreements on their own and nobody asked them to put those rules out."[36]

Following Evans's testimony, John Wahwassuck engaged in a brisk dialogue with Senator Watkins over such issues as allotment, taxation, and federal supervision of Indian affairs. Wahwassuck denounced land allotment, which had caused severe hardship on the Potawatomi reserve. Under the allotment program, Indian agents had connived with "land-graft men" and "racketeers" to usurp Indian lands:

The Indians, they were swindled out of what land they really actually had, all of the good land. That is why I say the white man is just like a fox. He is a fox, and he will take all of the good land which the poor Indians have. I am still poor. All we have been living on all of these years is promises, and promises and promise upon promise. We still haven't accomplished anything yet.

Senator Watkins then asked why, if federal agents were not trustworthy and the Kansas lands were worthless, did Wahwassuck and the others oppose lifting federal supervision? Why did the Indians worry about paying taxes on unproductive land? The answer to these questions should have been obvious to Watkins and the other advocates of termination. The Indians had little faith in promises that termination was for their benefit. "The only thing that I am proud of," Wahwassuck replied, "is that we have got a home, whether the land is worth anything or not, we have got a place to go."[37]

Indeed, they still had a home in Kansas, a home their ancestors had fought for, a home the Potawatomis, Kickapoos, and the others did not want to lose. Fortunately for them, the termination policy was never implemented in Kansas. By the late 1950s, facing Indian protest and opposition from states concerned about losing federal funds, Congress had lost interest in implementing the termination program.[38]

Although it remained official policy until the late 1960s, termination was no longer a priority. For Indians, however, many of the old problems remained, as poverty and disease still haunted the nation's reservations. The federal government's attempts to better conditions on the reservations often made matters worse. Reductions in federal services forced the closing of schools and medical facilities. During the 1950s, moreover, while Congress debated termination, the Bureau of Indian Affairs actively pursued a program of "relocating" Indians to the cities. Bureau officials believed that to attain an adequate standard of living, it was likely "that more than half of all Indians would have to seek their livelihood off [the] reservation." Relocation centers were established in cities such as Chicago, Cincinnati, Denver, and Los Angeles—sites far removed from the Indian homelands. Despite opposition to the program from the leaders of the Kansas bands, many jobless Kickapoos, Potawatomis, and others took advantage of the bureau's offer and left their homes seeking employment during the 1950s and 1960s.[39]

Although the years of termination and relocation were difficult for the Kansas bands, the 1970s proved to be a decade of renewal and hope. President Lyndon Johnson's War on Poverty had provided some relief, but it was Richard Nixon's call for Indian self-determination that provided the biggest boost for the Kansas bands. In a message to Congress on July 8, 1970, President Nixon announced that federal officials must now "act on the basis of what the Indians themselves have long been telling us. The time has come to break decisively with the past and to create the conditions for a new era in which the Indian future is determined by Indian acts and Indian decisions." Finally, the Indian Self-Determination and Education Act of 1975 provided for increased Indian participation in administering service programs, Indian control of reservation schools, and additional federal funds to promote the economic development of the reservations.[40]

A change for the better was immediately felt in Kansas, especially on the Kickapoo reservation. During the 1970s, the Kickapoos acquired federal funds to build new homes and to buy land. With federal loans, they managed to reacquire more than twenty-four hundred reservation acres that had previously fallen into white hands; by the early 1980s, the band held about thirty-five hundred acres in common, with an

"Sophia Keesis, Kickapoo, operates a disc on her father, Jesse Keesis', farm. In this rural area, the Indians are nearly all farmers and lately, through revolving credit loans, have managed to improve their farms and equipment. Now they are adding considerably to the food production of the nation. So many of the young men have gone into the military services, it is necessary for the women and girls to help in the fields." So read the original caption for this photograph, which was taken in 1943 for the Bureau of Indian Affairs. (Courtesy of the National Archives, Washington, D.C)

additional thirty-six hundred acres owned by allottees. The Kickapoos also constructed a water treatment plant, printing press, gymnasium, senior citizens' center, library, trading post, youth center, day-care facility, and tribal farm. The rapid development of the reservation led to expanded economic opportunity and, as a result, many Indians returned from the cities to their homelands. The reservation population soared to nearly six hundred souls in the 1980s—a turn of events that would have pleased the old prophet, Kenekuk.[41]

Unfortunately, President Ronald Reagan came to office in 1981 with "new" ideas on governmental relations with Indians. According to

Reagan, the old methods had been counterproductive, and state and local governments should take over many responsibilities for Indian affairs. "Instead of fostering and encouraging self-government," he announced, "federal policies have by and large inhibited the political and economic development of the tribes." The secretary of the Interior, James Watt, was even more emphatic in denouncing past governmental policy. "If you want an example of the failure of socialism," Watt advised television audiences, "don't go to Russia, come to America and go to the Indian reservations." Drug abuse, alcoholism, unemployment, and other social problems among Indians have been fostered "because of socialistic government policies." The secretary also blamed tribal leaders who "are interested in keeping this group of people assembled in a desert environment where there are no jobs, no agricultural potential, no water, because if Indians were allowed to be liberated, they'd go and get a job and that guy wouldn't have his handout as a paid government Indian official."[42]

The Reagan solution was to make drastic cuts in federal expenditures for American Indians—cuts that have almost completely reversed the economic fortunes of the Kickapoos and the other Kansas bands. Donald D. Stull, a University of Kansas anthropologist who worked closely with the Kansas bands in their striving toward self-sufficiency, reported that the Reagan administration's budget cuts have brought the Kickapoo "tribal economy to its knees. The number of tribal employees plunged from an all-time high of 142 in August 1980 to 16 in January 1982—in a mere 18 months the unemployment rate had soared from 34 percent to 93 percent!" In addition, lack of funding forced the closing of the Kickapoo gymnasium (except on weekends for bingo), the library, and the trading post; several tribal buildings have been abandoned and many houses need repair.[43]

Like the Kickapoos, the Sacs, Iowas, and Potawatomis enjoyed a brief economic recovery as a result of the Self-Determination Act. But the "Reagan revolution" has brought severe problems for them as well. The business office of the Sacs, for example, is full of empty desks for lack of federal grants to pay secretaries and managers. Although the more fortunate Iowas have managed to pay their bills, their reservation road maintenance has fallen behind and other services have been reduced. The Potawatomis have also suffered; in 1982 they borrowed federal funds to repurchase fifteen-hundred acres of their reservation to start a tribal farm. Operations had just gotten under way when a massive downturn in the national farm economy put a severe strain on the band's financial resources, which were already feeling the effects of the federal budget cuts. Despite such problems, the Potawatomis stayed with the farming project, barely scraping together enough funds to continue. "We don't want to give up on farming," a council member reported in February 1987, "but we're leaning that way."[44]

Despite these setbacks and problems, the Kansas bands are determined to persevere. The Indians realize that the struggle will be as difficult as it was for their ancestors. They intend to stick with the basic strategies that those ancestors taught them—strategies that allowed the Indians of Kansas to acculturate without assimilating into white society. Their strategies have enabled them to find the middle ground between complete acceptance of white ways and observance of cherished traditional customs. Despite overwhelming odds, the Kickapoos, Potawatomis, Iowas, Sacs, and others have managed to survive.[45] The nineteenth century had seen tremendous pressures placed upon them to become a part of white society. The twentieth century brought different but no less severe pressures, and many American Indians have succumbed, losing their customs and lands.

Yet there are many more who have retained their essential identity as Indians; for this, possessing the reservations has been vital, even for those who work elsewhere. This is especially true of the Kansas Potawatomis and Kickapoos; the Iowas and Missouri Sacs live much like their white Kansas neighbors, but their tribal councils and yearly powwows reinforce a sense of their Indian heritage.[46] The Chippewas and Munsees have far weaker ties to the old ways, for they live among whites who might not even be aware that their neighbors are Indians. But they, like members of the other tribes, are proud to recall that their ancestors were the first American pioneers to settle Kansas. To them, Eshtonoquot, White Cloud, No Heart, Nesourquoit, Mokohoko, Nozhakum, and Wahquahboshkuk—names unfamiliar to white Americans—remain heroic figures who carved homelands out of the wilderness and in the face of insuperable odds preserved at least a part of those homelands for their descendants. Since their arrival in Kansas, the Kickapoos, Chippewas, Munsees, Iowas, Sacs, and Potawatomis have loved their homes, have viewed their lands with reverence, and have resisted every effort to evict them from the state. For them, the end of Indian Kansas was unacceptable; they have remained on the lands that they had once been promised were theirs forever.

NOTES

CHAPTER 1. INTRODUCTION

1. I recognize that the use of the term "white" may be construed as a simplistic generalization that does not adequately distinguish the particular Euro-American with whom the Indians came into contact. Historically, the Indians who settled Kansas had encountered the French, the Spanish, and the British and had dealt with Americans of various ethnic backgrounds. Some of these "whites" were settlers, farmers, and other ordinary citizens; some were businessmen such as fur traders, merchants, land speculators, and railroad operators. Others were federal and state politicians, agents, commissioners, and other governmental employees. There were also Methodist, Presbyterian, Baptist, Catholic, and other missionaries. When pertinent and feasible, I will specify the particular ethnic background of the individuals in this story. However, I believe that the term "white," under certain circumstances, is useful when referring to Euro-Americans as a group who generally held the same attitudes and opinions of themselves and of the Indians. Reginald Horsman points out that nineteenth-century Americans, as well as the British, the French, and other western Europeans, thought of themselves as Anglo-Saxons. Ignoring logical inconsistencies and contradictions, these whites believed themselves to be an "innately superior people." Anglo-Saxon government, religion, and other institutions were also considered superior. Indians and other peoples of color, as well as their cultures and institutions, were deemed innately inferior. Americans especially, writes Horsman, believed themselves to be the chosen people, who by the 1830s and 1840s used their ideology of racial superiority to force political, economic, and social conformity upon immigrants and to justify the exploitation of blacks, Indians, and Mexicans. For an astute analysis of nineteenth-century attitudes, including the prevailing scientific conclusions that "proved" Indian racial inferiority, see Horsman, *Race and Manifest Destiny: The Origins of American Racial Anglo-Saxonism* (Cambridge, Mass., and London: Harvard University Press, 1981), 1–6, 116–186; see also Robert E. Bieder, *Science Encounters the Indian, 1820–1880: The Early Years of American Ethnology* (Norman and London: University of Oklahoma Press, 1986), 3–15, 60–103.

2. Scholars are now arguing that the use of the term "Indian" may also be misleading. Some writers draw attention to the fact that Columbus misnamed America's original inhabitants, who should be called Native Americans. In an attempt at clarity, some scholars have begun using such contrived terms as

"Amerind" and "Amerindian." But even these labels can project false meaning. James A. Clifton rightly asserts that a writer's "uncritical use of culturally derived terms such as White, Indian, and Black for individuals and groups is a misleading and intellectually inhibiting practice. To assume automatically that such nomenclature denotes separate, immutable groups of humans in North America effectively blocks understanding." Clifton writes that since the nineteenth century many people for various reasons have laid claim to Indian status based on a real or imaginary percentage of Indian "blood." Since the early days of Indian-white contact, as Clifton explains, there has been much "interbreeding" between peoples, producing large numbers of so-called mixed-bloods. These offspring have possessed mixed cultural heritages, a fact that has had a great impact on them and the particular European and Indian cultures with which they interacted (see Clifton, "Alternate Identities and Cultural Frontiers," in *Being and Becoming Indian: Biographical Studies of North American Frontiers*, edited by James A. Clifton [Chicago: Dorsey Press, 1989], 1–37).

My study will use the term "Indian" as it refers to ethnic identity; one who identified with a particular Indian band and cherished the customs and religion of that band and who, in turn, was accepted by the majority of the band as a member will be designated as Indian. Most of the Indians in this study were members of patrilineal tribes, and, as Clifton points out, they did not easily accept as members those bicultural individuals who had white fathers and Indian mothers. The mixed-bloods (those who identified with two or more cultures) in this study, however, will also be designated as Indian as long as they called themselves such and were accepted by most others of a particular band as members of that band.

3. Most scholars are vague in their definitions and use the terms "acculturation" and "assimilation" interchangeably. My intention is to demonstrate that many American Indians have resisted their absorption into the so-called American melting pot and, therefore, a clarification of these terms is necessary. The Indians of Kansas have willingly adopted the trappings of Euro-American culture, but they have consciously remained separate from mainstream society. They have always seen themselves as Indians of one particular tribe or another, with a culture and heritage distinct from those of other American ethnic groups.

Anthropologist Charlotte Seymour-Smith has recently pointed out that twentieth-century ethnologists have usually defined acculturation as a phenomenon that results when two or more groups come into firsthand contact, with subsequent changes in the original cultural patterns of each group. She defines assimilation as one of the outcomes of acculturation; assimilation occurs when one group is absorbed by the other and becomes culturally indistinguishable from it. She notes that many recent analyses of cultural interaction and change have focused on the "strategic use of cultural elements in contact situations" (see Seymour-Smith, *Dictionary of Anthropology* [Boston: G. K. Hall & Company, 1986], 1, 18). My study will demonstrate how the various Kansas bands strategically utilized their syncretic cultures in order to survive in a hostile Kansas social environment.

4. Agent Daniel Vanderslice to A. Cumming, superintendent of Indian affairs at St. Louis, Mo., 6 Sept. 1854, Letters Received, Great Nemaha Agency, 1848–1876, Bureau of Indian Affairs, Record Group 75, National Archives, Microcopy 234, Roll 308 (hereafter cited as LR, Great Nemaha Agency, BIA, RG75, M234, R[300–314]).

5. Edward H. Spicer presents an excellent account of Jesuit attitudes and methods in *Cycles of Conquest: The Impact of Spain, Mexico, and the United States on the Indians of the Southwest, 1533–1960* (Tucson: University of Arizona Press, 1962), 308–324. For the Jesuit approach to mission work, see Peter Duignan, "Early Jesuit Missionaries: A Suggestion for Further Study," *American Anthropologist* 60 (Aug. 1958): 725–732; James P. Ronda, "The European Indian: Jesuit Civilization Planning in New France," *Church History* 41 (Sept. 1972): 388–393; Robert C. Carriker, "Joseph M. Cataldo, S.J.: Courier of Catholicism to the Nez Percés," in *Churchmen and the Western Indians, 1820–1920,* edited and with an introduction by Clyde A. Milner II and Floyd A. O'Neil (Norman and London: University of Oklahoma Press, 1985), 109–139. Robert H. Keller, Jr., points out that most Protestant missionaries rejected the Jesuit practice of incorporating and remolding Indian rituals into Christian rites (see Keller, *American Protestantism and United States Indian Policy, 1869–82* [Lincoln and London: University of Nebraska Press, 1983], 155–158).

6. For discussions of missionaries in Indian country, see Robert F. Berkhofer, *Salvation and the Savage: An Analysis of Protestant Missions and American Indian Response, 1787–1862* (New York: Atheneum, 1976), 1–15, and James P. Ronda and James Axtell, *Indian Missions: A Critical Bibliography* (Bloomington: Indiana University Press, 1978), 1–50. Pratt is quoted in Jack W. Manning, "John Gill Pratt: Missionary, Printer, Physician, Teacher, and Statesman" (Ph.D. dissertation, Central Baptist Theological Seminary, Kansas City, Kan., 1951), 23–24.

7. For the Methodist minister's thoughts on the Kickapoo prophet, see Jerome C. Berryman to Agent Richard Cummins, [?] Oct. 1839, Letters Received, St. Louis Superintendency, 1824–1841, Bureau of Indian Affairs, Record Group 75, National Archives, Microcopy 234, Roll 752 (hereafter cited as LR, St. Louis Superintendency, BIA, RG75, M234, R[747 – 752]); Berryman to Cummins, 15 Aug. 1842, *Senate Executive Documents,* 27th Cong., 3d sess., ser. 413, pp. 488–489; and Berryman, "A Circuit Rider's Frontier Experiences," *Kansas State Historical Society Collections* 16 (1923–1925): 216–217.

8. The unidentified Kickapoo is quoted in Charles Augustus Murray, *Travels in North America during the Years 1834, 1835, and 1836,* 2 vols. (London: Richard Bently, 1839), 2:80.

9. Hoecken was undoubtedly referring to an Indian shaman, a traditional spiritual healer who uses special powers to communicate with spirits, treat patients, control events, or divine hidden objects; Eshtonoquot, or Francis McCoonse, of the Kansas Chippewas possessed such shamanistic traits. An Indian prophet may hold similar powers; but a prophet proclaims a revelatory message and carries a moral mandate to the people. Possessing a vision of historical destiny, prophets such as Kenekuk of the Kickapoos work to help solve a crisis facing their people. For a concise analysis and comparison of such religious leaders, see James R. Lewis, "Shamans and Prophets: Continuities and Discontinuities in Native American New Religions," *American Indian Quarterly* 12 (Summer 1988): 221–228. Hoecken is quoted in Arthur T. Donohue, "A History of the Early Jesuit Missions in Kansas" (Ph.D. dissertation, University of Kansas, Lawrence, 1931), 200.

10. For Coffin's remarks, see *Minutes of Kansas Yearly Meeting of Friends, Held at Lawrence, Kansas* (1873) (Lawrence: Journal Steam Book and Job Printing House, 1873), 36–37.

11. Johnston Lykins to commissioner of Indian affairs, 30 Sept. 1849, quoted in

William E. Connelley, "The Prairie Band of Pottawatomie Indians," *Kansas State Historical Society Collections* 14 (1915–1918): 495.

12. Douglas is quoted in Patricia Nelson Limerick, *The Legacy of Conquest: The Unbroken Past of the American West* (New York and London: W. W. Norton & Company, 1987), 92–93.

13. For the development of the federal reservation system, see Robert A. Trennert, Jr., *Alternative to Extinction: Federal Indian Policy and the Beginnings of the Reservation System, 1846–1851* (Philadelphia: Temple University Press, 1975), 1–15, 40–60, 152–153, and Robert M. Utley, *The Indian Frontier of the American West, 1846–1890* (Albuquerque: University of New Mexico Press, 1984), 31–63. Trennert correctly maintains that federal officials developed the general reservation system in the late 1840s; however, he overlooks the fact that, beginning in the 1820s, the Indians of Kansas had been placed on reservations, under federal supervision, and were expected to confine most of their activities to their particular reservation. These early reservations were nearly identical to the kind established in the 1850s and after.

14. George W. Manypenny, *Our Indian Wards* (Cincinnati: Robert Clarke and Company, 1880; reprint New York: Da Capo Press, 1972), 126; Francis Paul Prucha, *The Great Father: The United States Government and the American Indians*, 2 vols. (Lincoln and London: University of Nebraska Press, 1986), 1:349.

15. T. H. Gladstone, *The Englishman in Kansas, or Squatter Life and Border Warfare*, introduction by Frederick Law Olmsted, with a foreword by James A. Rawley (Lincoln: University of Nebraska Press, 1971), 202.

16. Vanderslice to Cumming, 6 Dec. 1853, LR, Great Nemaha Agency, BIA, RG75, M234, R308.

17. For a complete discussion of the various Indian rings and their efforts to usurp Indian lands, see H. Craig Miner and William E. Unrau, *The End of Indian Kansas: A Study of Cultural Revolution, 1854–1871* (Lawrence: University Press of Kansas, 1978). For more information on the Indians and their problems, see Unrau, *The Emigrant Indians of Kansas: A Critical Bibliography* (Bloomington: Indiana University Press, 1979), 1–43; and Grant Foreman, *The Last Trek of the Indians* (New York: Russell & Russell, 1946), 182–263.

In his book describing the actions of corporations in Indian Territory, H. Craig Miner points out that the dispossession of the Five Civilized Tribes was a very complex matter with no clear villains or heroes. "The corporation was both the chief despoiler of Indian sovereignty and its most powerful supporter," Miner writes. "The Indian was both a promoter and an opponent of corporate privilege—even a single Indian might be each at different times, in different situations, or at different levels of perception. The government was often simultaneously friend and foe of a development and worked at cross purposes within itself" (see Miner, *The Corporation and the Indian: Tribal Sovereignty and Industrial Civilization in Indian Territory, 1865–1907* [Columbia: University of Missouri Press, 1976], 207–208). Although Miner provides a thorough analysis of corporations and their interactions with "progressive" Indians, he pays little attention to the more traditional or "conservative" Indians, most of whom rejected corporate interference in tribal affairs and defended their people's interests and, in many cases, should be considered the true voice of their people. The corporations, at least in Kansas, were primarily interested in profits and were little concerned with Indian welfare.

18. Lewis Henry Morgan, *The Indian Journals, 1859–62*, edited by Leslie A. White (Ann Arbor: University of Michigan Press, 1959), 102.

19. An excellent description of the Ottawa land swindle can be found in William E. Unrau's "The Ottawa Indian University: C. C. Hutchinson, Baptists, and Land Fraud in Kansas," *Arizona and the West* 25 (Autumn 1983): 229–244. For a comprehensive discussion of the Baptist fraud, see Unrau and H. Craig Miner, *Tribal Dispossession and the Ottawa Indian University Fraud* (Norman: University of Oklahoma Press, 1985).

20. Most of these individuals were mixed-bloods, or bicultural people, such as Edward McCoonse of the Chippewas, Henry Donohoe of the Munsees, Moses Keokuk of the Sacs, and Eli Nadeau of the Potawatomis. These men possessed mixed Indian and Euro-American cultural heritages and lived on the margins of two or more cultural frontiers. They knew the ways of white society and frequently used this knowledge for political and economic gain. Gary Clayton Anderson points out that such "cultural marginals" were tied to tribes through marriage and/or descent. Through the generations, they had become involved in a set of mutual obligations and rights that had "evolved into a distinctly bicultural pattern of values and sentiments neither traditional Indian nor European in character" (see Anderson, "Joseph Renville and the Ethos of Biculturalism," in *Being and Becoming Indian*, 60–63).

James Axtell is one of many scholars who argue in favor of using the "neutral" French word *métis* in place of mixed-blood, which causes confusion and is pejorative (see Axtell, "Forked Tongues: Moral Judgments in Indian History," American Historical Association *Perspectives* 25 [Feb. 1987]: 13). Although métis may be a useful term to define some peoples of mixed descent, it is not appropriate for the Indians of Kansas. French-English dictionaries, moreover, invariably translate métis as "half-breed," an ethnocentric term.

21. For Romig's statement, see Joseph Romig to Brother John Jacobsen, 4 Aug. 1863, Moravian Mission Records, Kansas Mission, Box 185, Folder 2, Item 2, Microfilm Roll 23, Moravian Church Archives, Bethlehem, Pa. (hereafter cited as Moravian Records, with box, folder, item, and microfilm roll numbers); Romig to Commissioner of Indian Affairs William P. Dole, 13 Feb. 1865, Letters Received, Sac and Fox Agency, 1859–1880, Bureau of Indian Affairs, Record Group 75, National Archives, Microcopy 234, Roll 735 (hereafter cited as LR, Sac and Fox Agency, BIA, RG75, M234, R[735–744]). For a thorough discussion of Romig's activities in Kansas, see Joseph B. Herring, "The Chippewa and Munsee Indians: Acculturation and Survival in Kansas, 1850s–1870," *Kansas History* 6 (Winter 1983/84): 212–220. For Martin's reference to Eshtonoquot, see Herring, "Chippewa and Munsee Indians," 215; for Mokohoko's dismissal, see Agent Henry W. Martin to superintendent of Indian affairs at St. Joseph, Mo., H. B. Branch, 20 Oct. 1863, *House Executive Documents*, 38th Cong., 1st sess., ser. 1182, pp. 371–372; "Talk between Acting Commissioner of Indian Affairs Charles E. Mix and Chiefs of the Sacs and Foxes," 24 May 1866, "Petition for Agent Martin's Removal," 16 July 1866, A. F. Chipman to Commissioner of Indian Affairs D. N. Cooley, 24 July 1866, and "Council of the Chiefs of the Sacs and Foxes," 6 Oct. 1866, LR, Sac and Fox Agency, BIA, RG75, M234, R736.

22. John C. Ewers, "Thomas M. Easterly's Pioneer Daguerreotypes of Plains Indians," *Bulletin of the Missouri Historical Society* 24 (July 1968): 333–336; Agent Alfred Vaughn to Thomas H. Harvey, superintendent of Indian affairs at St. Louis, Mo., 24 Feb. 1849, LR, Great Nemaha Agency, BIA, RG75, M234, R308; Samuel Irvin to Walter Lowrie, 20 Apr. 1854, American Indian Correspondence, Presbyterian Historical Society Collection of Missionary Letters,

1833–1893, Greenwood Press, Philadelphia, Microfilm, Box 3, Volume 2, Letter 66.

23. Vaughn to Harvey, 1 June 1848, Bvt. Maj. James H. Caileton to Col. E. V. Sumner, [?] Sept. 1849, and Vaughn to Harvey, 27 Oct. 1848, LR, Great Nemaha Agency, BIA, RG75, M234, R308.

24. Vaughn to David D. Mitchell, 19 Sept. 1849, and Caileton to Sumner, [?] Sept. 1849, LR, Great Nemaha Agency, BIA, RG75, M234, R308.

25. Agent J. A. Scott to commissioner of Indian affairs, 19 Apr. 1893, Outgoing Letters of the Potawatomi Agency, 1887–1900, Bureau of Indian Affairs, Record Group 75, Federal Record Center, Kansas City, Mo., vol. 11 (hereafter cited as OL, Potawatomi Agency, vols. [6 – 25], KCFRC). For two accounts of Wahquahboshkuk's efforts, see James A. Clifton, *The Prairie People: Continuity and Change in Potawatomi Indian Culture, 1665–1965* (Lawrence: University Press of Kansas, 1977), 353–355, 395–403; Anonymous, "The Prairie Potawatomie: Resistance to Allotment," *Indian Historian* 9 (Fall 1976): 27–31.

CHAPTER 2. REMOVAL TO "KANSAS"

1. The Missouri Sacs are usually referred to as the Missouri Sacs and Foxes. At the time of the band's removal to Kansas in 1837, there were small numbers of Foxes associated with the band. Over the years, however, most of the Foxes left to join kinfolk in Iowa and elsewhere. I believe, therefore, that a more appropriate name for this band is the Missouri Sacs.

2. See Bert Anson, "Variations of the Indian Conflict: The Effects of the Emigrant Indian Removal Policy, 1830–1854," *Missouri Historical Review* 59 (Oct. 1964): 65–67.

3. Jerome O. Steffen disagrees with writers who find continuity between the Jeffersonian approach toward Indians and the later removal policy of Andrew Jackson. According to Steffen, acquisition of land and Indian assimilation were mutually dependent ideas in the minds of Jeffersonians such as William Clark. The Jeffersonians hoped that assimilation of Indians would open surplus tribal lands and make removal unnecessary; the Jeffersonians, as believers in human progress, thought that the Indians had the potential of equality with whites. If the assimilation process proceeded too slowly, however, removal to isolated regions away from interfering white settlers would provide enough time for Indians to become civilized. Jacksonians believed, on the other hand, that Indians were savages and incapable of advancement. Assimilation, therefore, was not an option because Indians were racially inferior to whites. Removal served the interests of politically powerful whites, and the Indians must move west to make way for progress and the growth of the American nation. See Steffen, *William Clark: Jeffersonian Man on the Frontier* (Norman: University of Oklahoma Press, 1977), 130–142, 166–168, 176; see also Steffen, "William Clark," in *Soldiers West: Biographies from the Military Frontier*, edited by Paul Andrew Hutton, with an introduction by Robert M. Utley (Lincoln and London: University of Nebraska Press, 1987), 21–22.

A thorough discussion of Jeffersonian concepts can be found in Bernard W. Sheehan, *Seeds of Extinction: Jeffersonian Philanthropy and the American Indian* (New York: W. W. Norton & Company, 1974). For detailed analyses of nineteenth-century views on the possibilities for Indian social progress, see

Reginald Horsman, "Scientific Racism and the American Indian in the Mid-Nineteenth Century," *American Quarterly* 27 (May 1975): 152–168; Horsman, *Race and Manifest Destiny: The Origins of American Racial Anglo-Saxonism* (Cambridge, Mass., and London: Harvard University Press, 1981), 116–138; Roy Harvey Pearce, *Savagism and Civilization: A Study of the Indian and the American Mind* (Baltimore: Johns Hopkins Press, 1967), 53–58, 66–73; Robert E. Bieder, *Science Encounters the Indian, 1820–1880: The Early Years of American Ethnology* (Norman and London: University of Oklahoma Press, 1986), 146–193.

4. Francis Paul Prucha argues convincingly that the governmental officials who engineered removal never intended to place Indians on desert wastelands. Officials knew that the fertile lands just beyond the borders of Iowa, Missouri, and Arkansas were suitable for farming (see Prucha, "Indian Removal and the Great American Desert," *Indiana Magazine of History* 59 [Dec. 1963]: 299–322). Wilcomb E. Washburn questions Prucha's contention that removal was administratively and historically inevitable. Washburn insists that other approaches could have been pursued and enforced by governmental officials; until removal was made official policy, the fundamental elements of federal policy included the protection of Indian rights to their land, the regulation of Indian trade, the control of liquor traffic, and the promotion of "civilization" and education of the Indians in order to assimilate them into American society. Washburn maintains that the removal policy was unjustifiable even by the standards of white morality in the nineteenth century (see Washburn, "Indian Removal Policy: Administrative, Historical, and Moral Criteria for Judging Its Success or Failure," *Ethnohistory* 12 [Summer 1965]: 274–278).

5. For information on Kansas' history and environment, see Robert W. Richmond, *Kansas: A Land of Contrasts*, 3d ed. (Arlington Heights, Ill.: Forum Press, 1989); William Frank Zornow, *Kansas: A History of the Jayhawk State* (Norman: University of Oklahoma Press, 1957); and Charles C. Howes, *This Place Called Kansas* (Norman: University of Oklahoma Press, 1952).

6. For information on Kansas provided by Lewis and Clark in 1804 and Pike's journey west in 1806, see Louise Barry, *The Beginning of the West: Annals of the Kansas Gateway to the American West, 1540–1854* (Topeka: Kansas State Historical Society, 1972), 48–50, 54–58.

7. George C. Sibley, "Extracts from the Diary of Major Sibley," *Chronicles of Oklahoma* 5 (June 1927): 196–200.

8. See "Part I of James' Account of S. H. Long's Expedition, 1819–1820," in *Early Western Travels, 1748–1846*, 32 vols., edited by Reuben Gold Thwaites (Cleveland: Arthur H. Clark Company, 1904–1907), 14:171–218; Prucha, "Indian Removal and the Great American Desert," 299–303; and Dale Van Every, *The Final Challenge: The American Frontier, 1804–1845* (New York: William Morrow and Company, 1964), 162–167.

9. For analyses of the justification for taking Indian lands based on the land-use argument, see Peter A. Thomas, "Contrastive Subsistence Strategies and Land Use as Factors for Understanding Indian-White Relations in New England," *Ethnohistory* 23 (Winter 1976): 3–5, 14–15; Wilcomb E. Washburn, "The Moral and Legal Justification for Dispossessing the Indians," in *Seventeenth Century America: Essays in Colonial History*, edited by James Morton Smith (New York: W. W. Norton & Company, 1972), 22–26; William T. Hagan, "Justifying Dispossession of the Indian: The Land Use Argument," in *American*

Indian Environments: Ecological Issues in Native American History, edited by Christopher Vecsey and Robert W. Venables (Syracuse, N.Y.: Syracuse University Press, 1980), 65–68; Francis Paul Prucha, "The Image of the Indian in Pre–Civil War America," in *Indian Policy in the United States: Historical Essays*, edited by Francis Paul Prucha (Lincoln and London: University of Nebraska Press, 1981), 52–54; Prucha, *The Great Father: The United States Government and the American Indians*, 2 vols. (Lincoln and London: University Press of Nebraska, 1986), 1:29–30, 195–196.

10. Charles Kappler, comp., *Indian Affairs, Laws and Treaties*, vol. 2 (Washington, D.C.: Government Printing Office, 1904), 145–155, 164, 168–174.

11. Monroe is quoted in Prucha, *Great Father*, 1:184; Secretary of War John C. Calhoun to Agent Benjamin Parke, 8 Sept. 1819, Records of the Secretary of War relating to Indian Affairs, Letters Sent, Bureau of Indian Affairs, Record Group 75, National Archives, Microcopy 15, Roll 4.

12. Reginald Horsman, "American Indian Policy and the Origins of Manifest Destiny," *University of Birmingham Historical Journal* 11 (Dec. 1968): 128–140.

13. See Ronald N. Satz, *American Indian Policy in the Jacksonian Era* (Lincoln: University of Nebraska Press, 1975), 1–6; for a description of Indian "social progress" in the South, see Dale Van Every, *Disinherited: The Lost Birthright of the American Indian* (New York: Avon Books, 1967), 18–22; Francis Paul Prucha discusses nineteenth-century justifications for dispossessing Indians in *American Indian Policy in the Formative Years: The Indian Trade and Intercourse Acts, 1790–1834* (Lincoln: University of Nebraska Press, 1973), 239–242.

14. For the attitude of western Indians, see Herman J. Viola, *Thomas L. McKenney, Architect of America's Early Indian Policy: 1816–1830* (Chicago: Swallow Press, 1974), 216. For Sibley's report, see William E. Unrau, "George Sibley's Plea for the 'Garden of Missouri' in 1824," *Bulletin of the Missouri Historical Society* 27 (Oct. 1970): 8.

15. The treaty with the Kansa, or Kaw, Indians can be found in William E. Unrau, *The Kansa Indians: A History of the Wind People, 1673–1873* (Norman: University of Oklahoma Press, 1971), 105–111; see also Unrau, "Removal, Death, and the Legal Reincarnation of the Kaw People," *Indian Historian* 9 (Winter 1976): 3–9. For the Osage treaty, see John Joseph Mathews, *The Osages: Children of the Middle Waters* (Norman: University of Oklahoma Press, 1961), 518–521; the story of the Shawnees' removal is discussed by Carl G. Klopfenstein, "Westward Ho: Removal of Ohio Shawnees, 1832–1833," *Bulletin of the Historical and Philosophical Society of Ohio* 15 (Jan. 1957): 3–5. See also Barry, *Beginning of the West*, 127–128, and Kappler, *Treaties*, 217–225, 262–264.

16. Paul Wallace Gates, "Indian Allotments Preceding the Dawes Act," in *The Frontier Challenge: Responses to the Trans-Mississippi West*, edited by John G. Clark (Lawrence: University Press of Kansas, 1971), 153–154.

17. William T. Hagan, *The Sac and Fox Indians* (Norman: University of Oklahoma Press, 1958), 16–47.

18. Agent Richard Graham to William Clark, superintendent of Indian affairs at St. Louis, Mo., 15 Jan. 1825, Letters Received, St. Louis Superintendency, 1824–1841, Bureau of Indian Affairs, Record Group 75, National Archives, Microcopy 234, Roll 747.

19. James Mooney, *The Ghost-Dance Religion and Wounded Knee* (New York: Dover Publications, 1973), 694–696; James H. Howard, "The Kenakuk Religion: An Early 19th Century Revitalization Movement 140 Years Later,"

Museum News 26 (Nov.–Dec. 1965): 8–12.

20. Quoted in William Miles, "'Enamoured with Colonization': Isaac McCoy's Plan of Indian Reform," *Kansas Historical Quarterly* 38 (Autumn 1972): 273.

21. See George A. Schultz, *An Indian Canaan: Isaac McCoy and the Vision of an Indian State* (Norman: University of Oklahoma Press, 1972); Lela Barnes, "Journal of Isaac McCoy for the Exploring Expedition of 1828," *Kansas Historical Quarterly* 5 (Aug. 1936): 227–277; Roscoe Wilmeth, "Kansa Village Locations in Light of McCoy's 1828 Journal," *Kansas Historical Quarterly* 26 (Summer 1960): 152–157; John Francis McDermott, ed., "Isaac McCoy's Second Exploring Trip in 1828," *Kansas Historical Quarterly* 13 (Aug. 1945): 400–462; Barnes, "Journal of Isaac McCoy for the Exploring Expedition of 1830," *Kansas Historical Quarterly* 5 (Nov. 1936): 339–377.

22. Robert V. Remini, *Andrew Jackson* (New York: Harper & Row, 1969), 108–109.

23. Francis Paul Prucha, "Thomas L. McKenney and the New York Indian Board," *Mississippi Valley Historical Review* 48 (Mar. 1962): 635–655; see also Viola, *Architect of America's Early Indian Policy*.

24. Satz, *Indian Policy in the Jacksonian Era*, 15–20, 41–43; for discussions of the typical missionary view of Indians during the nineteenth century, see Robert F. Berkhofer, Jr., *Salvation and the Savage: An Analysis of Protestant Missions and American Indian Response, 1787–1862*, (New York: Atheneum, 1976), 99–102, and Henry Warner Bowden, *American Indians and Christian Missions: Studies in Cultural Conflict* (Chicago and London: University of Chicago Press, 1981), 164–197.

25. Satz, *Indian Policy in the Jacksonian Era*, 19–20; "Message of Andrew Jackson to the Two Houses of Congress," *Senate Executive Documents*, 21st Cong., 2d sess., ser. 203, 1830, p. 19.

26. "Message of Andrew Jackson," ibid. Prucha argues unconvincingly that because the Jacksonians took a paternalistic approach toward a dependent people whom they considered inferior, they carried out the removal policy with the best interests of the Indians at heart. "Christian statesmen and their missionary allies," writes Prucha, "looked upon Indians as children toward whom they had a parental or paternal responsibility. It was the duty of parents to provide what was best for their minor children, look out for their best interests (which the children themselves could not judge), and assist the children to move to full maturity" (see Prucha, *The Indians in American Society: From the Revolutionary War to the Present* [Berkeley, Los Angeles, and London: University of California Press, 1985], 10–16; see also Prucha, "Andrew Jackson's Indian Policy: A Reassessment," in *The Indian in American History*, edited by Francis Paul Prucha [Hinsdale, Ill.: Dryden Press, 1971], 67–74).

Although men such as Thomas Jefferson and Thomas McKenney probably were truly concerned about uplifting the "savage," Jackson's actions appear far more politically motivated than Prucha admits. Southern and western voters were more important than Indians, and the harsh removal policy, carried out during Jackson's presidency, demonstrates most emphatically where Jackson's sentiments lay. For analyses of Jackson's attitudes toward Indians that differ from Prucha's, see Steffen, *William Clark*, 130–142, 166–168, 176; Remini, *Andrew Jackson*, 128–130; and Glyndon G. Van Deusen, *The Jacksonian Era, 1828–1848* (New York: Harper & Row, 1963), 48–50.

27. Satz, *Indian Policy in the Jacksonian Era*, 64–65, 97–115.

28. For Isaac McCoy's views on the matter, see *History of Baptist Indian Missions* (Washington, D.C., and New York: W. M. Morrison and H. & S. Rayner, 1840), 400.

29. See James C. Malin, *Indian Policy and Westward Expansion*, Bulletin of the University of Kansas Humanistic Studies, vol. 2, no. 3 (Lawrence: University of Kansas, 1921), 11–14.

30. Anthony F. C. Wallace, "Prelude to Disaster: The Course of Indian-White Relations Which Led to the Black Hawk War of 1832," in *The Black Hawk War, 1831–1832*, 3 vols., edited by Ellen M. Whitney (Springfield: Illinois State Historical Library, 1970), 1:36–38.

31. For examples of citizen outrage that resulted from the Black Hawk uprising, see Ninian Edwards to Sens. Elias K. Kane and I. M. Robinson, 19 Apr. 1832 and 5 June 1832, in Ninian W. Edwards, *History of Illinois from 1778 to 1833; and Life and Times of Ninian Edwards* (New York: Arno Press, 1975), 367–372; *Vandalia Whig and Illinois Intelligencer*, 13 June 1832; *St. Louis Beacon*, 31 May 1832; *St. Joseph Beacon* (Indiana), 6 June 1832, quoted in Ella Lonn, "Ripples of the Black Hawk War in Northern Indiana," *Indiana Magazine of History* 20 (Sept. 1924): 303–304.

32. Clark to Kenekuk, 31 Aug. 1832, and Clark to Kenekuk, 16 Jan. 1833, History, Indians, Kickapoo File, Manuscript Division, Kansas State Historical Society, Topeka.

33. Ibid.

34. Kappler, *Treaties*, 365–367.

35. James A. Clifton, *The Prairie People: Continuity and Change in Potawatomi Indian Culture, 1665–1965* (Lawrence: University Press of Kansas, 1977), 231–245; William E. Connelley, "The Prairie Band of Pottawatomie Indians," *Kansas State Historical Society Collections* 14 (1915–1918): 488–490.

36. Clifton, *Prairie People*, 183–185. R. David Edmunds shows how unscrupulous traders helped dispossess Indian lands in his article " 'Designing Men Seeking a Fortune': Indian Traders and the Potawatomi Claims Payment of 1836," *Indiana Magazine of History* 77 (June 1981): 109–122.

37. Benjamin F. Stuart, "The Deportation of Menominee and His Tribe of Pottawattomie Indians," *Indiana Magazine of History* 18 (Sept. 1922): 255–265.

38. Barry, *Beginning of the West*, 314–315; Kappler, *Treaties*, 468–470.

39. *Examiner* (London), 25 Jan. 1835; *Times* (London), 26 Mar. 1835. An 1897 letter by Michigan resident Steven Rose describes Eshtonoquot, or Francis McCoonse (see Grace C. Skinner and Elmer L. Skinner, *History Stories of New Baltimore* [New Baltimore, Mich.: New Baltimore Public Library, 1979], 248–252). For information on Eshtonoquot, see Joseph B. Herring, "The Chippewa and Munsee Indians: Acculturation and Survival in Kansas, 1850s–1870," *Kansas History* 6 (Winter 1983/84): 212–220. An unpublished manuscript entitled "Letters from Westport: To Kansas by Difficult Ways," by John A. Sturm of Ann Arbor, Michigan, also provides information on McCoonse.

40. Eshtonoquot to Henry Schoolcraft, 29 Nov. 1839, Letters Received by the Office of Indian Affairs, Michigan Superintendency, 1834, Bureau of Indian Affairs, Record Group 75, National Archives, Record Group 75, Microcopy 1, Roll 38.

41. Herring, "Chippewa and Munsee Indians," 212–220.

42. De Smet is quoted in Malin, *Indian Policy and Westward Expansion*, 53; for the governmental approach toward the immigrant Indians living along the

Lower Missouri River, see Robert A. Trennert, Jr., *Alternative to Extinction: Federal Indian Policy and the Beginnings of the Reservation System, 1846–1851* (Philadelphia: Temple University Press, 1975), 131–159.

CHAPTER 3. THE VERMILLION KICKAPOOS

1. Some of the material in this chapter, especially detail on the Kickapoo prophet, has already been covered in my other publications; no book about the emigrant tribes of Kansas, however, can exclude this information. Much additional material, not previously published, is also included here. See Joseph B. Herring, "The Vermillion Kickapoos of Illinois: The Prophet Kenekuk's Peaceful Resistance to Indian Removal, 1819–1833," *Selected Papers in Illinois History 1983* (1985): 28–38; "The Prophet Kenekuk, and the Vermillion Kickapoos: Acculturation without Assimilation," *American Indian Quarterly* 9 (Summer 1985): 295–307; *Kenekuk, the Kickapoo Prophet* (Lawrence: University Press of Kansas, 1988).

2. Ann Ruth Willner and Dorothy Willner define charisma as a particular leader's capacity to elicit deference, devotion, and awe toward himself as the source of authority within the group. A charismatic leader (such as Kenekuk) is seen by his followers to possess almost supernatural powers; he becomes associated with the sacred symbols of the society. The charismatic leader's appeal, however, is limited to those who share the traditions of a given culture. See Willner and Willner, "The Rise and Role of Charismatic Leaders," *Annals of the American Academy of Political and Social Science* 358 (Mar. 1965): 77–88.

3. For the story of Kenekuk's youth, see James H. Howard, "The Kenakuk Religion: An Early 19th Century Revitalization Movement 140 Years Later," *Museum News* 26 (Nov.–Dec. 1965): 4–5. Kenekuk's date of birth is estimated to be about 1790. Kenekuk's name first appears in official governmental records on the Kickapoos' 1816 peace treaty; see Charles Kappler, comp., *Indian Affairs, Laws and Treaties,* vol. 2 (Washington, D.C.: Government Printing Office, 1904), 131.

4. Kenekuk and his followers had begun a revitalization of their Kickapoo culture and society similar to that of Handsome Lake and the Seneca Indians of the early 1800s. Revitalization movements have been studied by anthropologists and historians for many years, and Fred W. Voget and Anthony F. C. Wallace provide two analyses. Voget would call the Vermillion Kickapoo experience positive nativism, meaning an attempt to attain social "reintegration through a selective rejection, modification and synthesis of both traditional and alien cultural components." Wallace would classify their movement as a "deliberate, organized, conscious effort by members of a society to construct a more satisfying culture." See Voget, "The American Indians in Transition: Reformation and Accommodation," and Wallace, "Revitalization Movements," *American Anthropologist* 58 (Apr. 1956): 249–263 and 264–281.

James R. Lewis has recently modified and added clarification to Wallace's definition. Lewis argues that no prophet could "deliberately" create an acceptable revelatory message. A successful prophet actually believes that the new message was revealed by a deity; the prophet then interprets and adapts the message to the culture's historical situation. Lewis maintains that the prophet's revelatory message is accepted by members of a society "as a new 'story' which expands or supplants a culture's previous stories (myths) about the way things are." The new story is most likely to be accepted during periods of severe societal stress. See Lewis, "Shamans and Prophets: Continuities and Discontinuities in Native American New Religions," *American Indian Quarterly* 12 (Summer 1988): 225–227.

5. Kickapoo tribal history and customs are discussed in Arrell M. Gibson, *The Kickapoos: Lords of the Middle Border* (Norman: University of Oklahoma Press, 1963), 1–51; Charles Callender, Richard K. Pope, and Susan M. Pope, "Kickapoo," in *Northeast*, vol. 15 of *Handbook of North American Indians*, edited by Bruce G. Trigger (Washington, D.C.: Smithsonian Institution, 1978), 656–667; George R. Nielsen, *The Kickapoo People* (Phoenix: Indian Tribal Series, 1975); Robert E. Ritzenthaler and Frederick A. Peterson, *The Mexican Kickapoo Indians* (Milwaukee: Milwaukee Public Museum Publications in Anthropology, 1956); Felipe A. Latorre and Delores L. Latorre, *The Mexican Kickapoo Indians* (Austin and London: University of Texas Press, 1976); Donald D. Stull, *Kiikaapoa: The Kansas Kickapoo* (Horton, Kans.: Kickapoo Tribal Press, 1984); Betty Ann Wilder Dillingham, "Oklahoma Kickapoo" (Ph.D. dissertation, University of Michigan, Ann Arbor, 1963), 72–275; Alice B. Kehoe, *North American Indians: A Comprehensive Account* (Englewood Cliffs, N.J.: Prentice-Hall, 1981), 305–307. For information on Algonquian political organizations, see Charles Callender, "Great Lakes–Riverine Sociopolitical Organization," in *Handbook of North American Indians*, 15:610–621.

6. By the 1830s Kenekuk had assumed the role as head chief. Although most of the band belonged to Kenekuk's church, some Vermillion Kickapoos chose to adhere to traditional beliefs and remained outside of the church while still retaining membership in the band.

7. Kenekuk is quoted in the New York newspaper of the Methodist Episcopal Church, the *Christian Advocate and Journal*, 4 Aug. 1837; reprinted in Nyle H. Miller and Edgar Langsdorf, eds., *Kansas in Newspapers* (Topeka: Kansas State Historical Society, 1963), 9–10.

8. See William D. Smith to Rev. E. P. Swift, 3 July 1833, American Indian Correspondence, Presbyterian Historical Society Collection of Missionary Letters, 1833–1893, Greenwood Press, Philadelphia, Microfilm, Box 3, Volume 1, Letter 5 (hereafter cited as Presbyterian Mission Letters, with box, volume, and letter numbers); Jerome C. Berryman, "A Circuit Rider's Frontier Experiences," *Kansas State Historical Society Collections* 16 (1923–1925): 177–226; Thomas Forsyth, "The Kickapoo Prophet," in *The Indian Tribes of the Upper Mississippi Valley and Region of the Great Lakes*, 2 vols., edited by Emma Helen Blair (Cleveland: Arthur H. Clark Company, 1911–1912), 1:280–281; Isaac McCoy, *History of Baptist Indian Missions* (Washington, D.C., and New York: W. M. Morrison and H. & S. Rayner, 1840), 458. Callender notes that the war chief usually assigned members of the warrior organization to enforce tribal regulations. Violators of tribal rules who resisted those men chosen to enforce the laws were subject to whippings, or even death (see *Callender*, "Great Lakes –Riverine Sociopolitical Organization," 619). By assigning men to whip violators, Kenekuk had assumed the responsibilities once held by the war chief.

9. Howard, "Kenakuk Religion," 22. For Kenekuk's quote on the fate of alcoholics and other sinners, see Gurdon S. Hubbard, "A Kickapoo Sermon," *Illinois Monthly Magazine* 1 (Oct. 1831): 474.

10. In keeping with Kickapoo tradition, Kenekuk initially worked to

strengthen the clans. He realized that adherence to clan membership rules had meant a stronger band that could better resist outside pressures. If the Kickapoos adhered to his teachings, Kenekuk promised that the clans would gain renewed strength. According to the prophet, the Great Spirit had spoken: " 'Our old men had totems [clans]. They were good and had many totems. Now you have scarcely any. If you follow my advice, you will soon have totems again' " (quoted in James Mooney, *The Ghost-Dance Religion and Wounded Knee* [New York: Dover Publications, 1973], 695–696). The clans never completely disappeared among either the adherents to Kenekuk's church or the other Kickapoo bands, and various Kickapoo informants tell me that the clans are still considered important on their Kansas reservation.

11. See George J. Remsburg, "Some Notes on the Kickapoo Indians," *Philatelic West* 36 (Apr. 30, 1907): 325–326; Howard, "Kenakuk Religion," 22; Charles Augustus Murray, *Travels in North America during the Years 1834, 1835, and 1836*, 2 vols. (London: Richard Bently, 1839), 2:78.

12. Smith to Swift, 3 July 1833, Presbyterian Mission Letters, Box 3, Volume 1, Letter 5.

13. Letter of W. W. Redman in *Christian Advocate and Journal*, 4 Aug. 1837; W. Patton to Rev. C. Elliott, 8 May 1843, *Western Christian Advocate*, June 9, 1843, 43, copy in Indian Missions File, Methodist, Manuscript Division, Kansas State Historical Society, Topeka.

14. Letter of W. W. Redman in *Christian Advocate and Journal*, 4 Aug. 1837; Smith to Swift, 3 July 1833, Presbyterian Mission Letters, Box 3, Volume 1, Letter 5; McCoy, *Baptist Indian Missions*, 457–458.

15. Elbert Herring to William Clark, 3 June 1833, Letters Sent by the Office of Indian Affairs, Bureau of Indian Affairs, Record Group 75, National Archives, Microcopy 21, Roll 10.

16. Callender, Pope, and Pope, "Kickapoo," 661–662.

17. John Dunbar and Samuel Allis, "Letters Concerning the Presbyterian Mission in Bellevue, Nebraska, 1831–1841," *Kansas State Historical Society Collections* 14 (1915–1918): 693. For reports on the strife that erupted between the two bands, see Agent Richard Cummins to Herring, 30 Sept. 1835, and Capt. Matthew Duncan to Col. Henry Dodge, 23 May 1835, Letters Received, Fort Leavenworth Agency, 1824–1851, Bureau of Indian Affairs, Record Group 75, National Archives, Microcopy 234, Roll 300 (hereafter cited as LR, Fort Leavenworth Agency, BIA, RG75, M234, R[300–303]; see also "Council with the Kickapoo," 13 June 1836, and Duncan to Gen. Henry Atkinson, 14 June 1836, Letters Received, St. Louis Superintendency, Bureau of Indian Affairs, Record Group 75, National Archives, Microcopy 234, Roll 751 (hereafter cited as LR, St. Louis Superintendency, BIA, RG75, M234, R751).

18. Herring's instructions to Ellsworth are quoted in John F. McDermott's edited reprint of John Treat Irving's *Indian Sketches, Taken during an Expedition to the Pawnee Tribes* [1833], 2 vols. (Philadelphia: Cary, Lea, and Blanchard, 1835; reprint, Norman: University of Oklahoma Press, 1955), 38–39, note 3.

19. According to one observer, the Kickapoos lived in a place "as attractive as any yet settled by civilized man." See the *Missouri Republican* (St. Louis), 28 May 1842; reprinted in "Bypaths of Kansas History," *Kansas Historical Quarterly* 10 (Aug. 1941): 324.

20. See the 1835 edition of Irving's *Indian Sketches*, 82–84, 87–88.

21. "Council of Ellsworth with the Kickapoo," 2 Sept. 1833, Letters Received,

Western Superintendency, Bureau of Indian Affairs, Record Group 75, National Archives, Microcopy 234, Roll 921 (hereafter cited as LR, Western Superintendency, BIA, RG75, M234, R921); Gibson, *Kickapoos*, 112–113. A description of the Kickapoo lands can be found in the "Report on the Expedition of Dragoons, under Colonel Henry Dodge, to the Rocky Mountains in 1835," in *Military Affairs*, vol. 7 of *American State Papers: Documents Legislative and Executive of the Congress of the United States* (Washington, D.C.: Gales & Seaton, 1836), p. 130.

22. Ibid.

23. Henry Ellsworth to Herring, 8 Nov. 1833, LR, Fort Leavenworth Agency, BIA, RG75, M234, R300; "E. A. Ellsworth in Council with Kenekuk at Fort Leavenworth," 13 Nov. 1833, and H. Ellsworth to the commissioner, [?] November 1833, LR, Western Superintendency, BIA, RG75, M234, R921.

24. For the traveler's description of the Prairie Kickapoos, see Charles F. Hoffman, *A Winter in the West, by a New Yorker* (New York: Harper & Brothers, 1835), 83–84.

25. For an example of the typical missionary attitude, see W. H. Goode's letter in J. J. Lutz, "The Methodist Missions among the Indian Tribes in Kansas," *Kansas State Historical Society Collections* 9 (1905–1906): 208.

26. Benedict Roux is quoted in Gilbert J. Garraghan, *Catholic Beginnings in Kansas City, Missouri: An Historical Sketch* (Chicago: Loyola University Press, 1920), 49–54.

27. Berryman is quoted in Lutz, "Methodist Missions among the Indian Tribes," 208–209; Berryman, "Frontier Experiences," 523–525, 538.

28. Thomas Johnson to the corresponding secretary of the Methodist Episcopal Church, 16 June 1835, in William W. Sweet, *The Methodists: A Collection of Source Materials*, vol. 4 in *Religion on the American Frontier, 1783–1840* (Chicago: University of Chicago Press, 1946), 516–518.

29. Van Quickenborne wrote about his journey to Kickapoo country in "Relations d'un voyage fait chez les tribus indiennes situées à l'ouest du missouri," 24 Sept. 1835, *Annales de la propagation de la foi* 9 (Sept. 1836): 99–101. See also Gilbert J. Garraghan, "The Kickapoo Mission," *St. Louis Catholic Historical Review* 4 (Jan.-Apr. 1922): 27–28; John M. Moeder, *History of the Diocese of Wichita* (Wichita, Kans.: By the author, 1963), 2–4; Richard Joseph Bollig, "History of Catholic Education in Kansas, 1836–1932" (Ph.D. dissertation, Catholic University of America, Washington, D.C., 1933), 1–12.

30. Garraghan, "Kickapoo Mission," 27–28.

31. "Council with the Kickapoo," 13 June 1836, and Matthew Duncan to Henry Atkinson, 14 June 1836, LR, St. Louis Superintendency, BIA, RG75, M234, R751.

32. Dale Van Every describes the Seminole victory in *Disinherited: The Lost Birthright of the American Indian*, (New York: Avon Books, 1967), 196–197; for information on the Seminole war, see Francis Paul Prucha, *The Sword of the Republic: The United States Army on the Frontier, 1783–1846* (New York: Macmillan Company, 1969), 273–300. For Pashishi's comments, see "Council with the Kickapoo," 13 June 1836, and Duncan to Atkinson, 14 June 1836, LR, St. Louis Superintendency, BIA, RG75, M234, R751.

33. Van Quickenborne to Father McSherry, 29 June 1836, and Van Quickenborne to McSherry, 1 July 1836, in Garraghan, "Kickapoo Mission," 32–33, 37–40; "Council with the Kickapoo," 13 June 1836, LR, St. Louis Superintendency, BIA, RG75, M234, R751.

34. Pashishi is quoted in Garraghan, "Kickapoo Mission," 47. The agency doctor certified that most of the Kickapoos had been vaccinated by Jerome Berryman; see J. A. Chute to Cummins, 23 July 1838, LR, Fort Leavenworth Agency, BIA, RG75, M234, R301

35. Pierre Jean De Smet, *Life, Letters, and Travels of Father Pierre Jean De Smet, S.J., 1801–1873*, 4 vols., edited by Hiram M. Chittenden and Alfred T. Richardson (New York: Francis P. Harper, 1905; reprint, New York: Kraus Reprint Company, 1969), 1:150–151, 162.

36. Cummins to the superintendent of Indian affairs in St. Louis, Joshua Pilcher, [?] Oct. 1839, *Senate Executive Documents*, 26th Cong., 1st sess., ser. 354, p. 502.

37. "Talk by the Kickapoo Chiefs," 31 Dec. 1838, LR, Fort Leavenworth Agency, BIA, RG75, M234, R301. For a discussion of the Prairie Kickapoos who left Kansas, see Joseph B. Herring, "Cultural and Economic Resilience among the Kickapoo Indians of the Southwest," *Great Plains Quarterly* 6 (Fall 1986): 263–275.

38. Cummins to Commissioner of Indian Affairs C. A. Harris, 25 Sept. 1838, LR, Fort Leavenworth Agency, BIA, RG75, M234, R301.

39. Berryman to Cummins, [?] Oct. 1839, LR, St. Louis Superintendency, BIA, RG75, M234, R752; Berryman to Cummins, 15 Aug. 1842, *Senate Executive Documents*, 27th Cong., 3d sess., ser. 413, pp. 488–489; Berryman, "Frontier Experiences," 537–539.

40. Nicolas Point, *Wilderness Kingdom: Indian Life in the Rocky Mountains, 1840–1847: The Journals and Paintings of Nicolas Point, S.J.*, translated and edited by Joseph P. Donnelly (New York: Holt, Rinehart and Winston, 1967), 23–24.

41. Garraghan, "Kickapoo Mission," 48–49.

42. De Smet, *Life, Letters, and Travels*, 1:150–151 and 162, and 3:1085–1086.

43. For reports on Kickapoo farming, see Cummins to St. Louis Superintendent of Indian Affairs D. D. Mitchell, 12 Sept. 1842, *Senate Executive Documents*, 27th Cong., 3d sess., ser. 413, p. 436; Cummins to Mitchell, 1 Oct. 1843, *Senate Executive Documents*, 28th Cong., 1st sess., ser. 431, p. 404.

44. For reports on the Kickapoos' work habits, see Nathaniel Talbott to John C. Spencer, 28 Jan. 1843, LR, Fort Leavenworth Agency, BIA, RG75, M234, R302; McCoy, *Baptist Indian Missions*, 458; David Kinnear to Cummins, 30 Sept. 1838, LR, Fort Leavenworth Agency, BIA, RG75, M234, R301; Samuel Mason to Cong. John C. Mason, 26 Dec. 1849, LR, Fort Leavenworth Agency, BIA, RG75, M234, R303; Cummins to St. Louis Superintendent of Indian Affairs William Clark, 31 Jan. 1838, Cummins to Clark, 16 May 1838, and Cummins to Commissioner of Indian Affairs Carey A. Harris, 23 Sept. 1838, LR, Fort Leavenworth Agency, BIA, RG75, M234, R301.

45. Cummins to Mitchell, 22 June 1843, and Thomas Harvey to the commissioner, 21 Feb. 1846, LR, Fort Leavenworth Agency, BIA, RG75, M234, R302.

46. Maj. B. F. Roberts to E. F. Sumner, commander at Fort Leavenworth, 13 Feb. 1849, and Mitchell to R. W. Wells, United States judge for Missouri, 8 Dec. 1850, LR, Fort Leavenworth Agency, BIA, RG75, M234, R303.

47. Richardson to Mitchell, 30 Sept. 1852, *Senate Executive Documents*, 32d Cong., 2d sess., ser. 658, p. 361; W. P. Badger to St. Louis Superintendent of Indian Affairs A. M. Robinson, 20 Sept. 1859, in the *Annual Report* of the commissioner of Indian affairs (Washington, D.C., 1859), 144; Louise Green Hoad, *Kickapoo Indian Trails* (Caldwell, Idaho: Caxton Printers, 1944), 52–53.

48. Richardson to Mitchell, 30 Sept. 1852, *Senate Executive Documents,* 32d Cong., 2d sess., ser. 658, p. 361.

49. Commissioner of Indian Affairs George Manypenny to Secretary of the Interior Robert McClelland, 9 Nov. 1853, *Senate Executive Documents,* 33d Cong., 1st sess., ser. 690, pp. 121–122.

50. Agent David Vanderslice to Manypenny, 25 Nov. 1853, Letters Received, Great Nemaha Agency, Bureau of Indian Affairs, Record Group 75, National Archives, Microcopy 234, Roll 308 (hereafter cited as LR, Great Nemaha Agency, BIA, RG75, M234, R308).

51. For information on the Preemption Law and other methods that whites used to acquire Kansas lands, see Homer E. Socolofsky, "How We Took the Land," in *Kansas: The First Century,* vol. 1, edited by John D. Bright (New York: Lewis Historical Publishing Company, 1956), 281–306; William Frank Zornow, *Kansas: A History of the Jayhawk State* (Norman: University of Oklahoma Press, 1957), 92–105; H. Craig Miner and William E. Unrau, *The End of Indian Kansas: A Study of Cultural Revolution, 1854–1871* (Lawrence: University Press of Kansas, 1978), 14; Unrau, "The Council Grove Merchants and Kansa Indians, 1855–1870," *Kansas Historical Quarterly* 34 (Autumn 1968): 266–269; Paul Wallace Gates, *Fifty Million Acres: Conflicts over Kansas Land Policy, 1854–1890* (Ithaca, N.Y.: Cornell University Press, 1954). Benjamin Harding is quoted in Louise Barry, *The Beginning of the West: Annals of the Kansas Gateway to the American West, 1540–1854* (Topeka: Kansas State Historical Society, 1972), 1202.

52. Kappler, *Treaties,* 614–626.

53. *Washington Daily Star,* 18 May 1854; *Washington National Intelligencer,* 19 May 1854; *Alexandria Gazette* (Virginia), 19 May 1854.

54. Kappler, *Treaties,* 634–636.

55. George W. Manypenny, *Our Indian Wards* (Cincinnati: Robert Clark and Company, 1880; reprint, New York: Da Capo Press, 1972), 122.

56. Both observers are quoted in Barry, *Beginning of the West,* 1227 and 1232.

57. Gates, *Fifty Million Acres,* 4; Gates is also quoted in Unrau, "Council Grove Merchants and Kansa Indians," 267.

58. *New York Times,* 15 July 1854; also quoted in Barry, *Beginning of the West,* 1230.

59. Royal Baldwin to superintendent of Indian affairs in St. Louis, A. Cumming, 7 Sept. 1853, Letters Received, Kickapoo Agency, Bureau of Indian Affairs, Record Group 75, National Archives, Microcopy 234, Roll 371 (hereafter cited as LR, Kickapoo Agency, BIA, RG75, M234, R371). The settler's description can be found in the "Reminiscences of William Honnell," no date, History, Indians, Kickapoo File, Manuscript Division, Kansas State Historical Society, Topeka.

60. Baldwin to Cumming, 31 Dec. 1855, and Baldwin to Cumming, 3 Apr. 1856, LR, Kickapoo Agency, BIA, RG75, M234, R371.

61. Baldwin to Cumming, 2 May 1856, LR, Kickapoo Agency, BIA, RG75, M234, R371; Baldwin to Cumming, 23 Oct. 1856, *Senate Executive Documents,* 34th Cong., 3d sess., ser. 875, pp. 662–664.

62. F. M. Williams, superintendent of the Methodist School, to Agent Charles B. Keith, 17 Sept. 1861, *Senate Executive Documents,* 36th Cong., 2d sess., ser. 1078, p. 661; Special Indian Inspector Edward Kenible to Commissioner of Indian Affairs E. P. Smith, 19 Nov. 1874, Reports of the Inspection of the Field Jurisdictions of the Office of Indian Affairs, Bureau of Indian Affairs, Record

Group 48, National Archives, Microcopy 1070, Roll 40 (hereafter cited as Field Jurisdiction Inspection Reports, BIA, RG48, M1070, R40).

63. Harry Kelsey, "William P. Dole and Mr. Lincoln's Indian Policy," *Journal of the West* 10 (July 1971): 487–489; Dean Banks, "Civil-War Refugees from Indian Territory, in the North, 1861–1864," *Chronicles of Oklahoma* 41 (Autumn 1963): 286–298; Edmund J. Danziger, Jr., "The Office of Indian Affairs and the Problem of Civil War Indian Refugees in Kansas," *Kansas Historical Quarterly* 35 (Autumn 1969): 257–275; James R. Mead, *Hunting and Trading on the Great Plains, 1859–1875*, edited by Schuyler Jones, with an introduction by Ignace Mead Jones (Norman: University of Oklahoma Press, 1986), 150–155; Annie Heloise Abel, *The American Indian as Participant in the Civil War*, vol. 2 of *The Slaveholding Indians* (Cleveland: Arthur H. Clark Company, 1919), 230. For a complete history of the effect of the Civil War on reservation Indians, see Edmund J. Danziger, Jr., *Indians and Bureaucrats: Administering the Reservation Policy during the Civil War* (Urbana: University of Illinois Press, 1974).

64. Gibson, *Kickapoos*, 124–140; Danziger, *Indians and Bureaucrats*, 163.

65. J. J. Lawler, clerk for the superintendent of Indian affairs at St. Joseph, Missouri, to Commissioner of Indian Affairs William Dole, 31 Mar. 1864, and Agent Abraham Bennett to the superintendent at St. Joseph, William Albin, 10 Aug. 1864, LR, Kickapoo Agency, BIA, RG75, M234, R372.

66. For the story of Pahkahka's death, see William Honnell's account in History, Indians, Kickapoo File; and John Winsea to George Remsburg, 25 May 1908, Remsburg Collection, Box 78:4, Manuscript Division, Kansas State Historical Society, Topeka.

67. Agent F. G. Adams to Central Superintendent of Indian Affairs Enoch Hoag, 6 Aug. 1869, *House Executive Documents*, 41st Cong., 2d sess., ser. 1414, pp. 807–812; Kenible to Smith, 19 Nov. 1874, Field Jurisdiction Inspection Reports, BIA, RG48, M1070, R40.

68. Agent M. H. Newlin to superintendent of Indian affairs at Lawrence, Kansas, William Nicholson, 1 Mar. 1876, and Newlin to Nicholson, 30 Sept. 1876, Letters Received relating to the Agency for Indians in Kansas (Potawatomi Agency) and the Kiowa Agency, 1876, Bureau of Indian Affairs, Record Group 75, National Archives, Microcopy 856, Roll 71; see also *Minutes of Kansas Yearly Meeting of Friends, Held at Lawrence, Kansas,* (1876), 33–34.

69. Inspector John McNeil to the commissioner, 9 Dec. 1878, Field Jurisdiction Inspection Reports, BIA, RG48, M1070, R40.

70. Newlin to Nicholson, 31 July 1877, Letters Received relating to the Cheyenne and Arapahoe and the Agency for Indians in Kansas (Potawatomi Agency), 1877, Bureau of Indian Affairs, Record Group 75, National Archives, Microcopy 856, Roll 79; see also *Minutes of Kansas Yearly Meeting of Friends, Held at Lawrence, Kansas,* (1877), 34.

CHAPTER 4. THE CHIPPEWAS AND MUNSEES

1. A treaty uniting the Chippewas and Munsees was concluded on 16 July 1859 (see Charles Kappler, comp., *Indian Affairs, Laws and Treaties*, vol. 2 (Washington, D.C.: Government Printing Office, 1904), 792–796.

2. Henry W. Martin to Commissioner of Indian Affairs D. N. Cooley, 26 June 1866, Letters Received, Sac and Fox Agency, 1859–1880, Bureau of Indian Affairs,

Record Group 75, National Archives, Microcopy 234, Roll 736 (hereafter cited as LR, Sac and Fox Agency, BIA, RG75, M234, R[734–744]).

3. See Lewis Henry Morgan, *The Indian Journals, 1859–62*, edited by Leslie A. White (Ann Arbor: University of Michigan Press, 1959), 59, 81–82. For a thorough sketch of Delaware Indian history and customs, see Ives Goddard, "Delaware," in *Northeast*, vol. 15 of *Handbook of North American Indians*, edited by Bruce G. Trigger (Washington, D.C.: Smithsonian Institution, 1978), 213–239; see also C. A. Weslager, *The Delaware Indians: A History* (New Brunswick, N.J.: Rutgers University Press, 1972), and *The Delawares: A Critical Bibliography* (Bloomington: Indiana University Press, 1978).

4. Louise Barry, ed., "Scenes in (and en route to) Kansas Territory, Autumn 1854: Five Letters by William H. Hunter," *Kansas Historical Quarterly* 35 (Autumn 1969): 319. For discussions of the interaction between Indians and Moravian missionaries, see Kenneth G. Hamilton, "Cultural Contributions of Moravian Missions among the Indians," *Pennsylvania History* 18 (Jan. 1951): 1–15; Marcie J. Kohnova, "The Moravians and Their Missionaries: A Problem in Americanization," *Mississippi Valley Historical Review* 19 (Dec. 1932): 349–354; Paul A. W. Wallace, "The Moravian Records," *Indiana Magazine of History* 48 (June 1952): 143–144.

5. See Morgan, *Indian Journals*, 59; Goddard, "Delaware," 216, 222, 225.

6. For an excellent analysis of this land swindle, see Paul Wallace Gates, "A Fragment of Kansas Land History: The Disposal of the Christian Indian Tract," *Kansas Historical Quarterly* 6 (Aug. 1937): 227–240.

7. Gates, "A Fragment of Kansas Land History," 233–240; G. F. Oehler to Rev. John Jacobsen, 7 Oct. 1858 and 13 Oct. 1858, Moravian Mission Records, Kansas Mission, Box 1853, Folder 3, Items 3 and 4, Microfilm Roll 24, Moravian Church Archives, Bethlehem, Pa. (hereafter cited as Moravian Records, with box, folder, item, and microfilm roll numbers).

8. Ibid.

9. For two excellent articles on individuals who served as a bridge between the Indian and white cultures, see Colin G. Calloway, "Simon Girty: Interpreter and Intermediary," and Gary Clayton Anderson, "Joseph Renville and the Ethos of Biculturalism," in *Being and Becoming Indian: Biographical Studies of North American Frontiers*, edited by James A. Clifton (Chicago: Dorsey Press, 1989), 38–58 and 59–81.

10. Henry Donohoe to Oehler, 27 Feb. 1862, Moravian Records, Box 185, Folder 1, Item 2, MR23.

11. For information on Chippewa culture and history, see E. S. Rogers, "Southeastern Ojibwa," in *Handbook of North American Indians*, 15: 760–771.

12. Francis Tymoney to Central Superintendent of Indian Affairs Alexander M. Robinson, 1 Sept. 1858, *House Executive Documents*, 35th Cong., 2d sess., ser. 997, pp. 472–474.

13. Ibid.

14. Morgan, *Indian Journals*, 82.

15. Ibid.

16. *Leavenworth Times*, 27 Aug. 1859.

17. Quoted in Ida M. Ferris, "The Sauks and Foxes in Franklin and Osage Counties, Kansas," *Kansas State Historical Society Collections* 11 (1909–1910): 362.

18. Friend Palmer, *Early Days in Detroit* (Detroit: Hunt and June, 1906),

150–152; Grace C. Skinner and Elmer L. Skinner, *History Stories of New Baltimore,* (New Baltimore, Mich.: New Baltimore Public Library, 1979), 249–252. According to E. S. Rogers, Chippewa "medicine men" possessed the "knowledge and ability to heal and to perform other functions. Their services were always paid for by a present made before they made a performance. To effect a cure, a medicine man with special training employed a rattle and 'sucking tubes.' " See Rogers, "Southeastern Ojibwa," 764.

19. See Morgan, *Indian Journals,* 82.

20. "Conditional Agreement between the Chippewa and Munsee Indians," 19 Mar. 1859, LR, Sac and Fox Agency, BIA, RG75, M234, R734; Kappler, *Treaties,* 792–795.

21. Clinton C. Hutchinson to H. B. Branch, superintendent of Indian affairs at St. Joseph, Mo., 1 Oct. 1861, *Senate Executive Documents,* 37th Cong., 2d sess., ser. 1117, p. 672.

22. Romig was a member of the Northern Province of the Moravian Church, headquartered in Bethlehem, Pennsylvania.

23. One reason federal officials permitted the Moravians to establish a mission among the tribes was that church elders agreed to finance the entire venture themselves. Even before Romig arrived on the reservation, however, Donohoe informed Moravian elders that the Indians might ask the government to give the Moravians permanent status on the reservation and allow the church to acquire tribal monies to support the school and mission. See Donohoe to Oehler, 27 Feb. 1862, and Joseph Romig to Brother S. Wolle, 24 Mar. 1862, Moravian Records, Box 185, Folder 1, Items 2 and 3, MR23.

24. Romig to Wolle, 24 Mar. 1862, Romig to Oehler, 24 Apr. 1862, Romig to Wolle, 23 June 1862, and Romig to Jacobsen, 9 Mar. 1863, Moravian Records, Box 185, Folder 1, Items 4, 5, and 6, and Folder 2, Item 1, MR23; Hutchinson to Branch, 17 Sept. 1862, *House Executive Documents,* 37th Cong., 3d sess., ser. 1157, pp. 253–254.

25. Francis McCoonse (Eshtonoquot) and others to Commissioner of Indian Affairs William P. Dole, 15 Feb. 1864, Letters Received, Ottawa Agency, 1863–1865, Bureau of Indian Affairs, Record Group 75, National Archives, Microcopy 234, Roll 656 (hereafter cited as LR, Ottawa Agency, BIA, RG75, M234, R656); Francis McCoonse and others to Dole, 6 Dec. 1864, and Francis McCoonse to commissioner, 10 Apr. 1866, LR, Sac and Fox Agency, BIA, RG75, M234, R735 and R736.

26. Romig to Jacobsen, 9 Mar. 1863, Moravian Records, Box 185, Folder 2, Item 1, MR23; Hutchinson to Dole, 20 Feb. 1864, LR, Ottawa Agency, BIA, RG75, M234, R656; Martin to Dole, 2 Jan. 1865, LR, Sac and Fox Agency, BIA, RG75, M234, R735.

27. Romig to Jacobsen, 4 Aug. 1863, Moravian Records, Box 185, Folder 2, Item 2, MR23; Romig to Dole, 13 Feb. 1865, LR, Sac and Fox Agency, BIA, RG75, M234, R735.

28. Hutchinson to Dole, 1 Dec. 1863, LR, Ottawa Agency, BIA, RG75, M234, R656; "Council of the Chippewa and Christian Indians," report signed by Henry Donohoe, Edward McCoonse, and others, 18 Jan. 1865, and Martin to Dole, 15 Mar. 1865, LR, Sac and Fox Agency, BIA, RG75, M234, R735; report of Commissioner Cooley, 31 Oct. 1865, *House Executive Documents,* 39th Cong., 1st sess., ser. 1248, pp. 212–213.

29. Romig to Wolle, 4 Apr. 1866, Moravian Records, Box 185, Folder 5, Item 2,

MR23; Romig to Martin, 6 Aug. 1866, LR, Sac and Fox Agency, BIA, RG75, M234, R736.

30. Donohoe to Jacobsen, 29 Jan. 1864, Hutchinson to Wolle, 30 Jan. 1864, Romig to Wolle, 12 Feb. 1864, Donohoe to Jacobsen, 15 Apr. 1864, and Oehler to Jacobsen, 5 May 1864, Moravian Records, Box 185, Folder 3, Items 2, 3, 4, 6, and 8, MR23.

31. Francis McCoonse and others to Dole, 15 Feb. 1864, LR, Ottawa Agency, BIA, RG75, M234, R656; Donohoe to Jacobsen, 15 Apr. 1864, and Romig to Wolle, 27 Apr. 1864, Moravian Records, Box 185, Folder 3, Items 6 and 7, MR23.

32. Romig to Jacobsen, 13 Dec. 1864, Moravian Records, Box 185, Folder 3, Item 13, MR23; "Council of the Chippewa and Christian Indians," 18 Jan. 1865, and Romig to Dole, 13 Feb. 1865, LR, Sac and Fox Agency, BIA, RG75, M234, R735. E. S. Rogers reports that the Chippewas believed that "medicine men could inflict as well as remove disorders (see "Southeastern Ojibwa," 764).

33. Romig to Wolle, 1 May 1865, Moravian Records, Box 185, Folder 4, Item 5, MR23.

34. The June 1865 census listed thirty-eight children, and Romig reported that twenty-nine were attending his school; see "Statement of the Number of Indians Belonging to the Sac and Fox Agency, Kansas, 30 June 1865," LR, Sac and Fox Agency, BIA, RG75, M234, R735; Romig to Martin, 8 Aug. 1865, *House Executive Documents*, 39th Cong., 1st sess., ser. 1248, p. 565.

35. Martin to Dole, 17 Mar. 1865 and Martin to Dole, 26 June 1865, LR, Sac and Fox Agency, BIA, RG75, M234, R735; report of Commissioner Cooley, 31 Oct. 1865, *House Executive Documents*, 39th Cong., 1st sess., ser. 1248, p. 213; Anna H. Abel, "Indian Reservations in Kansas and the Extinguishment of Their Title," *Kansas State Historical Society Collections* 8 (1903–1904): 99; Romig to Wolle, 1 May 1865, and Romig to Jacobsen, 3 Aug. 1865, Moravian Records, Box 185, Folder 4, Items 5 and 2, MR23.

36. Francis McCoonse to the secretary of the Interior, 29 June 1866, Donohoe and others to Martin, 24 June 1866, and Martin to Cooley, 26 June 1866, LR, Sac and Fox Agency, BIA, RG75, M234, R736.

37. Albert Wiley to the commissioner of Indian affairs, 6 June 1867, LR, Sac and Fox Agency, BIA, RG75, M234, R737; Wiley to Central Superintendent of Indian Affairs Thomas Murphy, 30 July 1867, *House Executive Documents*, 40th Cong., 2d sess., ser. 1326, p. 300; "Report of the Acting Commissioner of Indian Affairs Charles E. Mix," 15 Nov. 1867, *House Executive Documents*, 40th Cong., 2d sess., ser. 1326, p. 17.

38. Edward McCoonse and others to Martin, 11 Jan. 1867, "Petition Opposing Removal from Kansas," signed by Francis McCoonse and members of the council, 19 Jan. 1867, and Eshtonoquot (Francis McCoonse) to commissioner of Indian affairs, 8 Feb. 1867, LR, Sac and Fox Agency, BIA, RG75, M234, R737.

39. For crop reports, see Wiley to Murphy, 30 July 1867, and Romig to Wiley, 31 July 1867, *House Executive Documents*, 40th Cong., 2d sess., ser. 1326, pp. 300, 302–303.

40. Romig to Wolle, 16 Feb. 1868 and 10 Mar. 1868, Moravian Records, Box 185, Folder 7, Items 3 and 4, MR23.

41. Romig to Wolle, 1 Apr. 1868 and 2 June 1868, ibid., Items 5 and 6, MR23; Murphy to commissioner of Indian Affairs, 1 June 1868, LR, Sac and Fox Agency, BIA, RG75, M234, R737.

42. "Treaty between the United States and the Swan Creek and Black River Chippewas and the Munsee or Christian Indians," 1 June 1868, Documents

relating to the Negotiation of Ratified and Unratified Treaties with Various Indian Tribes, 1868–1869, Bureau of Indian Affairs, Record Group 75, National Archives, Microcopy-T494, R10.

43. In 1871 the United States Congress discontinued the practice of making treaties with American Indian tribes.

44. Romig to Wolle, 25 Aug. 1868 and 12 Oct. 1869, Moravian Records, Box 185, Folder 7, Item 10, and Folder 8, Item 1, MR23.

45. Report of Commissioner of Indian Affairs Ely S. Parker, 23 Dec. 1869, *House Executive Documents,* 41st Cong., 2d sess., ser. 1414, p. 474.

46. Romig to Brother Kampman, 7 Jan. 1870, and Romig to Wolle, 9 Aug. 1870, Moravian Records, Box 185, Folder 9, Items 1 and 4, MR23.

47. Romig to Wiley, 7 July 1869, *House Executive Documents,* 41st Cong., 2d sess., ser. 1414, p. 806; Romig to Wolle, 9 Aug. 1870, Moravian Records, Box 185, Folder 9, Item 3, MR23; William Nicholson, "A Tour of Indian Agencies in Kansas and the Indian Territory in 1870," *Kansas Historical Quarterly* 3 (Aug. 1934): 309.

48. It is not clear how many Chippewas actually became Christians at this time. E. S. Rogers reports that even if a Chippewa converts to Christianity, he or she does not abandon the traditional belief system (see "Southeastern Ojibwa," 766).

49. C. R. Kinsey to Rev. E. de Schweinitz, 27 May 1881, Moravian Records, Box 185, Folder 9B, Item 1, MR23.

50. Nicholson, "Tour of Indian Agencies," 308.

51. Although the Indians did not receive patents in fee simple until 1900, individuals could sell their land before that time if they were declared competent by a court. During the 1850s and 1860s, there was much fraud connected with this process and many Indians from other tribes lost their holdings. See Grant Foreman, *The Last Trek of the Indians* (Chicago: University of Chicago Press, 1946), 228, note 3.

CHAPTER 5. THE IOWAS AND THE MISSOURI SACS

1. The Missouri Sacs are usually referred to as the Sacs and Foxes of the Missouri; this was the official United States government designation for them. Because very few Foxes ever associated with this band, however, this chapter will refer to them either as the Missouri Sacs or simply as the Sacs.

2. Charles Kappler, comp., *Indian Affairs, Laws and Treaties,* vol. 2 (Washington, D.C.: Government Printing Office, 1904), 468–469; Agent Andrew Hughes to Henry Dodge, superintendent of Indian affairs in Wisconsin, 12 May 1837, Letters Received, Great Nemaha Agency, 1848–1876, Bureau of Indian Affairs, Record Group 75, National Archives, Microcopy 234, Roll 314 (hereafter cited as LR, Great Nemaha Agency, BIA, RG75, M234, R[300–314]). The Sacs and Iowas settled on what became known as the Great Nemaha Agency or reservation, which included lands in what later became Kansas and Nebraska. Since the two tribes settled partially in Kansas, I believe that they should be included in this story.

3. Agent W. P. Richardson to David D. Mitchell, superintendent of Indian affairs at St. Louis, Mo., 4 Oct. 1843, *House Executive Documents,* 28th Cong., 2d sess., ser. 439, pp. 403–405.

4. For information on Iowa culture, see Martha Royce Blaine, *The Ioway*

Indians (Norman: University of Oklahoma Press, 1979), 7–15, 121–126; Roy W. Meyer, "The Iowa Indians, 1836–1885," *Kansas Historical Quarterly* 28 (Autumn 1962): 273–300; Alanson Skinner, "A Summer among the Sauk and Ioway Indians," *Yearbook of the Public Museum of the City of Milwaukee* 2 (Aug. 1923): 6–22; Skinner, "Societies of the Iowa, Kansa, and Ponca Indians," *Anthropological Papers of the American Museum of Natural History* 9 (1915): 683–740; Duane Anderson, "Ioway Ethnohistory: A Review," *Annals of Iowa* 41 (Spring 1973): 1228–1241 (part 1) and 42 (Summer 1973): 41–59 (part 2).

5. For information on the Sacs, see Alanson Skinner, *Observations on the Ethnology of the Sac Indians* (Westport, Conn.: Greenwood Press, 1970), 6–181; Charles Callender, "Sauk," in *Northeast*, vol. 15 of Handbook of North American Indians, edited by Bruce G. Trigger (Washington, D.C.: Smithsonian Institution, 1978), 648–655.

6. T. H. Gladstone, *The Englishman in Kansas, or Squatter Life and Border Warfare*, introduction by Frederick Law Olmsted, with a foreword by James A. Rawley (Lincoln: University of Nebraska Press, 1971), 201; Vanderslice to A. Cumming, 30 Nov. 1854, LR, Great Nemaha Agency, BIA, RG75, M234, R308; William Hamilton to Walter Lowrie, 5 Feb. 1839 and 1 Apr. 1840, American Indian Correspondence, Presbyterian Historical Society Collection of Missionary Letters, 1833–1893, Greenwood Press, Philadelphia, Microfilm, Box 8, Volume 1, Letters 36 and 54 (hereafter cited as Presbyterian Mission Letters, with box, volume, and letter numbers).

7. Rudolph Friederich Kurz, *Journal of Rudolph Friederich Kurz: An Account of His Experiences among Fur Traders and American Indians*, edited by J. N. B. Hewitt (Lincoln: University of Nebraska Press, 1970), 33–43.

8. See Aurey Ballard to Samuel Thompson, 28 Feb. 1837, and Samuel Irvin to Presbyterian Mission Secretary Walter Lowrie, 31 May 1841, Presbyterian Mission Letters, Box 3, Volume 1, Letter 83, and Box 8, Volume 1, Letter 71; Vaughn to Harvey, 1 June 1848, LR, Great Nemaha Agency, BIA, RG75, M234, R308.

9. Agent W. P. Richardson to Harvey, 6 Oct. 1844, *Senate Executive Documents*, 28th Cong., 2d sess., ser. 449, pp. 445–448.

10. Hughes to Capt. E. A. Hitchcock, disbursement officer at the St. Louis Superintendency, 14 Mar. 1838, LR, Great Nemaha Agency, BIA, RG75, M234, R314.

11. Aurey Ballard to Samuel Thompson, 30 Mar. 1837, Presbyterian Mission Letters, Box 3, Volume 1, Letter 185; William Hamilton to Walter Lowrie, 16 Dec. 1837 and 12 Feb. 1838, and Samuel Irvin to Lowrie, 22 Oct. 1838, Presbyterian Mission Letters, Box 8, Volume 1, Letters 4, 5, and 28; for information on Hamilton and Irvin's work among the Indians, see Joseph B. Herring, "Presbyterian Ethnologists among the Iowa and Sac Indians, 1837–1853," *American Presbyterians: Journal of Presbyterian History* 65 (Fall 1987): 195–203.

12. Samuel Irvin and William Hamilton, "Iowa and Sac Tribes," in Henry R. Schoolcraft, *Information respecting the History, Condition and Prospects of the Indian Tribes of the United States*, 6 vols. (Philadelphia: Lippincott, Grambo & Company, 1851–1857), 3:267–268.

13. Diaries of Samuel M. Irvin, 1841–1848, 7 Jan. 1841, p. 5, Manuscript Division, Kansas State Historical Society, Topeka, Microfilm Box 89, pp. 22–23 (hereafter cited as Irvin's Diary, with the date and page numbers); Irvin to Lowrie, 7 Feb. 1839, Presbyterian Mission Letters, Box 8, Volume 1, Letter 37.

14. The Presbyterian school building has been restored and is located near Highland, Kansas.

15. Irvin to Agent Richardson, 10 May 1843, Presbyterian Mission Letters, Box 8, Volume 1, Letter 106.

16. Hamilton, "Iowa and Sac Mission," Presbyterian Mission Letters, Box 3, Volume 2, Letter 11; Hamilton to Richardson, 30 Sept. 1843, *House Executive Documents*, 28th Cong., 1st sess., ser. 439, pp. 324–327; Irvin's Diary, 12 Apr. 1841, p. 71.

17. Hamilton to Lowrie, 28 Mar. 1843, Presbyterian Mission Letters, Box 8, Volume 1, Letter 105.

18. Irvin and Hamilton to Lowrie, 18 Feb. 1851, Presbyterian Mission Letters, Box 3, Volume 2, Letter 15.

19. Irvin's Diary, 8 June 1841, p. 118.

20. Irvin's Diary, 28 Feb. 1841, pp. 39–40; 7 Mar. 1842, p. 33; 12 Apr. 1842, p. 55; 9 Aug. 1842, p. 142; 19 and 20 Aug. 1842, pp. 151–152; 22 Aug. 1842, pp. 152–153; 29 Jan. 1844, p. 22.

21. "Journal of William Hamilton," Jan. 1841, and "Communication from Rev. William Hamilton," 21 Mar. 1842, and "Journal of S. M. Irvin," Aug. 1841, Presbyterian Mission Letters, Box 8, Volume 1, Letters 79, 83, and 76; for detailed information on the sacred packs, see M. R. Harrington, "Sacred Bundles of the Sac and Fox Indians," *University of Pennsylvania Anthropological Publications* 4 (1914): 125–262.

22. "Communication from Hamilton," 21 Mar. 1842, and "Journal of William Hamilton," Aug. 1840, Presbyterian Mission Letters, Box 8, Volume 1, Letters 83 and 62.

23. Irvin to Lowrie, 31 May 1841, Presbyterian Mission Letters, Box 8, Volume 1, Letter 71.

24. Irvin's Diary, 2 Feb. 1842, p. 28; Irvin to Lowrie, 16 Feb. 1842, and "Journal of William Hamilton," Feb. 1842, Presbyterian Mission Letters, Box 8, Volume 1, Letters 81 and 84.

25. Irvin's Diary, 18 Aug. 1842, pp. 149–151; Herring, "Presbyterian Ethnologists among the Iowa and Sac Indians," 199–202.

26. Hamilton to Lowrie, 29 Apr. 1839, and 2 Feb. 1841, Presbyterian Mission Letters, Box 8, Volume 1, Letters 40 and 69.

27. Hamilton, "Ioway and Sac Mission," 14 Nov. 1850, Irvin and Hamilton to Lowrie, 18 Feb. 1851, and Irvin to Lowrie, 29 Jan. 1852, Presbyterian Mission Letters, Box 3, Volume 2, Letters 11, 15, and 29.

28. Agent David Vanderslice to superintendent of Indian affairs at St. Louis, Mo., Alfred Cumming, 6 Sept. 1854, LR, Great Nemaha Agency, BIA, RG75, M234, R308; Edward McKinney to Rev. Moderator Presbytery at Carlisle, n.d. (probably 1847 or 1848), Edward McKinney Collection, Manuscript Division, Kansas State Historical Society, Topeka.

29. Hamilton to Richardson, 30 Sept. 1843, 28th Cong., *House Executive Documents*, 2d sess., ser. 439, pp. 324–327.

30. Thomas L. McKenney and James Hall, *The Indian Tribes of North America, with Biographical Sketches and Anecdotes of the Principal Chiefs*, vol. 1 (Edinburgh, Scot.: John Grant, 1933), 301.

31. George Catlin, *Notes on Eight Years' Travels and Residence in Europe: England, France, and Belgium*, vol. 2 (London: By the author, 1848), 167.

32. Ibid., 185.

33. Ibid., 39–42; George Catlin, *Life among the Indians* (London: Gall and Inglis, n.d.), 338–339.

34. Preston Richardson to W. P. Richardson, 30 Sept. 1845, *House Executive Documents,* 29th Cong., 1st sess., ser. 480, p. 559.

35. W. P. Richardson to Mitchell, 4 Oct. 1843, *House Executive Documents,* 28th Cong., 2d sess., ser. 439, pp. 403–405; Alfred Vaughn to superintendent of Indian affairs at St. Louis, Mo., Thomas Harvey, 24 Feb. 1849, LR, Great Nemaha Agency, BIA, RG75, M234, R308.

36. "Journal of S. M. Irvin," 28 Aug. 1841, Presbyterian Mission Letters, Box 8, Volume 1, Letter 76.

37. Kendall's exploits were reprinted by the *New York Times,* 15 Oct. 1851; James R. Mead, *Hunting and Trading on the Great Plains, 1859–1875,* edited by Schuyler Jones, with an introduction by Ignace Mead Jones (Norman: University of Oklahoma Press, 1986), 182–189.

38. Vaughn to Harvey, 1 June 1848 and 27 Oct. 1848, LR, Great Nemaha Agency, BIA, RG75, M234, R308.

39. For descriptions of Indian lacrosse, see *Junction City Union,* 9 Aug. 1879, and *Leavenworth Times,* 10 Dec. 1859, as well as items reprinted in the *Kansas Historical Quarterly* 18 (Aug. 1950): 328 and 10 (Feb. 1944): 99; see also James H. Vandergriff, ed., *The Indians of Kansas* (Emporia, Kans.: Teachers College Press, 1973), 109–110. For a discussion of the game as played by modern Indians, see Robert E. Ritzenthaler and Frederick A. Peterson, *The Mexican Kickapoo Indians* (Milwaukee: Milwaukee Public Museum Publications in Anthropology, 1956), 50–51; and Robert E. Ritzenthaler, "The Potawatomi Indians of Wisconsin," *Bulletin of the Public Museum of the City of Milwaukee* 19 (Feb. 1953): 164.

40. Donald Stull and James Divney, *Discussion Leader's Guide for Neshnabek: The People* (Lawrence: Kansas University Printing Service, 1980), 21. *Neshnabek: The People* is a film about the Prairie Potawatomis of Kansas distributed by the University of California Extension Media Center, Berkeley.

41. John Treat Irving, Jr., *Indian Sketches Taken during an Expedition to the Pawnee Tribes* [1833], 2 vols., edited by John F. McDermott (Philadelphia: Carey, Lea and Blanchard, 1835; reprint, Norman: University of Oklahoma Press, 1955), 40–41.

42. George Allen Root Collection, Potawatomi File, Manuscript Division, Kansas State Historical Society, Topeka.

43. Catlin is quoted in Stewart Culin, *Games of the North American Indians* (Washington, D.C.: Government Printing Office, 1907; reprint, New York: Dover Publications, 1975), 615.

44. Irvin's Diary, 5 Feb. 1842, pp. 22–23.

45. Vanderslice to Cumming, 6 Dec. 1853, LR, Great Nemaha Agency, BIA, RG75, M234, R308.

46. "Council of Commissioner George Manypenny and the Missouri Sacs and Foxes," 12 Sept. 1853, and Sac chiefs to Manypenny, 7 Oct. 1853, LR, Great Nemaha Agency, BIA, RG75, M234, R308.

47. Irvin to Lowrie, 20 Apr. 1854, Presbyterian Mission Letters, Box 3, Volume 2, Letter 66.

48. Irvin to Lowrie, 8 Oct. 1853, 20 Apr. 1854, and 2 June 1854, Presbyterian Mission Letters, Box 3, Volume 2, Letters 55, 66, and 67.

49. The Sacs walked to the commissioner's office accompanied by the Ver-

million Kickapoos. Details of their experience—encountering millions of dead mayflies on the streets and sidewalks as a result of the previous day's storm—are discussed in Chapter 3. The Sac chiefs' feelings at the time were never recorded, but at least two of the deeply religious delegates later had second thoughts about selling half of their reservation that day. To them, the forces of nature had signaled the Great Spirit's obvious displeasure at their actions. For details on the treaty proceedings, see Kappler, *Treaties*, 628–633; Vanderslice to Manypenny, 19 May 1854, LR, Great Nemaha Agency, BIA, RG75, M234, R308; the storm and its aftermath are described in the *Washington Daily Star*, 18 May 1854, and the *Washington National Intelligencer*, 19 May 1854.

50. The Iowa interpreter, John B. Roy, received three hundred twenty acres of reservation land for "services" rendered. Curiously, his acres passed quickly into the hands of the former government-employed farmer for the Sacs and the current licensed trader to the Great Nemaha tribes, John W. Forman (see Forman to Irvin, 24 June 1854, Presbyterian Mission Letters, Box 3, Volume 2, Letter 69).

51. Irvin to Lowrie, 7 Aug. 1852, Presbyterian Mission Letters, Box 3, Volume 2, Letter 34.

52. Vanderslice to Cumming, 6 Oct. 1854, LR, Great Nemaha Agency, BIA, RG75, M234, R308. For an insight into Vanderslice's unscrupulous land deal-ings, see Lewis Henry Morgan, *The Indian Journals*, edited by Leslie A. White (Ann Arbor: University of Michigan Press, 1959), 139–140; Martha B. Caldwell, ed., "Records of the Squatter Association of Whitehead District, Doniphan County," *Kansas Historical Quarterly* 13 (Feb. 1944): 20–24.

53. Lt. Col. George Cooke to Maj. O. F. Winship, 20 Dec. 1854, and Joseph Tesson and S. G. Karney to commissioner of Indian affairs, 6 Mar. 1857, LR, Great Nemaha Agency, BIA, RG75, M234, R308 and R309.

54. Vanderslice to Cumming, 30 Dec. 1854, and Vanderslice to Agent Royal Baldwin, 20 Sept. 1856, LR, Great Nemaha Agency, BIA, RG75, M234, R308.

55. Vanderslice to Cumming, 30 Nov. 1854, LR, Great Nemaha Agency, BIA, RG75, M234, R308.

56. Petition of Nesourquoit, Mokohoko, and other Sac chiefs, 21 Oct. 1856, LR, Great Nemaha Agency, BIA, RG75, M234, R308.

57. Tesson and Karney to commissioner, 6 Mar. 1857, and Petaokemah, Moless, Nokowat, and others to commissioner, 25 Dec. 1857, LR, Great Nemaha Agency, BIA, RG75, M234, R309.

58. Herman J. Viola, *Diplomats in Buckskins: A History of Indian Delega-tions in Washington City* (Washington, D.C.: Smithsonian Institution, 1981), 179–180.

59. Interview between Acting Commissioner of Indian Affairs Charles Mix and Nesourquoit and his companions, 20 Jan. 1858, LR, Great Nemaha Agency, BIA, RG75, M234, R309.

60. Ibid.

61. Ibid.

62. Second interview between Mix and Nesourquoit, 28 Jan. 1858, LR, Great Nemaha Agency, BIA, RG75, M234, R309.

63. Council of Sac Chiefs Petaokemah, Moless, Nesourquoit, and others, 26 Apr. 1859, LR, Great Nemaha Agency, BIA, RG75, M234, R309. Mokohoko was not present at this council.

64. By June 1860 Vanderslice had taken the necessary steps to acquire for himself the valuable Sac and Iowa farms—model farms that governmental

employees had supervised. Both farms had plowed fields, barns and other outbuildings, streams for irrigation, and timber; the Sac farm included a trading post. Although it cannot be proven for certain that Vanderslice violated state or federal laws, his methods were highly suspect. He managed to purchase both farms at prices far under market value. See Vanderslice to Commissioner of Indian Affairs A. B. Greenwood, 28 June 1860, and Petaokemah, Nesourquoit, Moless, and others to Greenwood, 28 June 1860, LR, Great Nemaha Agency, BIA, RG75, M234, R310; Morgan, *Indian Journals*, 139–140.

65. The Sac census of 1863 counted 99 tribespeople; in September 1864 there were 293 Iowas. For information on the numbers of Sacs and Iowas, see Sac and Fox of the Missouri annuity payment, 7 Feb. 1863, and Agent John A. Burbank to W. M. Albin, superintendent of Indian affairs at St. Joseph, 30 Sept. 1864, LR, Great Nemaha Agency, BIA, RG75, M234, R311; see also Morgan, *Indian Journals*, 137.

66. Vanderslice to A. M. Robinson, superintendent of Indian affairs at St. Joseph, Mo., 21 Jan. 1860, LR, Great Nemaha Agency, BIA, RG75, M234, R310.

67. For information on the impact of the great Kansas drought of 1860, see George W. Glick, "The Drought of 1860," *Kansas State Historical Society Collections* 9 (1905–1906): 480–485.

68. Petition of Petaokemah, Nesourquoit, Moless, and others, 12 Dec. 1860, and memorial of the Sac and Iowa chiefs, 13 Dec. 1860, LR, Great Nemaha Agency, BIA, RG75, M234, R310.

69. Kappler, *Treaties*, 811–814. Sac Chiefs Petaokemah, Nesourquoit, and Moless received their land patents in November 1863 (see Burbank to Commissioner of Indian Affairs William P. Dole, 21 Nov. 1863, and Dole to Secretary of the Interior J. P. Usher, 25 Nov. 1863, LR, Great Nemaha Agency, BIA, RG75, M234, R311).

70. Morgan, *Indian Journals*, 137; Burbank to Robinson, 26 Apr. 1861, council of the Iowa chiefs, 27 Apr. 1861, Burbank to superintendent of Indian affairs at St. Joseph, Mo., 14 May 1861, Burbank to Branch, 4 Jan. 1862, Burbank to Branch, 6 Jan. 1862, council with the Iowas, 3 Mar. 1862, and Burbank to Branch, 20 Jan. 1863, LR, Great Nemaha Agency, BIA, RG75, M234, R310 and R311.

71. Quoted in Anderson, "Ioway Ethnohistory" (part 2), 56.

72. Sac chiefs to Dole, 19 Oct. 1863, LR, Great Nemaha Agency, BIA, RG75, M234, R311.

CHAPTER 6. "VAGABOND TRESPASSERS": MOKOHOKO'S BAND OF SAC INDIANS

1. Like their Missouri Band kinfolk, the makeup of the Mississippi Sacs and Foxes was predominantly Sac; since the late 1840s, when they first arrived in Kansas, most of the Fox bands had drifted back to Iowa where the Foxes had repurchased some of their old lands. Because federal officials continued to lump them together as one tribe, the Sacs and Foxes, I will occasionally use the same designation. In most cases, however, they appear here simply as the Sacs.

2. Donald Fixico, "The Black Hawk–Keokuk Controversy," in *Indian Leaders: Oklahoma's First Statesmen*, edited by H. Glenn Jordan and Thomas M. Holm (Oklahoma City: Oklahoma Historical Society, 1979), 64–78.

3. For a briefer version of the Mokohoko story previously published by the

author, see "Indian Intransigency in Kansas: Government Bureaucracy vs. Mokohoko's Sacs and Foxes," *Western Historical Quarterly* 17 (Apr. 1986): 185–200.

4. Chiefs and headmen of Mokohoko's band to President Ulysses S. Grant, 1 May 1873, Letters Received, Sac and Fox Agency, 1859–1880, Bureau of Indian Affairs, Record Group 75, National Archives, Microcopy 234, Roll 739 (hereafter cited as LR, Sac and Fox Agency, BIA, RG75, M234, R[734–744]).

5. William Hamilton to Walter Lowrie, 28 Mar. 1843, American Indian Correspondence, Presbyterian Historical Society Collection of Missionary Letters, 1833–1893, Greenwood Press, Philadelphia, Pa., Microfilm, Box 8, Volume 1, Letter 105.

6. Agent Perry Fuller to A. M. Robinson, superintendent of Indian affairs at St. Joseph, Mo., 8 May 1860, and Keokuk and other Sac and Fox chiefs of the Mississippi to Commissioner of Indian Affairs A. B. Greenwood, 5 July 1860, LR, Sac and Fox Agency, BIA, RG75, M234, R734; petition of Petaokama, Nesourquoit, and others, 17 July 1860, Letters Received, Great Nemaha Agency, 1848–1876, Bureau of Indian Affairs, Record Group 75, National Archives, Microcopy 234, Roll 310 (hereafter cited as LR, Great Nemaha Agency, BIA, RG75, M234, R[300–314]).

7. For the 1861 treaty, see Charles Kappler, comp., *Indian Affairs, Laws and Treaties*, vol. 2 (Washington, D.C.: Government Printing Office, 1904), 811–814. In the fall of 1863, the Missouri chiefs each received patents in fee simple to one hundred sixty acres (see Agent John A. Burbank to Commissioner of Indian Affairs William P. Dole, 21 Nov. 1863, LR, Great Nemaha Agency, BIA, RG75, M234, R311).

8. "Council of the Chiefs of the Sacs and Foxes of the Mississippi," 6 Oct. 1866, LR, Sac and Fox Agency, BIA, RG75, M234, R736.

9. Charles R. Green, *Early Days in Kansas: Tales and Traditions of the Marais des Cygnes Valley* (Olathe, Kans.: By the author, 1914), 79.

10. Agent Henry W. Martin to H. B. Branch, superintendent of Indian affairs at St. Joseph, Mo., 20 Oct. 1863, *House Executive Documents*, 38th Cong., 1st sess., ser. 1182, pp. 371–372; Green, *Tales and Traditions of the Marais des Cygnes Valley*, 73–74.

11. Agent Henry W. Martin to superintendent of Indian affairs at St. Joseph, Mo., H. B. Branch, 20 Oct. 1863, *House Executive Documents*, 38th Cong., 1st sess., ser. 1182, pp. 371–372; "Talk between Acting Commissioner of Indian Affairs Charles E. Mix and Chiefs of the Sacs and Foxes," 24 May 1866, "Petition for Agent Martin's Removal," 16 July 1866; A. P. Chipman to Commissioner of Indian Affairs D. N. Cooley, 24 July 1866, and "Council of the Chiefs of the Sacs and Foxes," 6 Oct. 1866, LR, Sac and Fox Agency, BIA, RG75, M234, R736. By the 1860s it was common practice for Indian agents to meddle into the internal affairs of a tribe; the agents had the power to dismiss chiefs — including hereditary chiefs — who refused to cooperate with the civilization program. Federal officials had appointed the younger Keokuk a government-recognized leader after his father's death many years earlier.

12. For information on the differences between Keokuk and Mokohoko, see William T. Hagan, *The Sac and Fox Indians* (Norman: University of Oklahoma Press, 1958), 233–235, 243–257; H. Craig Miner and William E. Unrau, *The End of Indian Kansas: A Study of Cultural Revolution, 1854–1871* (Lawrence: University Press of Kansas, 1978), 62–64, 104–106, 135–137.

13. See headmen of the Sac and Fox Tribe to commissioner, 12 Apr. 1866, LR, Sac and Fox Agency, BIA, RG75, M234, R736.

14. See Ida M. Ferris, "The Sauks and Foxes in Franklin and Osage Counties, Kansas," *Kansas State Historical Society Collections* 11 (1909–1910): 335–336; Hagan, *Sac and Fox Indians*, 233–234; "Talk between Mix and Sacs and Foxes," 24 May 1866, and "Council of the Sacs and Foxes," 6 Oct. 1866, LR, Sac and Fox Agency, BIA, RG75, M234, R736.

15. Martin to Cooley, 18 May 1866, LR, Sac and Fox Agency, BIA, RG75, M234, R736.

16. Keokuk and others to the commissioner, 23 June 1865, and "A Petition of Mokohoko and 145 Other Sac and Fox Men," July 1866, LR, Sac and Fox Agency, BIA, RG75, M234, R736.

17. Ida Ferris wrote that the government built a "mansion" for Moses Keokuk, "the hall and stairway being finished in solid, polished walnut, which is to this day [1909–1910] most beautiful" (see Ferris, "Sacs and Foxes in Franklin and Osage Counties," 358).

18. "Council of the Sacs and Foxes," 6 Oct. 1866, "A General Council of the Sacs and Foxes of the Mississippi," 7 Oct. 1866, and Special Agent W. R. Irwin to Cooley, 9 Oct. 1866, LR, Sac and Fox Agency, BIA, RG75, M234, R736.

19. Ibid.

20. Kappler, *Laws and Treaties*, 951–956; Special Commissioners Vital Jarrot and H. W. Farnsworth to Commissioner of Indian Affairs L. V. Bogy, 26 Feb. 1867, LR, Sac and Fox Agency, BIA, RG75, M234, R737.

21. Wiley had replaced Martin as agent shortly after the treaty proceedings, possibly as an attempt to mollify Mokohoko and to make him more agreeable to the new treaty. As an agent, however, Wiley was no more honest than Martin. Miner and Unrau point out that Wiley was a partner in a real-estate firm in Quenemo, Kansas, and was interested in buying Indian lands (see Miner and Unrau, *End of Indian Kansas*, 61).

22. Annual report of Agent Albert Wiley, 31 July 1867, in Records of the Shawnee Indian Agency, Records of the Sac and Fox Agency in Kansas, 1855–1879, Bureau of Indian Affairs, Record Group 75, Federal Record Center, Fort Worth, Tex., E2; recollections of Dr. Elbridge B. Fenn, in Charles R. Green, *Early Days in Kansas: In Keokuk's Time on the Kansas Reservation* (Olathe, Kans.: By the author, 1913), 42.

23. Green, *Tales and Traditions of the Marais des Cygnes Valley*, 80–81.

24. Central Superintendent of Indian Affairs Enoch Hoag to Commissioner of Indian Affairs Ely S. Parker, 3 Sept. 1869, LR, Sac and Fox Agency, BIA, RG75, M234, R738; Green, *Tales and Traditions of the Marais des Cygnes Valley*, 81.

25. Wiley to superintendent of Indian affairs at Atchison, Kans., Thomas Murphy, 12 Jan. 1869, Wiley to Murphy, 26 Jan. 1869, Wiley to Murphy, 9 Feb. 1869, A. C. Farnham to Commissioner of Indian Affairs N. G. Taylor, 11 Mar. 1869, Murphy to Charles Whiting, U.S. marshal at Topeka, Kans., 15 Apr. 1869, and Hoag to Parker, 3 Sept. 1869, LR, Sac and Fox Agency, BIA, RG75, M234, R738; "Mokohoko's Noted Speech," in Charles R. Green, *Sac and Fox Indians in Kansas: Mokohoko's Stubbornness* (Olathe, Kans.: By the author, 1914), no pag.; Green, *Tales and Traditions of the Marais des Cygnes Valley*, 81.

26. Hoag to Parker, 1 Dec. 1869, Warner Craig to Hoag, 29 Dec. 1869, Hoag to Parker, 11 Apr. 1870, Hoag to Parker, 5 May 1870, William Whistler to Hoag, 15 Aug. 1870, and Farnham to Parker, 27 Aug. 1870, LR, Sac and Fox Agency, BIA,

RG75, M234, R738; Agent Thomas Miller to Hoag, 18 Aug. 1870, *House Executive Documents*, 41st Cong., 3d sess., ser. 1449, pp. 733–735; *Guilford Citizen* (Fredonia, Kans.), 21 Apr. 1870. For a description of the 1869 removal and a discussion of Sac and Fox customs, see Grant Foreman, *The Last Trek of the Indians* (New York: Russell & Russell, 1946), 222–228.

27. Farnham to Parker, 27 Aug. 1870, LR, Sac and Fox Agency, BIA, RG75, M234, R738; *Osage Chronicle* (Burlingame, Kans.), 16 Apr. 1870.

28. Hoag to Parker, 11 Mar. 1871, Hoag to Acting Commissioner of Indian Affairs H. R. Clum, 2 Aug. 1871, Hoag to Clum, 8 Aug. 1871, Hoag to Clum, 17 Aug. 1871, Hoag to Commissioner of Indian Affairs E. P. Smith, 20 Aug. 1873, and Hoag to E. P. Smith, 10 Nov. 1874, LR, Sac and Fox Agency, BIA, RG75, M234, R739 and R740; for information on Edward McCoonse's character, see Joseph B. Herring, "The Chippewa and Munsee Indians: Acculturation and Survival in Kansas, 1850–1870," *Kansas History* 6 (Winter 1983/84): 212–220.

29. For information on the successes and failures of Grant's Indian Peace Policy, see Henry G. Waltmann, "Circumstantial Reformer: President Grant and the Indian Problem," *Arizona and the West* 13 (Winter 1971): 323–342; Robert M. Utley, *The Indian Frontier of the American West, 1846–1890* (Albuquerque: University of New Mexico Press, 1984), 129–155; Robert H. Keller, Jr., *American Protestantism and United States Indian Policy, 1869–82* (Lincoln and London: University of Nebraska Press, 1983); Clyde A. Milner II, *With Good Intentions: Quaker Work among the Pawnees, Otos, and Omahas in the 1870s* (Lincoln and London: University of Nebraska Press, 1982); Brian W. Dippie, *The Vanishing American: White Attitudes and U.S. Indian Policy* (Middletown, Conn.: Wesleyan University Press, 1982), 144–146; Francis Paul Prucha, *The Great Father: The United States Government and the American Indians*, 2 vols. (Lincoln and London: University of Nebraska Press, 1986), 1:479–483, 501–533.

30. Dippie points out that Grant's policy rested on "the outmoded isolationist philosophy represented by the reservation system." This old policy was on the verge of collapse, however, and would soon be replaced with the "new" concepts of land allotment, assimilation, and citizenship. See Dippie, *Vanishing American*, 149–151.

31. Information on the Board of Indian Commissioners can be found in Prucha, *Great Father*, 1:501–512; Keller, *American Protestantism and United States Indian Policy*, 72–89.

32. For information on Hoag and other Quaker appointees in Kansas, see Milner, *With Good Intentions*, 20–21; Keller, *American Protestantism and United States Indian Policy*, 46–49; Lawrie Tatum, *Our Red Brothers and the Peace Policy of President Ulysses S. Grant*, with an introduction by Thomas C. Battey (Philadelphia: John C. Winston & Company, 1899), 22–25.

33. Green, *Tales and Traditions of the Marais des Cygnes Valley*, 19–26, 63–68, 83–87.

34. Ibid., 26 and 51.

35. Ibid.

36. For information on withheld annuity payments, see Hoag to Clum, 17 Aug. 1871; Edward McCoonse to Special Indian Commissioner Vincent Colyer, 4 Nov. 1871; and Hoag to E. P. Smith, 28 Oct. 1873, LR, Sac and Fox Agency, BIA, RG75, M234, R739. Discussions of the Kansas Sac and Fox customs and way of life can be found in Green, *Sac and Fox Indians*, no pag.; Green, *Keokuk's Time on the Kansas Reservation*, 8–43; Charles R. Green, *Early*

Days in Kansas: Pioneer Narratives of the First Twenty-five Years of Kansas History (Olathe, Kans.: by the author, 1912), passim; R. Morton House, " 'The Only Way' Church and the Sac and Fox Indians," *Chronicles of Oklahoma* 43 (Winter 1965/66): 456, note 9. For Cochran's note, see Green, *Tales and Traditions of the Marais des Cygnes Valley*, 40.

37. Chiefs and headmen of Mokohoko's band to President Grant, 1 May 1873, LR, Sac and Fox Agency, BIA, RG75, M234, R739.

38. Mokohoko and others to Hoag, 1 Aug. 1873, Cyrus Case to Grant, 28 Feb. 1874, "Superintendent Hoag's Remarks to Mokohoko Indians," 16 Nov. 1875, LR, Sac and Fox Agency, BIA, RG75, M234, R739, R740, and R741.

39. Hoag to E. P. Smith, 28 Oct. 1873, and Hoag to Smith, 10 Nov. 1874, LR, Sac and Fox Agency, BIA, RG75, M234, R739 and R740. Mokohoko quoted in Green, *Sac and Fox Indians*, no pag.

40. Hoag to E. P. Smith, 10 Nov. 1874, and Pawshepawho and Mayapit to the commissioner, 1 Feb. 1875, LR, Sac and Fox Agency, BIA, RG75, M234, R740.

41. "Council with Delegation of Sac and Fox Indians of Kansas Known as Mokohoko's Band," 1 Feb. 1875, LR, Sac and Fox Agency, BIA, RG75, M234, R740.

42. "Council with Delegation of Sac and Fox Indians of Kansas Known as Mokohoko's Band," 4 Feb. 1875, LR, Sac and Fox Agency, BIA, RG75, M234, R740; *New York Times*, 5 Feb. 1875.

43. Hoag to Agent Levi Woodard, 9 Nov. 1875, and "Superintendent Hoag's Remarks to Mokohoko's Indians," 16 Nov. 1875, LR, Sac and Fox Agency, BIA, RG75, M234, R741.

44. Woodard to Hoag, 25 Dec. 1875, LR, Sac and Fox Agency, BIA, RG75, M234, R741; *Topeka Commonwealth*, 9 Dec. 1875.

45. John H. Pickering to Commissioner of Indian Affairs J. Q. Smith, 12 Dec. 1875, Letters Received relating to the Quapaw and Sac and Fox agencies, 1875, Records of the Central Superintendency of Indian Affairs, Bureau of Indian Affairs, Record Group 75, National Archives, Microcopy 856, Roll 64 (hereafter cited as LR, Central Superintendency, BIA, RG75, M856, R64); Woodard to J. Q. Smith, 4 Mar. 1876, Woodard to the superintendent of Indian affairs at Lawrence, Kans., William Nicholson, 29 Mar. 1876. Letters Received relating to the Sac and Fox and the Union agencies, 1876, Records of the Central Superintendency of Indian Affairs, Bureau of Indian Affairs, Record Group 75, National Archives, Microcopy 856, Roll 74 (hereafter cited as LR, Central Superintendency, BIA, RG75, M856, R74); Chief Clerk of the Central Superintendency George Nicholson to Woodard, 14 Apr. 1876, Letters Sent to Agents, 1 Feb. 1876–3 Mar. 1877, Records of the Central Superintendency of Indian Affairs, Bureau of Indian Affairs, Record Group 75, National Archives, Microcopy 856, Roll 100 (hereafter cited as LS Central Superintendency, BIA, RG75, M856, R100).

46. Hoag to J. Q. Smith, 22 Jan. 1876, and Hoag to J. Q. Smith, 29 Feb. 1876, LR, Sac and Fox Agency, BIA, RG75, M234, R741; Woodard to commissioner, 31 Aug. 1876, *House Executive Documents*, 44th Cong., 2d sess., ser. 1749, p. 471; Woodard to William Nicholson, 18 Apr. 1876, LR, Central Superintendency, BIA, RG75, M856, R74; *Minutes of Kansas Yearly Meeting of Friends, Held at Lawrence, Kansas* (1876), 36.

47. McCoonse to Secretary of the Interior Carl Schurz, [?] Aug. 1878, John Parkinson to U.S. Sen. P. B. Plumb, 19 May 1879, and "Petition to Commissioner Hayt," [?] June 1879, LR, Sac and Fox Agency, BIA, RG75, M234, R742–743.

48. Prucha, *Great Father*, 1:583–589; Loring Benson Priest discusses the failure of the Indian Peace Policy and the rampant corruption in the Indian service (see Priest, *Uncle Sam's Stepchildren: The Reformation of United States Indian Policy, 1865–1887* [Lincoln: University of Nebraska Press, 1975], 28–41, 66–75).

49. A discussion of the *Standing Bear v. Crook* case can be found in James King, "'A Better Way': General George Crook and the Ponca Indians," *Nebraska History* 50 (Fall 1969): 239–256; Thomas Henry Tibbles, *Buckskin and Blanket Days* (Garden City, N.Y.: Doubleday, 1957); see also Frederick E. Hoxie, *A Final Promise: The Campaign to Assimilate the Indians, 1880–1920* (Lincoln and London: University of Nebraska Press, 1984), 4–11.

50. Report of Commissioner J. D. C. Atkins, 1 Nov. 1886, *House Executive Documents*, 49th Cong., 2d sess., ser. 2467, p. 122. For a discussion of the dispute between Schurz and the humanitarians, see Prucha, *Great Father*, 1:566–571.

51. Atkins to secretary of the Interior, 15 Sept. 1886, Letters Received by the Office of the Adjutant General (Main Series), File 5269, Record Group 94, National Archives, Microcopy 689, Roll 483 (hereafter cited as LR, Adjutant General, RG94, M689, R483).

52. Ibid.

53. Report of Commissioner Atkins, 1 Nov. 1886, *House Executive Documents*, 49th Cong., 2d sess., ser. 2467, pp. 122–123; Secretary of the Interior L. Q. C. Lamar to U.S. Indian Inspector E. D. Bannister, 6 Aug. 1886, and Lamar to Bannister, 29 Sept. 1886, Letters Sent by the Indian Division of the Office of the Secretary of the Interior, Bureau of Indian Affairs, Record Group 48, National Archives, Microcopy 606, Rolls 46–47; Lamar to the secretary of war, 29 Sept. 1886, LR, Adjutant General, RG94, M689, R483.

54. For descriptions of the 1886 removal, see Secretary of War William Endicott to the secretary of the Interior, 15 Dec. 1886, Letters Sent by the Secretary of War relating to Military Affairs, Records of the Office of the Secretary of War, Record Group 107, National Archives, Microcopy 6, Roll 98 (hereafter cited as LS, Secretary of War, RG107, M6, R98); Green, *Sac and Fox Indians*, no pag.

55. Lt. J. T. Haines to assistant adjutant general, Department of the Missouri, 26 Nov. 1886, LR, Adjutant General, RG94, M689, R483; Endicott to secretary of the Interior, 15 Dec. 1886, LS, Secretary of War, RG107, M6, R98.

56. Bannister to secretary of the Interior, 12 Nov. 1886, Lamar to secretary of war, 17 Nov. 1886, Capt. E. M. Hayes to assistant adjutant general, Department of the Missouri, 24 Nov. 1886, LR, Adjutant General, RG94, M689, R483.

57. The 1887 journey to Washington is discussed by Agent Moses Neal to George Powers, 19 Apr. 1887, and Neal to John V. MacKnight, 4 May 1887, Letters Sent from the Sac and Fox-Shawnee Agency (SF-SA), Bureau of Indian Affairs, Record Group 75, National Archives, Oklahoma Historical Society Microfilm Publications, SF-SA9; Neal to commissioner, 25 Aug. 1887, *House Executive Documents*, 50th Cong., 1st sess., ser. 2542, p. 177.

58. See Hagan, *Sac and Fox Indians*, 249–261; Harry B. Gilstrap, Jr., "Colonel Samuel Lee Patrick," *Chronicles of Oklahoma* 46 (Spring 1968): 60–62; J. Y. Brice, "Some Experiences in the Sac and Fox Reservation," *Chronicles of Oklahoma* 4 (Dec. 1926): 309–311; U.S. Indian Inspector Robert S. Gardner to secretary of the Interior, 23 Apr. 1887, and U.S. Indian Inspector Paul F. Faison to secretary of the Interior, 28 Dec. 1894 and 5 Nov. 1895, Reports of Inspection of the Field Jurisdictions of the Office of Indian Affairs, Bureau of Indian Affairs, Record Group 48, National Archives, Microcopy 1070, Roll 45.

CHAPTER 7. THE PRAIRIE POTAWATOMIS AND
THE STRUGGLE AGAINST LAND ALLOTMENT

1. The following description of Wahquahboshkuk and the Prairie Potawatomis differs substantially from that portrayed by James A. Clifton in *The Prairie People: Continuity and Change in Potawatomi Indian Culture, 1665–1965*, published in 1977 by the University Press of Kansas, Lawrence. *The Prairie People* depicts Wahquahboshkuk as a shallow and callous Indian who used his leadership position unwisely and to his own advantage. The author rejects the tribal oral account of Wahquahboshkuk, which acclaims the old leader as a hero who fought against overwhelming odds on behalf of his people. Clifton points out that this version merely represents "Potawatomi, not American, historiography. It is basically a morality tale based on traditional interpretations of a long series of complex historical events with numerous individual actors." His version argues that Wahquahboshkuk and his followers resorted to "magical devices" instead of common sense in their fight against land allotment during the late nineteenth century (see Clifton, *Prairie People*, 354, 362–363, 395).

A careful examination of the historical record reveals, however, that the Potawatomi oral accounts of their own history are closer to the truth than Clifton may realize. Anthropologist Alfonso Ortiz has recently argued that a true picture of the American Indian cannot be drawn until scholars evaluate the Indians as "multidimensional" human beings and understand their "side of the historical encounter and tell their story fully" (see Ortiz, "Indian/White Relations: A View from the Other Side of the 'Frontier,' " in *Indians in American History*, edited by Frederick E. Hoxie [Arlington Heights, Ill.: Harlan Davidson, 1988], 1). This chapter attempts to follow Ortiz's prescription for writing Indian history.

2. H. C. Linn to commissioner, 10 Sept. 1881, *House Executive Documents*, 46th Cong., 3d sess., ser. 2018, pp. 164–167; Lt. J. C. Gresham to assistant adjutant general, Missouri, 26 Aug. 1891, Letters Received by the Bureau of Indian Affairs, 1881–1907, Bureau of Indian Affairs, Record Group 75, National Archives, Letter 33021 (hereafter cited as LR, BIA, RG75, NA, Letter 33021).

3. Without providing documentable evidence, Clifton argues that the "powerfully charismatic if benign" Wahquahboshkuk was not a Potawatomi by birth but was of "Sauk origin." He adds that Wahquahboshkuk was merely one of a long line of men of various backgrounds—French-speaking métis, Anglo-Saxons, Scots-Irish, and "dispossessed" members of other tribes and bands—who assumed positions of leadership among the Prairie Potawatomis (see *Clifton, Prairie People*, 354, 395). Nothing in the records of the National Archives or elsewhere indicates that Wahquahboshkuk was a Sac; the archival evidence consistently demonstrates, however, that he was indeed of Potawatomi origin.

4. J. A. Scott to commissioner, 14 Apr. 1893 and 14 July 1893, Outgoing Letters of the Potawatomi Agency, 1887–1900, Bureau of Indian Affairs, Record Group 75, Federal Record Center, Kansas City, Mo., vol. 11 (hereafter cited as OL, Potawatomi Agency, BIA, RG75, vols. [6–25], KCFRC).

5. Bands of these Potawatomis had also settled in Michigan and Canada. Prior to the 1850s, the Prairie bands had been referred to as the United Potawatomis, Chippewas, and Ottawas. By the 1840s, the makeup of that "united" band was predominantly Potawatomi. For brief discussions of the Potawatomis' early history and political composition, see Thomas G. Conway, "Potawatomi Poli-

tics," *Journal of the Illinois State Historical Society* 65 (Winter 1972): 395–418; and James A. Clifton, "Potawatomi," in *Northeast,* vol. 15 of *Handbook of North American Indians,* edited by Bruce G. Trigger (Washington, D.C.: Smithsonian Institution, 1978), 725–742.

6. See Charles Kappler, comp., *Indian Affairs, Laws and Treaties,* vol. 2 (Washington, D.C.: Government Printing Office, 1904), 557–560; Clifton, *Prairie People,* 318, 329–342.

7. Louise Barry, ed., "Scenes in (and en route to) Kansas Territory, Autumn, 1854: Five Letters by William H. Hunter," *Kansas Historical Quarterly* 35 (Autumn 1969): 320.

8. Commissioner of Indian affairs to U.S. Representative John C. Mason, 19 Jan. 1850, Letters Sent by the Office of Indian Affairs, Bureau of Indian Affairs, Record Group 75, National Archives, Microcopy 21, Roll 42. In reality, there were no firm barriers separating members of one band from another. Clan membership, which transcended that of the band, was still viable during the nineteenth century, and individual Potawatomis, through intermarriage and other means, often moved from one band to another.

9. Agent Richard Cummins to St. Louis Superintendent of Indian Affairs Thomas Harvey, 26 Sept. 1848, *House Executive Documents,* 30th Cong., 2d sess., ser. 537, p. 447.

10. See Clifton, *Prairie People,* 279–280.

11. According to Clifton, Nozhakum and his Potawatomi followers were in two different places at the same time. They abandoned Illinois in 1819 and eventually were settled in Mexico by 1834. However, Clifton also locates Nozhakum and his people in Kansas in 1834 (see Clifton, *Prairie People,* 236–237, 284). Actually, the Nozhakum to whom Clifton refers probably never set foot in Mexico, although several of Nozhakum's followers settled there in 1864. Archival sources reveal that few, if any, Potawatomis had settled in Mexico before the Civil War.

12. Harvey to commissioner, 8 June 1844, and "Potawatomi Petition to Remain with the Kickapoo," 8 June 1844, Letters Received, Fort Leavenworth Agency, 1824–1851, Bureau of Indian Affairs, Record Group 75, National Archives, Microcopy 234, Roll 302 (hereafter cited as LR, Fort Leavenworth Agency, BIA, RG75, M234, R[300–303]).

13. Harvey to Commissioner of Indian Affairs T. Hartley Crawford, 8 June 1844, LR, Fort Leavenworth Agency, BIA, RG75, M234, R302.

14. Nozhakum and other Potawatomi chiefs to Commissioner of Indian Affairs J. M. Armstrong, 22 Dec. 1849, and Samuel Mason to John C. Mason, 26 Dec. 1849, LR, Fort Leavenworth Agency, BIA, RG75, M234, R303.

15. "Petition by the Kickapoo Chiefs in the Presence of John Collier (Justice of the Peace at Weston, Missouri)," 8 Feb. 1851, "Petition by the Potawatomi Chiefs in the Presence of John Collier," 10 Feb. 1851, and Collier to David Mitchell, 10 Feb. 1851, LR, Fort Leavenworth Agency, BIA, RG75, M234, R303; Mitchell to Commissioner of Indian Affairs Luke Lea, 25 Oct. 1851, *Senate Executive Documents,* 32d Cong., 1st sess., ser. 613, p. 323; "Keotuck on behalf of the Potawatomis Living upon the Kickapoo Reserve," 27 Feb. 1857, History, Indians, Potawatomi File, Manuscript Division, Kansas State Historical Society, Topeka.

16. Royal Baldwin to A. Cumming, 8 July 1857, Letters Received, Kickapoo Agency, 1855–1876, Bureau of Indian Affairs, Record Group 75, National Ar-

chives, Microcopy 234, Roll 371 (hereafter cited as LR, Kickapoo Agency, BIA, RG75, M234, R[371–374]); "Keotuck on behalf of the Potawatomis," 27 Feb. 1857, History, Indians, Potawatomi File, KSHS.

17. George A. Root, "Sketch of Kickapoo History," unpublished document, George Allen Root Collection, Kickapoo Indians File, Manuscript Division, Kansas State Historical Society, Topeka; Baldwin to Cumming, 23 Oct. 1856, *House Executive Documents,* 34th Cong., 3d sess., ser. 893, pp. 663–664; Agent W. P. Badger to Superintendent of Indian Affairs at St. Louis, Mo., A. M. Robinson, 20 Sept. 1859, *Senate Executive Documents,* 36th Cong., 1st sess., ser. 1023, pp. 144–147.

18. The disruption was intensified when over five hundred Potawatomis from Wisconsin began arriving on the reservation in the early 1850s (see Robert A. Trennert, "The Business of Indian Removal: Deporting the Potawatomi from Wisconsin, 1851," *Wisconsin Magazine of History* 63 [Autumn 1979]: 36–50). Many of these Indians joined forces with the Prairie Band; many others simply returned over the years to Wisconsin.

19. John Duerinck to Rev. Pierre Jean De Smet, 31 Dec. 1850, in Pierre Jean De Smet, *Western Missions and Missionaries: A Series of Letters* (New York: P. J. Kenedy, 1859), 336. For a favorable view of Jesuit efforts at St. Mary's, see Richard Joseph Bollig, "History of Catholic Education in Kansas, 1836–1932" (Ph.D. dissertation, Catholic University of America, Washington, D.C., 1933), 12–28.

20. The report of Maurice Gaillard can be found in Hubert Jacobs, ed., "The Potawatomi Mission 1854," *Mid-America* 36 (Oct. 1954): 246; Duerinck to Clarke, 1 Oct. 1855, Commissioner of Indian Affairs *Annual Report* (Washington, D.C., 1855), 97–99.

21. George W. Clarke to Cumming, 17 Oct. 1855, Commissioner of Indian Affairs *Annual Report* (1855), 102.

22. Quoted in *Proceedings of the Eighth Annual Meeting of the Lake Mohonk Conference of Friends of the Indian (1890)* (Lake Mohonk, N.Y.: Lake Mohonk Conference, 1890), 145. For accounts of the Catholic mission culled from newspaper reports of the 1850s and early 1860s, see "Some Contemporary References to St. Mary's Mission," *Mid-America* 17 (Apr. 1935): 84–103.

23. For information on Potawatomi religious practices, see Clifton, "Potawatomi," 733–734. Clifton points out that the Potawatomi clans were grouped into six phratries: Water, Bird, Buffalo, Wolf, Bear, and Man (ibid., 732–733). In 1859, Potawatomi informants gave Lewis Henry Morgan the names of the following tribal clans: Wolf, Bear, Beaver, Elk, Loon, Eagle, Black Hawk, Sturgeon, Sucker, Bald Eagle, Thunder, Hare or Rabbit, Crow, Fox, and Turkey (see Morgan, *The Indian Journals, 1859–62,* edited by Leslie A. White (Ann Arbor: University of Michigan Press, 1959), 58.

24. For the history of the Baptist school, see Thomas P. Barr, "The Pottawatomie Baptist Manual Labor Training School," *Kansas Historical Quarterly* 43 (Winter 1977): 377–431.

25. Ibid., 330–335.

26. For Duerinck's ideas, see Arthur T. Donohue, "A History of the Early Jesuit Missions in Kansas," (Ph.D. dissertation, University of Kansas, Lawrence, 1931), 146–148; Duerinck to Agent George W. Clarke, 1 Oct. 1855, Commissioner of Indian Affairs *Annual Report* (1855), 103–104.

27. Mitchell is quoted in William E. Connelley, "The Prairie Band of Pot-

tawatomie Indians," *Kansas State Historical Society Collections* 14 (1915–1918): 497; Vanderslice to Cumming, 29 Sept. 1853, *Senate Executive Documents*, 33d Cong., 1st sess., ser. 690, pp. 329–330; Agent Royal Baldwin to Cumming, 23 Oct. 1856, *Senate Executive Documents*, 34th Cong., 3d sess., ser. 875, pp. 662–664; Clarke to Cumming, 17 Oct. 1855, Commissioner of Indian Affairs *Annual Report* (1856), 96–101.

28. Agent William Murphy to superintendent of Indian affairs at St. Louis, Mo., John Haverty, 15 Sept. 1857, *Senate Executive Documents*, 35th Cong., 1st sess., ser. 919, p. 463; Murphy to Haverty, 24 Nov. 1857, and Murphy to Robinson, 21 May 1858, Letters Received, Potawatomi Agency, 1857–1880, Bureau of Indian Affairs, Record Group 75, National Archives, Microcopy 234, Roll 681 (hereafter cited as LR, Potawatomi Agency, BIA, RG75, M234, R[681–695]).

29. Shagwee and other chiefs to commissioner, 14 Mar. 1860, and Agent William W. Ross to commissioner, 29 Nov. 1861, LR, Potawatomi Agency, BIA, RG75, M234, R683.

30. Shagwee is quoted in Donohue, "Early Jesuit Missions," 148–153.

31. Ibid.

32. Kappler, *Treaties*, 824–828.

33. In 1863 the name of this railroad was changed to the Union Pacific Railway (Eastern Division). For information on the company's efforts to acquire Potawatomi lands, see Secretary of the Interior James Harlan to John P. Devereux, 13 Oct. 1865, Acting Commissioner of Indian Affairs R. B. Vanvalkenburg to Harlan, 20 Sept. 1865, Secretary of the Interior O. H. Browning to John D. Perry, 7 Jan. 1867, and Perry to Browning, 20 Apr. 1867, Special Files relative to Negotiations with Indians, Land Matters, Investigations, and Other Subjects, Bureau of Indian Affairs, Record Group 48, National Archives, File 14 (Potawatomi Land Matters); see also John D. Cruise, "Early Days on the Union Pacific," *Kansas State Historical Society Collections* 11 (1909–1910): 529–549; O. P. Byers, "When Railroading Outdid the Wild West Stories," *Kansas State Historical Society Collections*, 17 (1926–1928): 339–348.

34. Ross to Dole, 19 Aug. 1864, LR, Potawatomi Agency, BIA, RG75, M234, R684; William Albin, superintendent of Indian affairs at St. Joseph, Mo., to Dole, 1 Oct. 1864, Letters Received by the Office of Indian Affairs, Central Superintendency, 1862–1873, Bureau of Indian Affairs, Record Group 75, National Archives, Microcopy 234, Roll 58 (hereafter cited as LR, Central Superintendency, BIA, RG75, M234, R[58–62]); Agent L. R. Palmer to superintendent of Indian affairs at Atchison, Kans., Thomas Murphy, 14 Sept. 1865, *House Executive Documents*, 39th Cong., 1st sess., ser. 1248, p. 559.

35. Potawatomi oral history reveals that Nozhakum's followers, including Chequmkego, had gone to Mexico (see Ruth Landes, *The Prairie Potawatomi: Tradition and Ritual in the Twentieth Century* [Madison: University of Wisconsin Press, 1970], 20). Arrell M. Gibson writes incorrectly that Chequmkego was a Kickapoo chief (see Gibson, *The Kickapoos: Lords of the Middle Border* [Norman: University of Oklahoma Press, 1963], 246–248). For additional information on the Indians' journey to Mexico, see George A. Root, ed., "No-ko-aht's Talk: A Kickapoo Chief's Account of a Tribal Journey from Kansas to Mexico and Return in the Sixties," *Kansas Historical Quarterly* 1 (Feb. 1932): 153–159; "Potawatomi Memorial to the Senate and House of Representatives," Apr. 1880, LR, Potawatomi Agency, BIA, RG75, M234, R695.

36. Quoted in Joseph Francis Murphy, "Potawatomi Indians of the West:

Origins of the Citizen Band" (Ph.D. dissertation, University of Oklahoma, 1961), 458.

37. Quoted in W. W. Graves, *Life and Letters of Rev. Father John Schoenmakers, S.J.: Apostle to the Osages* (Parsons, Kans.: The Commercial Publishers, 1928), 90.

38. Palmer to Thomas Murphy, 17 Sept. 1866, *House Executive Documents*, 39th Cong., 2d sess., ser. 1284, pp. 263–264.

39. When Thomas Murphy, the superintendent of Indian affairs at Lawrence, Kansas, paid out the band's $340,709 in head-right money in the fall of 1868 (each member of the Citizen Band received $610), the Bertrands, Bourassas, and the Eli Nadeau family each obtained several payments. See Murphy to commissioner, 24 Nov. 1868, and "Potawatomi Head-Right List, 1868," Special Cases, 1821–1907, Bureau of Indian Affairs, Record Group 75, National Archives, Special Case 120, (Mexican Potawatomis), box 102 (hereafter cited as BIA, RG75, SC120 [Mexican Potawatomis], Box 102).

40. Kappler, *Treaties*, 970–974.

41. Quoted in Murphy, "Origins of the Citizen Band," 488.

42. Anna H. Abel, "Indian Reservations in Kansas and the Extinguishment of Their Title," *Kansas State Historical Society Collections* 8 (1903–1904): 102–103; Kappler, *Treaties*, 972–973.

43. For an insight on this swindle, see Joseph Bourassa, George L. Young, and Eli G. Nadeau to Commissioner E. S. Parker, 10 Feb. 1871, BIA, RG75, SC120, (Mexican Potawatomis), Box 102; Commissioner of Indian Affairs Hiram Price to secretary of the Interior, 27 Mar. 1882, *House of Representatives Committee Reports*, 47th Cong., 1st sess., H. Rpt. 1149, ser. 2068. Perry A. Armstrong discusses the actions of Young and Payne in *The Sauks and the Black Hawk War* (Springfield, Ill.: H. W. Rokker, 1887), 606.

44. For further information on this complex case and its aftermath, see *United States v. Kah-w-sot, Jacob Smith, and John R. Mulvane,* 29 July 1876, *United States v. Mazhe-nah-num-nuk-okuk and Ferdinand Abbles,* 15 July 1876, *United States v. Te-bah-suy and Jacob Smith,* 15 July 1876, and *United States v. Ze-be-qua, Jacob Smith, and John R. Mulvane,* 15 July 1876, Records of the United States Circuit Court for the District of Kansas, 1st Division, Topeka, Law and Equity Cases (1862–1912), Box 116, Federal Record Center, Kansas City, Mo.; see also "Potawatomi Memorial," Apr. 1880, LR, Potawatomi Agency, BIA, RG75, M234, R695.

45. "Depredations on the Frontier of Texas," *House Executive Documents*, 43d Cong., 1st sess., 1873–1874, ser. 1615, p. 17; Joseph B. Herring, "Cultural and Economic Resilience among the Kickapoo Indians of the Southwest, *Great Plains Quarterly* 6 (Fall 1986): 271–272.

46. John D. Miles to Superintendent Hoag, 13 July 1871, LR, Kickapoo Agency, BIA, RG75, M234, R373. Loring Benson Priest writes that Miles "was more successful than other Quaker representatives because he frequently sacrificed his principles to necessity" (see Priest, *Uncle Sam's Stepchildren: The Reformation of United States Indian Policy, 1865–1887,* [Lincoln: University of Nebraska Press, 1975], 28–40). For an assessment of Grant's Indian Peace Policy, see Robert H. Keller, Jr., *American Protestantism and United States Indian Policy, 1869–82* (Lincoln and London: University of Nebraska Press, 1983), 149–166, 205–216.

47. Quoted in Gibson, *Kickapoos*, 243; see also Ernest Wallace and Adrian S. Anderson, "R. S. Mackenzie and the Kickapoos: The Raid into Mexico in 1873," *Arizona and the West* 7 (Summer 1965): 105–126; Ernest Wallace, *Ranald S. Mackenzie on the Texas Frontier* (Lubbock: West Texas Museum Association, 1964), 92–114; J'Nell L. Pate, "Ranald S. Mackenzie," in *Soldiers West: Biographies from the Military Frontier*, edited by Paul Andrew Hutton (Lincoln and London: University of Nebraska Press, 1987), 180–181.

48. See Albert Turpe's testimony in "Depredations on the Frontier of Texas," *House Executive Documents*, 43d Cong., 1st sess., 1873–1874, ser. 1615, p. 23.

49. Thomas G. Williams and Henry M. Atkinson to Commissioner of Indian Affairs Edward P. Smith, 14 June 1873, LR, Kickapoo Agency, BIA, RG75, M234, R374; Atkinson and Williams to Smith, 8 Oct. 1873, Commissioner of Indian Affairs *Annual Report* (1873), 169–173.

50. See Archie F. McGrew and C. D. Ward to the superintendent of Indian affairs at Lawrence, Kans., 6 May 1872, McGrew and Ward to superintendent, 24 June 1872, sworn statement of A. F. McGrew, 9 July 1872, and McGrew to President U. S. Grant, 8 Aug. 1872, Special Files relative to Negotiations with Indians, Land Matters, Investigations, and Other Subjects, Bureau of Indian Affairs, Record Group 48, National Archives, File 6 (Mexican Kickapoos).

51. Council with the Mexican Kickapoos and Potawatomis, 25 Aug. 1873, LR, Central Superintendency, BIA, RG75, M234, R62.

52. Agent M. H. Newlin to Hoag, 4 Apr. 1873, LR, Potawatomi Agency, BIA, RG75, M234, R691; Atkinson and Williams to E. P. Smith, 8 Oct. 1873, Commissioner of Indian Affairs Annual Report (1873), 171; Atkinson and Williams to Smith, 30 June 1873 and 11 July 1873, LR, Central Superintendency, BIA, RG75, M234, R62; Atkinson and Williams to Smith, 14 July 1873, LR, Kickapoo Agency, BIA, RG75, M234, R374.

53. Council with the Mexican Kickapoos and Potawatomis, 25 Aug. 1873, LR, Central Superintendency, BIA, RG75, M234, R62.

54. Atkinson and Williams to E. P. Smith, 8 Oct. 1873, Commissioner of Indian Affairs *Annual Report* (1873), 172; Newlin to Smith, 1 Sept. 1874, *House Executive Documents*, 43d Cong., 2d sess., ser. 1639, p. 525; Newlin to Hoag, 10 July 1874, and Hoag to commissioner, 26 Aug. 1874, BIA, RG75, SC120 (Mexican Potawatomis) Box 102.

55. For further information, see "Potawatomi Memorial," Apr. 1880, LR, Potawatomi Agency, BIA, RG75, M234, R695. *New York Times* and other eastern papers agreed that certain governmental officers must "have been guilty of complicity" in the swindle. Editors of the *Times* demanded that a thorough investigation be carried out. The Indian "lands are inalienable, under the treaty by which they were allotted in severalty," the editors wrote. "But it will be seen that it is comparatively easy to cheat the Indian out of his property, notwithstanding the vaunted theory that the allotment plan is an impregnable defense against the invasion of the white man" (*New York Times*, 29 Mar. 1880).

56. J. H. Morris to Hoag, 1 Sept. 1871, *House Executive Documents*, 42d Cong., 2d sess., ser. 1505, p. 912.

57. Joseph Bourassa to Hoag, summer 1873 and 1 Aug. 1873, LR, Potawatomi Agency, BIA, RG75, M234, R691.

58. The Quaker school averaged about forty students during the mid-1870s. For information on the school and the Potawatomi accommodation to other

white ways, see the annual *Minutes of Kansas Yearly Meeting of Friends, Held at Lawrence, Kansas* (1873), 31–32; (1874), 19; (1875), 22–23; (1876), 32–33; (1877), 32–33; (1878), 30–31.

59. Newlin was one of the Quakers appointed as part of Grant's Indian Peace Policy.

60. Newlin to E. P. Smith, 1 Sept. 1874, *House Executive Documents*, 44th Cong., 1st sess., ser. 1680, p. 525.

61. See *Minutes of Kansas Yearly Meeting of Friends* (1876), 33.

62. W. W. Letson to Sen. John J. Ingalls, 31 May 1879, LR, Potawatomi Agency, BIA, RG75, M234, R694; Newlin to commissioner, 1 Sept. 1877, *House Executive Documents*, 45th Cong., 2d sess., ser. 1800, p. 515.

63. See Helen Hunt Jackson, *A Century of Dishonor: The Early Crusade for Indian Reform*, edited by Andrew F. Rolle (New York, Evanston, and London: Harper Torchbooks, 1965).

64. For information on the Friends of the Indian and the movement for allotment, see Francis Paul Prucha, *American Indian Policy in Crisis: Christian Reformers and the Indian, 1865–1900* (Norman: University of Oklahoma Press, 1976), 132–168; Robert Winston Mardock, *The Reformers and the American Indian* (Columbia: University of Missouri Press, 1971), 192–228; Henry E. Fritz, *The Movement for Indian Assimilation, 1860–1890* (Philadelphia: University of Pennsylvania Press, 1963), 185–221; Frederick E. Hoxie, *A Final Promise: The Campaign to Assimilate the Indians, 1880–1920* (Lincoln and London: University of Nebraska Press, 1984), 1–81; Patricia Nelson Limerick, *The Legacy of Conquest: The Unbroken Past of the American West* (New York and London: W. W. Norton & Company, 1987), 196–200.

65. For the thoughts of Painter and Dawes, see *Proceedings of the Fourth Annual Meeting of the Lake Mohonk Conference of Friends of the Indian* (1886) (Philadelphia: Indian Rights Association, 1887), 18–34; Hayt is quoted in Francis Paul Prucha, ed., *Americanizing the American Indians: Writings by "Friends of the Indian," 1880–1900* (Cambridge, Mass.: Harvard University Press, 1973), 80.

66. Prucha, *Americanizing the American Indians*, 136–137.

67. See George W. Manypenny, "Shall We Persist in a Policy That Has Failed?" in Wilcomb E. Washburn, *The Assault on Indian Tribalism: The General Allotment Law (Dawes Act) of 1887*, edited by Harold M. Hyman (Philadelphia: J. B. Lippincott Company, 1975), 61–67.

68. Ibid., 67.

69. Welsh is quoted in the *Proceedings of the Fourth Annual Meeting of the Lake Mohonk Conference*, 11.

70. Washburn, *Assault on Indian Tribalism*, 3–73; Francis Paul Prucha, *The Great Father: The United States Government and the American Indians*, 2 vols. (Lincoln and London: University of Nebraska Press, 1986), 2:666–686. Prucha points out that the Burke Act of 1906 "provided that citizenship should not be granted and the Indians should not be subject to state and territorial laws until the expiration of the trust period and the issuing of the patents in fee" (see Prucha, *American Indian Policy in Crisis: Christian Reformers and the Indian, 1865–1900*, [Norman: University of Oklahoma Press, 1976], 255, note 61).

71. *Proceedings of the Fifth Annual Meeting of the Lake Mohonk Conference of Friends of the Indian* (1887) (Philadelphia: Sherman & Company, Printers, 1887), 12–13; Dawes' speech can also be found in Prucha, ed., *Americanizing the American Indians*, 102–103.

72. William T. Hagan writes that on their visit among the Sioux in May 1882, Herbert Welsh and Henry S. Pancoast, two reformers from Philadelphia, came "most often in contact with 'progressive' Sioux, those associated with the schools and missions of the agencies" (see Hagan, *The Indian Rights Association: The Herbert Welsh Years, 1882–1904* [Tucson: University of Arizona Press, 1985], 6–7). The experiences of Welsh and Pancoast were typical of most other reformers inspecting conditions on the reservations.

73. Robert Gardner to secretary of the Interior, 6 Nov. 1885, Reports of the Inspection of the Field Jurisdictions of the Office of Indian Affairs, Interior Department, Record Group 48, National Archives, Microcopy 1070, Roll 40 (hereafter cited as Reports of the Field Jurisdictions, RG48, M1070, R40).

74. Gardner to secretary of the Interior, 10 Apr. 1887, ibid.

75. Agent Charles H. Grover to commissioner, 20 June 1887, OL, Potawatomi Agency, vol. 6, KCFRC; Grover to commissioner, 5 Sept. 1887, *House Executive Documents*, 50th Cong., 1st sess., ser. 2542, p. 205.

76. The reference here is to the traditional council of Potawatomi elders, not to the government–recognized council that normally expressed the wishes of its federal sponsors.

77. Wahquahboshkuk's age is noted as fifty-four for both 1893 and 1895 in Agent George James to Commissioner, 7 May 1898, LR, BIA, RG75, Letter 21702. A Potawatomi informant, Sam Bosley, told anthropologist Alanson Skinner that Wahquahboshkuk was "a chief of the Fish clan" (see Skinner, "The Mascoutens or Prairie Potawatomi Indians," *Bulletin of the Public Museum of the City of Milwaukee* 6 [Jan. 1927]: 392). Wahquahboshkuk was probably a member of the Sturgeon clan.

78. Wahquahboshkuk, John Half Day, and Sam Field to A. B. Upham, acting commissioner of Indian affairs, 15 June 1886, LR, BIA, RG75, Letter 16203.

79. Grover to Commissioner of Indian Affairs J. D. C. Atkins, 26 June 1888, OL, Potawatomi Agency, vol. 7, KCFRC; *New York Times*, 10 Sept. 1889.

80. Agent John Blair to commissioner, 19 Aug. 1889, *House Executive Documents*, 51st Cong., 1st sess., ser. 2725, p. 217; see also Special Agent Henry J. Aten to Commissioner T. J. Morgan, 3 Sept. 1891, LR, BIA, RG75, Letter 32450.

81. Gardner to commissioner, 30 Oct. 1891, Reports of the Field Jurisdictions, RG48, M1070, R40.

82. Aten to Morgan, 15 July 1891, LR, BIA, RG75, Letter 25746.

83. Scott to Gresham, 27 Aug. 1891, and Scott to Morgan, 17 Dec. 1891, OL, Potawatomi Agency, vol. 9, KCFRC.

84. Gresham to assistant adjutant general, 26 Aug. 1891, Gen. Nelson A. Miles to adjutant general, 17 Sept. 1891, and Scott to Morgan, 17 Dec. 1891, LR, BIA, RG75, Letters 33021 and 34803 (1891) and 9866 (1893).

85. Scott to Morgan, 29 Aug. 1891, OL, Potawatomi Agency, vol. 9, KCFRC; Scott to Gresham, 26 Aug. 1891, LR, BIA, RG75, Letter 33021.

86. Scott to Capt. Henry Jackson, 29 Aug. 1891, Scott to commissioner, 17 Sept. 1891, and Scott to Morgan, 21 Dec. 1891, OL, Potawatomi Agency, vol. 9, KCFRC; see also Anonymous, "The Prairie Potawatomie Resistance to Allotment," *Indian Historian* 9 (Fall 1976): 27–31.

87. Scott to Morgan, 20 Apr. 1892, OL, Potawatomi Agency, vol. 10, KCFRC; Benjamin Miller to secretary of the Interior, 11 June 1892, Reports of the Field Jurisdictions, RG48, M1070, R40.

88. Clifton asserts that because Wahquahboshkuk could read and write Eng-

lish, he was more effective than traditional Potawatomis in dealing with traders, missionaries, and federal officials. According to Clifton, Wahquahboshkuk was a "literate man whose prose and spelling was about the same quality as that of George Rogers Clark." The Indian habitually signed his letters with the title "Gentil Brave" (see Clifton, *Prairie People*, 395). It is very doubtful that Wahquahboshkuk spoke English; there is no archival evidence that bears this out. Indeed, the Potawatomi leader needed the services of an interpreter when he dealt with white officials, and he signed his name to letters and documents with the traditional "X" mark. The evidence clearly demonstrates, moreover, that others (literate white and Indian sympathizers) translated and wrote letters in his behalf.

89. In one instance, an acting commissioner of Indian affairs told the Potawatomi leader that he had come to Washington without authorization and was to return immediately. The official refused to listen to anything Wahquahboshkuk had to say (see the transcript of the conference of Wahquahboshkuk, James Thompson, and Frank Topash with the acting commissioner, 18 Mar. 1893, and Scott to commissioner, 29 Apr. 1893, LR, BIA, RG75, Letters 9944 and 15982). Wahquahboshkuk again left for Washington in January 1894, accompanied by two men from the Kickapoo reservation in Oklahoma. These two were probably former Mexican Potawatomis (see Scott to commissioner, 30 Jan. 1894, LR, BIA, RG75, Letter 5129).

90. These religious ceremonies are discussed in greater detail in the next chapter.

91. Scott to Morgan, 31 Oct. 1892, and Scott to commissioner, 19 Apr. 1893 and 17 May 1893, OL, Potawatomi Agency, vols. 10 and 11, KCFRC.

92. Scott to Morgan, 3 Dec. 1892, and Scott to commissioner, 14 Apr. 1893, 19 Apr. 1893, and 17 May 1893, OL, Potawatomi Agency, vol. 11, KCFRC.

93. Scott to Commissioner of Indian Affairs D. M. Browning, 14 July 1893, ibid.; Agent George W. James to commissioner, 24 Aug. 1897, *House Executive Documents*, 55th Cong., 2d sess., ser. 3641, pp. 153–154.

94. Wahquahboshkuk, James Thompson, and Martha Gosline to Interior Secretary Hoke Smith, 3 Feb. 1894, LR, BIA, RG75, Letter 5104. Martha Gosline was serving as interpreter for Wahquahboshkuk; she was a Citizen Potawatomi who had lived among the Kickapoos for many years (see Scott to commissioner, 6 Aug. 1894, LR, BIA, RG75, Letter 30540).

95. See Aten to Morgan, 3 Sept. 1891, LR, BIA, RG75, Letter 32450; L. F. Pearson to superintendent of Indian schools, 14 Feb. 1895, OL, Potawatomi Agency, vol. 14, KCFRC.

96. Scott to commissioner, 3 Aug. 1894, OL, Potawatomi Agency, vol. 13, KCFRC.

97. Report of the commissioner of Indian affairs, 14 Sept. 1894, *House Executive Documents*, 53d Cong., 3d sess., ser. 3306, p. 21; "Potawatomie Resistance to Allotment," 30.

98. Weshkeenoo, Wahquahboshkuk, and others to D. M. Browning, 5 Feb. 1896, LR, BIA, RG75, Letter 5649.

99. Clerk Frederick Luther to commissioner, 13 Feb. 1896, OL, Potawatomi Agency, vol. 16, KCFRC; Pearson to the commissioner, 23 Mar. 1896, LR, BIA, RG75, Letter 11351; Pearson to commissioner, 19 Sept. 1896, *House Executive Documents*, 54th Cong., 2d sess., ser. 3489, p. 164; Agent George W. James to commissioner, 8 June 1898, LR, BIA, RG75, Letter 26520.

100. Clifton asserts that Wahquahboshkuk failed because his "tactics and

techniques were obsolescent." Because of their leader's inadequacies, writes Clifton, the Prairie Potawatomis entered the twentieth century "culturally deflated and impoverished" (see Clifton, *Prairie People*, 372, 386, 396). Clifton's assessment of Wahquahboshkuk and the Prairie Potawatomis, however, is based on an inadequate search of the available archival materials. Just because the Potawatomis were forced to accept allotments, moreover, does not mean that they failed as a people, as Clifton insinuates. Indeed, their Indian customs, religions, and kinship networks remained strong, and their cultural autonomy helped carry them through the hardships of the twentieth century.

101. Agent W. R. Honnell to Merrill E. Gates, secretary of the Board of Indian Commissioners, 15 Jan. 1900, OL, Potawatomi Agency, vol. 25, KCFRC; *A Compilation of the Messages and Letters of the Presidents*, 20 vols. (New York: Bureau of National Literature, 1897–1927), 14:6674.

CHAPTER 8. THE TRIUMPH OF INDIAN KANSAS

1. C. C. Isely, "Democracy in the Primitive," unpublished document, History, Indians, Kickapoo File, Manuscript Division, Kansas State Historical Society, Topeka.

2. Ibid.

3. Agent John Blair to commissioner, 26 Aug. 1890, *House Executive Documents*, 51st Cong., 2d sess., ser. 2841, p. 110.

4. "Report on Indians Taxed and Not Taxed in the United States (except Alaska) at the Eleventh Census: 1890," *House Miscellaneous Document*, 52d Cong., 1st sess., no. 340, pt. 15, Doc. 3016, p. 327; Agent L. F. Pearson to commissioner, 19 Dec. 1896, Outgoing Letters of the Potawatomi Agency, 1887–1900, Bureau of Indian Affairs, Record Group 75, Federal Record Center, Kansas City, Mo., vol. 14 (hereafter cited as OL, Potawatomi Agency, BIA, RG75, vols. [6–25], KCFRC). For information on the deaths of Edward McCoonse and Lewis Gokey, see the Moravian Mission Logbook, 9 May 1888 and 3 Sept. 1889, Moravian Mission Records, Kansas Mission, Moravian Church Archives, Bethlehem, Pa., Box 185, Folder 13, Item 1, Microfilm Roll 23 (hereafter cited as Moravian Records, with box, folder, item, and microfilm roll numbers).

5. Agent W. R. Honnell to commissioner, 12 Sept. 1899, *House Executive Documents*, 56th Cong., 1st sess., ser. 3915, pp. 203–204; report of Commissioner D. M. Browning, 15 Sept. 1896, ibid., 54th Cong., 2d sess., ser. 3489, pp. 82–83.

6. C. A. Weslager, "Enrollment List of Chippewa and Delaware Munsies in Franklin County, Kansas, May 31, 1900," *Kansas Historical Quarterly* 40 (Summer 1974): 234–235; Romig, "Final Payment and Issuing of Patents," 8 Nov. 1900, and Romig communication, 12 Apr. 1903, Moravian Records, Box 185, Folder 13, Item 1, MR23; Honnell to commissioner, 29 Aug. 1901, *House Executive Documents*, 57th Cong., 1st sess., ser. 4290, p. 245; Romig to George Martin, secretary of the Kansas State Historical Society, 13 May 1907, 1 Oct. 1907 and 27 May 1910, History, Indians, Chippewa and Munsee File, Manuscript Division, Kansas State Historical Society, Topeka; Joseph Romig, "The Chippewa and Munsee (or Christian) Indians of Franklin County, Kansas," *Kansas State Historical Society Collections* 11 (1909–1910): 314–323.

7. "Indians Taxed and Not Taxed," 327–328; Agent J. A. Scott to Commis-

sioner T. J. Morgan, 9 Feb. 1892 and 8 June 1892, OL, Potawatomi Agency, BIA, RG75, vols. 9 and 10.

8. Blair to commissioner, 26 Aug. 1890, *House Executive Documents,* 51st Cong., 2d sess., ser. 2841, p. 110; Duane Anderson, "Ioway Ethnohistory: A Review," *Annals of Iowa* 42 (Summer 1973): 57 (part 2).

9. J. Neale Carman and Karl S. Pond, "The Replacement of the Indian Languages of Kansas by English," *Transactions of the Kansas Academy of Science* 58 (Summer 1955): 147–150; Alanson Skinner, "A Summer among the Sauk and Ioway Indians," *Yearbook of the Public Museum of the City of Milwaukee* 2 (Aug. 1923): 6–22; Roy W. Meyer, "The Iowa Indians, 1836–1885," *Kansas Historical Quarterly* 38 (Autumn 1962): 298–300.

10. Agent Samuel L. Patrick to commissioner, 1 Sept. 1892, *House Executive Documents,* 52d Cong., 2d sess., ser. 3088, p. 403.

11. Agent Lee Patrick to commissioner, 23 Aug. 1897, ibid., 55th Cong., 2d sess., ser. 3641, p. 248; Lee Patrick to commissioner, 31 Aug. 1898, ibid., 55th Cong., 3d sess., ser. 3757, pp. 250–251; Lee Patrick to commissioner, 31 Aug. 1899, ibid., 56th Cong., 1st sess., ser. 3915, pp. 306–307; Agent Ross Guffin, 27 Aug. 1903, ibid., 58th Cong., 2d sess., ser. 4645, p. 278; Agent W. C. Kohlenberg to commissioner, 6 Aug. 1904, ibid., 58th Cong., 3d sess., ser. 4798, p. 307; Kohlenberg to commissioner, 19 Aug. 1905, ibid., 59th Cong., 1st sess., ser. 4959, pp. 320–321; Kohlenberg to commissioner, 6 Aug. 1906, ibid., 59th Cong., 2d sess., ser. 5118, p. 322.

12. Blair to commissioner, 26 Aug. 1890, *House Executive Documents,* 51st Cong., 2d sess., ser. 2841, p. 110. For a report on the Kickapoo religious leaders, see Newlin to superintendent of Indian affairs at Lawrence, Kans., William Nicholson, 6 Sept. 1876, in Letters Received relating to the Quapaw and Sac and Fox agencies, 1875, Records of the Central Superintendency of Indian Affairs, Bureau of Indian Affairs, Record Group 75, National Archives, Microcopy 856, Roll 71 (hereafter cited as LR, Central Superintendency, BIA, RG75, M856, R71).

13. James H. Howard, "The Kenakuk Religion: An Early 19th Century Revitalization Movement 140 Years Later," *Museum News* 26 (Nov.-Dec. 1965): 38–40."Indians Taxed and Not Taxed," 326; questionnaire of George J. Remsburg completed by John Masquequa, November 1906, Remsburg Collection, box 78:3, Manuscript Division, Kansas State Historical Society, Topeka.

14. For information on the Drum Dance, see James A. Clifton, "Sociocultural Dynamics of the Prairie Potawatomi Drum Cult," *Plains Anthropologist* 14 (May 1969): 85–93.

15. Agent H. C. Linn to commissioner, 10 Sept. 1884, *House Executive Documents,* 48th Cong., 2d sess., ser. 2287, p. 146; Agent I. W. Patrick, 20 Aug. 1885, ibid., 49th Cong., 1st sess., ser. 2379, p. 337; "Sworn Statement of Wilson Stuve, Agency Physician, to Inspector E. D. Bannister," 17 Feb. 1888, Reports of the Inspection of the Field Jurisdictions of the Office of Indian Affairs, Bureau of Indian Affairs, Record Group 48, National Archives, Microcopy 1070, Roll 40 (hereafter cited as Reports of the Field Jurisdictions, BIA, RG48, M1070, R40).

16. Agent Henry Aten reported that the Potawatomis and Kickapoos considered their opposition to allotment "a religious duty" (see Aten to Morgan, 3 Sept. 1891, Letters Received by the Bureau of Indian Affairs, 1881–1907, Bureau of Indian Affairs, Record Group 75, National Archives, Letter 32450 (hereafter cited as LR, BIA, RG75, Letter 32450).

17. Special Indian Agent Reuben Sears reported from the Kickapoo reservation

in the summer of 1890 that allotment would prove "disastrous to Indian tribes." The citizen Kickapoos had "squandered their property, and are now living with the tribe on the reservation, and are a burden upon them, in fact half-way paupers, who are not counted as members of the tribe, but only as poor dependents" (see "Indians Taxed and Not Taxed," 326).

18. Scott to commissioner, 7 Oct. 1892, 20 Oct. 1892, 31 Oct. 1892, and 17 May 1893, OL, Potawatomi Agency, BIA, RG75, vols. 10 and 11, KCFRC; Scott to commissioner, 27 Aug. 1893, *House Executive Documents,* 53d Cong., 2d sess., ser. 3210, p. 161.

19. For information on the various Indian religions, see James A. Clifton, *The Prairie People: Continuity and Change in Potawatomi Indian Culture, 1665–1965* (Lawrence: University Press of Kansas, 1977), 382–386; Robert L. Bee, "Potawatomi Peyotism: The Influence of Traditional Patterns," *Southwestern Journal of Anthropology* 22 (Summer 1966): 194–205; James H. Howard, "When They Worship the Underwater Panther: A Prairie Potawatomi Bundle Ceremony," *Southwestern Journal of Anthropology* 16 (Summer 1960): 217–224; Howard, "Kenakuk Religion," 29–40; Donald D. Stull, *Kiikaapoa: The Kansas Kickapoo* (Horton: Kans.: Kickapoo Tribal Press, 1984), 96.

20. Agent George W. James to commissioner, 24 Aug. 1897, *House Executive Documents,* 55th Cong., 2d sess., ser. 3641, p. 154.

21. Milton M. Thorne to A. R. Snyder, 15 July 1919, and Snyder to Thorne, 18 July 1919, Religion and Missions File, Box A-60, Bureau of Indian Affairs, Record Group 75, Federal Record Center, Kansas City, Mo.

22. For information on Indian education, see Margaret Szasz, *Education and the American Indian: The Road to Self-Determination, 1928–1973* (Albuquerque: University of New Mexico Press, 1974); see also Francis Paul Prucha, *The Great Father: The United States Government and the American Indians,* 2 vols. (Lincoln and London: University of Nebraska Press, 1986), 2:818–840. For information on the state of Indian education up to 1928, see Lewis Meriam et al., *The Problem of Indian Administration* (Baltimore: Johns Hopkins Press, 1928); this is popularly known as the Meriam Report. For an excellent visual demonstration of the effects of schooling on Indians, see *Another Wind Is Moving: The Off-Reservation Indian Boarding School,* produced by Donald Stull and directed by David M. Kendall (Lawrence, Kans.: Kickapoo Nation School, 1985; Berkeley: University of California Media Extension Center, gen. release, 1987), VHS, 59 min. Historian Frederick E. Hoxie makes the point that assimilating Indians had taken on a new meaning by the 1920s. Federal officials and other concerned whites no longer advocated full equality for Indians or other minorities; Indians would remain on the periphery of mainstream society and a more "practical" governmental policy would unfold, allowing Indians to follow their own customs and assimilate gradually, while whites bought or leased tribal lands and officials forced Indian children to learn manual skills (see Hoxie, *A Final Promise: The Campaign to Assimilate the Indians, 1880–1920,* [Lincoln and London: University of Nebraska Press, 1984], 184–244).

23. The Prairie Potawatomis had already reestablished a seven-member tribal council in 1932 that handled the business affairs of the band. These Potawatomis did not trust governmental policies designed for their "benefit," and they preferred to remain independent of BIA supervision. They refused to restructure their council according to Indian Reorganization Act guidelines. Officially, the government allowed their existing council to exercise only an

advisory role. Finally, in 1961, the Potawatomis caved in to governmental pressure and adopted a democratically elected business council based on Collier's model (see Clifton, *Prairie People*, 406–410; Stull, *Kansas Kickapoo*, 109–110). For information on Collier and the Indian Reorganization Act, see Kenneth R. Philp, *John Collier's Crusade for Indian Reform* (Tucson: University of Arizona Press, 1977), 159–186; Prucha, *Great Father*, 2:954–1012; Lawrence C. Kelly, "The Indian Reorganization Act: The Dream and the Reality," *Pacific Historical Review* 44 (Aug. 1975): 291–312; Kelly, *The Assault on Assimilation: John Collier and the Origins of Indian Policy Reform* (Albuquerque: University of New Mexico Press, 1983); James S. Olson and Raymond Wilson, *Native Americans in the Twentieth Century* (Urbana and Chicago: University of Illinois Press, 1984), 107–132.

24. "Testimony of Minnie Evans, Chairman of the Tribal Council of the Prairie Band of Potawatomi Indians," 18 Feb. 1954, *Termination of Federal Supervision over Certain Tribes of Indians*, Joint Hearing before the Subcommittees on Interior and Insular Affairs, 83d Cong., 2d sess., S. 2743 and H. 7318, pt. 11 (Sac and Fox, Kickapoo, and Potawatomi tribes) (Washington, D.C.: Government Printing Office, 1954), 1341 (hereafter cited as *Termination Hearings*, with page numbers).

25. For a thorough discussion of termination, see Donald L. Fixico, *Termination and Relocation: Federal Indian Policy, 1945–1960* (Albuquerque: University of New Mexico Press, 1986); see also Prucha, *Great Father*, 2:1023–1084; Olson and Wilson, *Native Americans in the Twentieth Century*, 131–153.

26. Hugh Butler to Sen. Frank Carlson, 3 Sept. 1953, *Termination Hearings*, 1348.

27. Fixico, *Termination and Relocation*, 111–133; Prucha, *Great Father*, 2:1049–1056.

28. *Termination Hearings*, 1400–1401.

29. *Topeka State Journal*, 6 Nov. 1953. The article containing this quotation is reprinted in *Termination Hearings*, 1345–1346.

30. Peter Iverson astutely points out that the termination proposal roused Indians to action; termination was an era "in which tribalism and Indian nationalism were reinforced. Indeed, to a significant degree, the threat and the enactment of terminationist policy often strengthened rather than weakened Indian institutions and associations" (see Iverson, "Building toward Self-Determination: Plains and Southwestern Indians in the 1940s and 1950s," *Western Historical Quarterly* 16 [Apr. 1985]: 163–173).

31. Evans's official title was Potawatomi tribal chairman. For the sake of clarity, I have changed "chairman" to the more modern "chairwoman."

32. *Topeka State Journal*, 15 Feb. 1954; reprinted in *Termination Hearings*, 1347.

33. *Termination Hearings*, 1387–1388. The Kickapoo tribal council had met in October 1953 to discuss termination. After consulting with other tribal members, the council passed a resolution on October 19 in opposition to the policy (see Stull, *Kansas Kickapoo*, 118–119).

34. The treaties that the "two old men" had defended were the treaties of 1861 and 1867.

35. For Evans's testimony, see *Termination Hearings*, 1327–1338.

36. Ibid.

37. For Wahwassuck's testimony, see *Termination Hearings*, 1353–1368.

38. Prucha, *Great Father*, 2:1056–1059.
39. Fixico, *Termination and Relocation*, 134–157; Prucha, *Great Father*, 2:1079–1084; Stull, *Kansas Kickapoo*, 121. Kenneth R. Philp points out that the relocation program had widespread support from Indians seeking to better their own economic fortunes (see Philp, "Stride toward Freedom: The Relocation of Indians to Cities, 1952–1960," *Western Historical Quarterly* 16 [Apr. 1985]: 175–190).
40. Stull, *Kansas Kickapoo*, 122–129; Prucha, *Great Father*, 2:1157–1162.
41. Stull, *Kansas Kickapoo*, 127–129.
42. *New York Times*, 19 Jan. 1983, 25 Jan. 1983, and 26 Jan. 1983. Watt's remarks were not appreciated by Indians, and there was a nationwide call for the secretary's resignation. The Kickapoo tribal chairman, John Thomas, reported that he wanted to "throw a bowling ball through the T.V. set" after listening to Watt's comments (see *Wichita Eagle-Beacon*, 20 Jan. 1983). Syndicated newspaper columnist Edwin Yoder best expressed the general outrage over the secretary's comments: "What is perhaps most objectionable about Watt's remark, apart from insensitivity, is a historical disorientation bordering on yahooism —an inability to frame distinctly American problems in appropriate terms" (see *Wichita Eagle-Beacon*, 25 Jan. 1983).
43. For a description of the Kickapoos' recent plight, see Donald D. Stull, Jerry A. Schultz, and Ken Cadue, Sr., "Rights without Resources: The Rise and Fall of the Kansas Kickapoo," *American Indian Culture and Research Journal* 10, 2 (1986): 41–59; see also Stull, Schultz, and Cadue, "In the People's Service: The Kansas Kickapoo Technical Assistance Project," in *Collaborative Research and Social Change: Applied Anthropology in Action*, edited by Donald D. Stull and Jean J. Schensul (Boulder, Colo.: Westview Press, 1987), 33–54.
44. *Wichita Eagle-Beacon*, 15 Feb. 1987.
45. On the four Kansas reservations, there are now about 620 Kickapoos, 500 Potawatomis, 590 Iowas, and 40 Sacs (*Wichita Eagle-Beacon*, 15 Feb. 1987). The 1980 federal census lists a total of 17,829 American Indians living in Kansas. This number includes reservation Indians and those living in Lawrence, Topeka, Wichita, Kansas City (Missouri and Kansas), and other cities and rural areas (see *Census of Population*, Vol. 1: *Characteristics of the Population, General Social and Economic Characteristics*, Part 18: *Kansas* [Washington, D.C.: Department of Commerce, 1983], 17).
46. Two excellent films describe in vivid fashion the lives of twentieth-century Potawatomis and Kickapoos in Kansas—see *Neshnabek: The People*, produced by Donald Stull and directed by Gene Bernofsky (Berkeley: University of California Extension Media Center, 1979, re-release, 1987), 16 mm, 30 min.; and *Return to Sovereignty: Self-Determination and the Kansas Kickapoo*, produced by Donald Stull and directed by David M. Kendall (Berkeley: University of California Extension Media Center, 1982, gen. release, 1987), VHS, 46 min.

SELECTED
BIBLIOGRAPHY

MANUSCRIPT MATERIALS

National Archives, Washington, D.C.

Record Group 48. Letters Sent by the Indian Division of the Office of the Secretary of the Interior. Microcopy 606. Roll 47.

———. Reports of the Inspection of the Field Jurisdictions of the Office of Indian Affairs. Microcopy 1070. Roll 40.

———. Special Files relative to Negotiations with Indians, Land Matters, Investigations, and Other Subjects, File 6 (Mexican Kickapoos) and File 14 (Potawatomi Land Matters).

Record Group 75. Documents relating to the Negotation of Ratified and Unratified Treaties with Various Indian Tribes, 1868–1869. T494. Roll 10.

———. E2. Records of the Sac and Fox Agency in Kansas, 1855–1879. Federal Record Center, Fort Worth, Texas.

———. Letters Received, Fort Leavenworth Agency, 1824–1851, Microcopy 234. Rolls 300–303.

———. Letters Received, Great Nemaha Agency, 1848–1876, Microcopy 234. Rolls 300–314.

———. Letters Received, Kickapoo Agency, 1855–1876, Microcopy 234. Rolls 371–374.

———. Letters Received, Ottawa Agency, 1863–1865, Microcopy 234. Roll 656.

———. Letters Received, Potawatomi Agency, 1857–1880, Microcopy 234. Rolls 681–695

———. Letters Received, Sac and Fox Agency, 1859–1880, Microcopy 234. Rolls 734–744.

———. Letters Received, St. Louis Superintendency, 1824–1841, Microcopy 234. Rolls 747–752.

———. Letters Received, Western Superintendency, 1832–1836, Microcopy 234. Roll 921.

———. Letters Received by the Bureau of Indian Affairs, 1881–1907.

———. Letters Received by the Office of Indian Affairs, Central Superintendency, 1862–1873. Microcopy 234. Rolls 58–62.

———. Letters Received by the Office of Indian Affairs, Michigan Superintendency, 1834. Microcopy 1. Roll 38.

———. Letters Received relating to the Agency for the Indians in Kansas (Potawatomi Agency) and the Kiowa Agency, 1876, Microcopy 856. Roll 71.

————. Letters Received relating to the Cheyenne and Arapahoe and the Agency for Indians in Kansas (Potawatomi Agency), 1877. Microcopy 856. Roll 79.

————. Letters Received relating to the Sac and Fox and the Union Agencies, 1876, Microcopy 856, Roll 74.

————. Letters Sent by the Office of Indian Affairs. Microcopy 21. Rolls 10 and 42.

————. Letters Sent from the Sac and Fox-Shawnee Agency (SF-SA), vols. 2 and 11A, Oklahoma Historical Society Microfilm Publications, SF-SA4 and SF-SA9.

————. Letters Sent to Agents (press copies), vols. 3 and 4, 1 Feb. 1876–3 Mar. 1877. Microcopy 856. Roll 100.

————. Outgoing Letters of the Potawatomi Agency, vols. 6–25, 1887–1900. Federal Record Center, Kansas City, Missouri.

————. Records of the Central Superintendency of Indian Affairs. Letters Received relating to the Quapaw and Sac and Fox Agencies, 1875. Microcopy 856. Roll 64.

————. Records of the Secretary of War relating to Indian Affairs. Letters Sent. Microcopy 15. Roll 4.

————. Religion and Missions File, Box A-60. Federal Record Center, Kansas City, Missouri.

————. Special Cases, 1821–1907, Special Case 120 (Mexican Potawatomis). Record Group 94. Letters Received by the Office of the Adjutant General (Main Series), File 5269, 1886. Microcopy 689. Roll 483.

Record Group 107. Letters Sent by the Secretary of War relating to Military Affairs. Records of the Office of the Secretary of War, vol. 115, 1 June–31 Dec. 1886. Microcopy 6. Roll 98.

Records of the United States Circuit Court for the District of Kansas, 1st Division, Topeka. Law and Equity Cases (1862–1912), 1876, Box 116. Federal Record Center, Kansas City, Missouri.

Kansas State Historical Society, Topeka, Manuscript Division

Diaries of Samuel M. Irvin, 1841–1848. Microfilm Box 89.
Edward McKinney Collection:
George Allen Root Collection, Potawatomi and Kickapoo Indian files.
History, Indians, Chippewa and Munsee File.
History, Indians, Kickapoo File.
History, Indians, Potawatomi File.
Indian Missions File, Methodist.
Remsburg Collection.

Other Archives

Moravian Church Archives, Bethlehem, Pa. Moravian Mission Records, Kansas Mission. Boxes 185 and 1853, Microfilm rolls 23 and 24.

Presbyterian Historical Society, American Indian Correspondence, Collection of Missionary Letters, 1833–1893. Greenwood Press, Philadelphia. Microfilm boxes 3 and 8.

ANNUAL REPORTS

Minutes of Kansas Yearly Meeting of Friends, Held at Lawrence, Kansas, 1873–1878. Various publishers.

Proceedings of the Annual Meeting of the Lake Mohonk Conference of Friends of the Indian, 1886, 1887, 1889, 1890, 1897. Various editors and publishers.

PUBLISHED GOVERNMENT DOCUMENTS

Census of Population. Vol. 1: *Characteristics of the Population, General Social and Economic Characteristics.* Part 18: *Kansas.* Washington, D.C.: Department of Commerce, 1983.

House Executive Documents. Washington, D.C.: Government Printing Office, 1843–1906.

House of Representatives Committee Reports, 47th Cong., 1st sess., H. Rpt. 1149, ser. 2068.

Kappler, Charles, comp. *Indian Affairs, Laws and Treaties,* vol. 2. Washington, D.C.: Government Printing Office, 1904.

"Report on Indians Taxed and Not Taxed in the United States (except Alaska) at the Eleventh Census: 1890." *House Miscellaneous Document* 340, pt. 15, 52d Cong., 1st sess., Doc. 3016.

"Report on the Expedition of Dragoons, under Colonel Henry Dodge, to the Rocky Mountains in 1835." *American State Papers: Documents Legislative and Executive of the Congress of the United States.* Vol. 7: *Military Affairs.* Washington, D.C.: Gales and Seaton, 1836.

Riker, Dorothy, and Gayle Thornbrough, eds. *Messages and Papers relating to the Administration of James Brown Ray, Governor of Indiana, 1825–1831.* Indianapolis: Indiana Historical Bureau, 1954.

Senate Executive Documents. Washington, D.C.: Government Printing Office, 1830–1861.

Termination of Federal Supervision over Certain Tribes of Indians. Joint Hearing before the Subcommittees on Interior and Insular Affairs, 83d Cong., 2d sess., S. 2743 and H. 7318, pt. 11 (Sac and Fox, Kickapoo, and Potawatomi tribes). Washington, D.C.: Government Printing Office, 1954.

NEWSPAPERS

Alexandria Gazette (Virginia)
Christian Advocate and Journal (New York)
Examiner (London)
Guilford Citizen (Fredonia, Kansas)
Junction City Union (Kansas)
Leavenworth Times
Missouri Republican (St. Louis)
New York Times
Osage Chronicle (Burlingame, Kansas)
St. Joseph Beacon (Indiana)
St. Louis Beacon

Times (London)
Topeka Commonwealth
Topeka State Journal
Vandalia Whig and Illinois Intelligencer
Washington Daily Star
Washington National Intelligencer
Washington Post
Western Christian Advocate
Wichita Eagle-Beacon

DISSERTATIONS

Bollig, Richard Joseph. "History of Catholic Education in Kansas, 1836–1932."
Ph.D. dissertation. Catholic University of America, Washington, D.C., 1933.
Dillingham, Betty Ann Wilder. "Oklahoma Kickapoo." Ph.D. dissertation. University of Michigan, Ann Arbor, 1963.
Donohoe, Arthur T. "A History of the Early Jesuit Missions in Kansas." Ph.D.
dissertation. University of Kansas, Lawrence, 1931.
Manning, Jack W. "John Gill Pratt: Missionary, Printer, Physician, Teacher, and
Statesman." Ph.D. dissertation. Central Baptist Theological Seminary, Kansas City, Kans., 1951.
Murphy, Joseph Francis. "Potawatomi Indians of the West: Origins of the Citizen Band." Ph.D. dissertation. University of Oklahoma, Norman, 1961.

VIDEORECORDINGS

Another Wind Is Moving: The Off-Reservation Indian Boarding School. Produced by Donald Stull. Directed by David M. Kendall. VHS, 59 min. Lawrence,
Kans.: Kickapoo Nation School, 1985; Berkeley: University of California
Media Extension Center, gen. release, 1987.
Neshnabek: The People. Produced by Donald Stull. Directed by Gene Bernofsky. 16 mm, 30 min. Berkeley: University of California Extension Media
Center, 1979, re-release, 1987.
Return to Sovereignty: Self-Determination and the Kansas Kickapoo. Produced
by Donald Stull. Directed by David M. Kendall. VHS, 46 min. Berkeley:
University of California Extension Media Center, 1982, gen. release, 1987.

BOOKS

Abel, Annie Heloise. *The Slaveholding Indians.* Vol. 2: *The American Indian
as Participant in the Civil War.* Cleveland: Arthur H. Clark Company, 1919.
Armstrong, Perry A. *The Sauks and the Black Hawk War.* Springfield, Ill.: H. W.
Rokker, 1887.
Barry, Louise. *The Beginning of the West: Annals of the Kansas Gateway to the
American West, 1540–1854.* Topeka: Kansas State Historical Society, 1972.
Barsh, Russel Lawrence, and James Youngblood Henderson. *The Road: Indian
Tribes and Political Liberty.* Berkeley: University of California Press, 1980.

Berkhofer, Robert F., Jr. *Salvation and the Savage: An Analysis of Protestant Missions and American Indian Response, 1787–1862*. New York: Atheneum, 1976.

Bieder, Robert E. *Science Encounters the Indian, 1820–1880: The Early Years of American Ethnology*. Norman and London: University of Oklahoma Press, 1986.

Blaine, Martha Royce. *The Ioway Indians*. Norman: University of Oklahoma Press, 1979.

Blair, Emma Helen, ed. *The Indian Tribes of the Upper Mississippi Valley and Region of the Great Lakes*. 2 vols. Cleveland: Arthur H. Clark Company, 1911–1912.

Bowden, Henry Warner. *American Indians and Christian Missions: Studies in Cultural Conflict*. Chicago and London: University of Chicago Press, 1981.

Cash, Joseph H. *The Potawatomi People (Citizen Band)*. Phoenix: Indian Tribal Series, 1976.

Catlin, George. *Life among the Indians*. London: Gall and Inglis, no date.

———. *Notes on Eight Years' Travels and Residence in Europe: England, France, and Belgium*. Vol. 2. London: By the author, 1848.

Clark, John G., ed. *The Frontier Challenge: Responses to the Trans-Mississippi West*. Lawrence: University Press of Kansas, 1971.

Clifton, James A. *The Prairie People: Continuity and Change in Potawatomi Indian Culture, 1665–1965*. Lawrence: University Press of Kansas, 1977.

Clifton, James A., ed. *Being and Becoming Indian: Biographical Studies of North American Frontiers*. Chicago: Dorsey Press, 1989.

Culin, Stewart. *Games of the North American Indians*. Washington, D.C.: Government Printing Office, 1907; reprint, New York: Dover Publications, 1975.

Danziger, Edmund J., Jr. *Indians and Bureaucrats: Administering the Reservation Policy during the Civil War*. Urbana: University of Illinois Press, 1974.

De Smet, Pierre Jean. *Life, Letters, and Travels of Father Pierre Jean De Smet, S.J., 1801–1873*. 4 vols. Edited by Hiram M. Chittenden and Alfred T. Richardson. New York: Francis P. Harper, 1905; reprint, New York: Kraus Reprint Company, 1969.

———. *Western Missions and Missionaries: A Series of Letters*. New York: P. J. Kenedy, 1859.

Dippie, Brian W. *The Vanishing American: White Attitudes and U.S. Indian Policy*. Middletown, Conn.: Wesleyan University Press, 1982.

Duir, E. *The Good Old Times in McLean County, Illinois*. Bloomington, Ill.: McKnight & McKnight Publishing Company, 1968.

Edmunds, R. David. *The Potawatomis: Keepers of the Fire*. Norman: University of Oklahoma Press, 1978.

———. *The Shawnee Prophet*. Lincoln: University of Nebraska Press, 1983.

———. *Tecumseh and the Quest for Indian Leadership*. Boston and Toronto: Little, Brown and Company, 1984.

Edwards, Ninian W. *History of Illinois from 1778 to 1833; and Life and Times of Ninian Edwards*. New York: Arno Press, 1975.

Fixico, Donald L. *Termination and Relocation: Federal Indian Policy, 1945–1960*. Albuquerque: University of New Mexico Press, 1986.

Foreman, Grant. *The Last Trek of the Indians*. Chicago: University of Chicago Press, 1946.

Fritz, Henry E. *The Movement for Indian Assimilation, 1860–1890*. Philadelphia: University of Pennsylvania Press, 1963.

Garraghan, Gilbert J. *Catholic Beginnings in Kansas City, Missouri: An Historical Sketch*. Chicago: Loyola University Press, 1920.

Gates, Paul Wallace. *Fifty Million Acres: Conflicts over Kansas Land Policy, 1854–1890*. Ithaca, N.Y.: Cornell University Press, 1954.

Gibson, Arrell M. *The Kickapoos: Lords of the Middle Border*. Norman: University of Oklahoma Press, 1963.

Gladstone, T. H. *The Englishman in Kansas, or Squatter Life and Border Warfare*. Introduction by Frederick Law Olmsted, with a foreword by James A. Rawley. Lincoln: University of Nebraska Press, 1971.

Graves, W. W. *Life and Letters of Rev. Father John Schoenmakers, S.J.: Apostle to the Osages*. Parsons, Kans.: Commercial Publishers, 1928.

Green, Charles R. *Early Days in Kansas: In Keokuk's Time on the Kansas Reservation*. Olathe, Kans.: By the author, 1913.

———. *Early Days in Kansas: Pioneer Narratives of the First Twenty-five Years of Kansas History*. Olathe, Kans.: By the author, 1912.

———. *Early Days in Kansas: Tales and Traditions of the Marais des Cygnes Valley*. Olathe, Kans.: By the author, 1914.

———. *Sac and Fox Indians in Kansas: Mokohoko's Stubbornness*. Olathe, Kans.: By the author, 1914.

Hagan, William T. *The Indian Rights Association: The Herbert Welsh Years, 1882–1904*. Tucson: University of Arizona Press, 1985.

———. *The Sac and Fox Indians*. Norman: University of Oklahoma Press, 1958.

Herring, Joseph B. *Kenekuk, the Kickapoo Prophet*. Lawrence: University Press of Kansas, 1988.

Hoad, Louise Green. *Kickapoo Indian Trails*. Cáldwell, Ida.: Caxton Printers, 1944.

Hoffman, Charles F. *A Winter in the West, by a New Yorker*. New York: Harper & Brothers, 1835.

Horsman, Reginald. *Race and Manifest Destiny: The Origins of American Racial Anglo-Saxonism*. Cambridge, Mass., and London: Harvard University Press, 1981.

Howes, Charles C. *This Place Called Kansas*. Norman: University of Oklahoma Press, 1952.

Hoxie, Frederick E. *A Final Promise: The Campaign to Assimilate the Indians, 1880–1920*. Lincoln and London: University of Nebraska Press, 1984.

Hutton, Paul Andrew. *Soldiers West: Biographies from the Military Frontier*. Introduction by Robert M. Utley. Lincoln and London: University of Nebraska Press, 1987.

Irving, John Treat, Jr. *Indian Sketches, Taken during an Expedition to the Pawnee Tribes [1833]*. 2 vols. Philadelphia: Carey, Lea, and Blanchard, 1835; reprint, edited by John F. McDermott, Norman: University of Oklahoma Press, 1955.

Jackson, Helen Hunt. *A Century of Dishonor: The Early Crusade for Indian Reform*. Edited by Andrew F. Rolle. New York, Evanston, and London: Harper Torchbooks, 1965.

Kehoe, Alice B. *North American Indians: A Comprehensive Account*. Englewood Cliffs, N.J.: Prentice-Hall, 1981.

Keller, Robert H., Jr. *American Protestantism and United States Indian Policy, 1869–82.* Lincoln and London: University of Nebraska Press, 1983.

Kelly, Lawrence C. *The Assault on Assimilation: John Collier and the Origins of Indian Policy Reform.* Albuquerque: University of New Mexico Press, 1983.

Kinney, J. P. *A Continent Lost—A Civilization Won.* Baltimore: Johns Hopkins Press, 1937; reprint, New York: Octagon Books, 1975.

Kinsella, Thomas. *The History of Our Cradle Land: Catholic Indian Missions and Missionaries of Kansas.* Kansas City, Kans.: Casey Printing Company, 1921.

Kurz, Rudolph Friederich. *Journal of Rudolph Friederich Kurz: An Account of His Experiences among Fur Traders and American Indians.* Edited by J. N. B. Hewitt. Lincoln: University of Nebraska Press, 1970.

Landes, Ruth. *The Prairie Potawatomi: Tradition and Ritual in the Twentieth Century.* Madison: University of Wisconsin Press, 1970.

Latorre, Felipe A., and Dolores L. Latorre. *The Mexican Kickapoo Indians.* Austin and London: University of Texas Press, 1976.

Limerick, Patricia Nelson. *The Legacy of Conquest: The Unbroken Past of the American West.* New York and London: W. W. Norton & Company, 1987.

McCoy, Isaac. *History of Baptist Indian Missions.* Washington, D.C., and New York: W. M. Morrison and H. & S. Rayner, 1840.

McKenney, Thomas L., and James Hall. *The Indian Tribes of North America, with Biographical Sketches and Anecdotes of the Principal Chiefs.* Vol. 1. Edinburgh, Scot.: John Grant, 1933.

Malin, James C. *Indian Policy and Western Expansion.* Bulletin of the University of Kansas Humanistic Studies, vol. 2, no. 3. Lawrence: University of Kansas, 1921.

Manypenny, George W. *Our Indian Wards.* Cincinnati: Robert Clarke and Company, 1880; reprint, New York: Da Capo Press, 1972.

Mardock, Robert Winston. *The Reformers and the American Indian.* Columbia: University of Missouri Press, 1971.

Mathews, John Joseph. *The Osages: Children of the Middle Waters.* Norman: University of Oklahoma Press, 1961.

Mead, James R. *Hunting and Trading on the Great Plains, 1859–1875.* Edited by Schuyler Jones. Introduction by Ignace Mead Jones. Norman: University of Oklahoma Press, 1986.

Meriam, Lewis, et al. *The Problem of Indian Administration.* Baltimore: Johns Hopkins Press, 1928.

Miller, Nyle H., and Edgar Langsdorf, eds. *Kansas in Newspapers.* Topeka: Kansas State Historical Society, 1963.

Milner, Clyde A., II. *With Good Intentions: Quaker Work among the Pawnees, Otos, and Omahas in the 1870s.* Lincoln and London: University of Nebraska Press, 1982.

Milner, Clyde A., II, and Floyd A. O'Neil, eds. *Churchmen and the Western Indians, 1820–1920.* Introduction by the editors. Norman and London: University of Oklahoma Press, 1985.

Miner, H. Craig. *The Corporation and the Indian: Tribal Sovereignty and Industrial Civilization in Indian Territory, 1865–1907.* Columbia: University of Missouri Press, 1976.

Miner, H. Craig, and William E. Unrau. *The End of Indian Kansas: A Study of Cultural Revolution, 1854–1871.* Lawrence: University Press of Kansas, 1978.

Moeder, John M. *History of the Diocese of Wichita*. Wichita, Kans.: By the author, 1963.

Mooney, James. *The Ghost-Dance Religion and Wounded Knee*. New York: Dover Publications, 1973.

Morgan, Lewis Henry. *The Indian Journals, 1859–62*. Edited by Leslie A. White. Ann Arbor: University of Michigan Press, 1959.

Murray, Charles Augustus. *Travels in North America during the Years 1834, 1835, and 1836*. 2 vols. London: Richard Bently, 1839.

Nielsen, George R. *The Kickapoo People*. Phoenix: Indian Tribal Series, 1975.

Olson, James S., and Raymond Wilson. *Native Americans in the Twentieth Century*. Urbana and Chicago: University of Illinois Press, 1984.

Otis, D. S. *The Dawes Act and the Allotment of Indian Lands*. Edited by Francis Paul Prucha. Norman: University of Oklahoma Press, 1973.

Palmer, Friend. *Early Days in Detroit*. Detroit: Hunt and June, 1906.

Pearce, Roy Harvey. *Savagism and Civilization: A Study of the Indian and the American Mind*. Baltimore: Johns Hopkins Press, 1967.

Philp, Kenneth R. *John Collier's Crusade for Indian Reform*. Tucson: University of Arizona Press, 1977.

Point, Nicolas. *Wilderness Kingdom: Indian Life in the Rocky Mountains, 1840–1847: The Journals and Paintings of Nicolas Point, S.J.* Translated and edited by Joseph P. Donnelly. New York: Holt, Rinehart and Winston, 1967.

Priest, Loring Benson. *Uncle Sam's Stepchildren: The Reformation of United States Indian Policy, 1865–1887*. Lincoln: University of Nebraska Press, 1975.

Prucha, Francis Paul. *American Indian Policy in Crisis: Christian Reformers and the Indian, 1865–1900*. Norman: University of Oklahoma Press, 1976.

————. *American Indian Policy in the Formative Years: The Indian Trade and Intercourse Acts, 1790–1834*. Lincoln: University of Nebraska Press, 1973.

————. *The Great Father: The United States Government and the American Indians*. 2 vols. Lincoln and London: University of Nebraska Press, 1986.

————. *The Indian in American History*. Hinsdale, Ill.: Dryden Press, 1971.

————. *The Indians in American Society: From the Revolutionary War to the Present*. Berkeley, Los Angeles and London: University of California Press, 1985.

————. *The Sword of the Republic: The United States Army on the Frontier, 1783–1846*. New York: Macmillan Company, 1969.

————, ed. *Americanizing the American Indians: Writings by "Friends of the Indian," 1880–1900*. Cambridge, Mass.: Harvard University Press, 1973.

————, ed. *Indian Policy in the United States: Historical Essays*. Lincoln and London: University of Nebraska Press, 1981.

Remini, Robert V. *Andrew Jackson*. New York: Harper & Row, 1969.

Richmond, Robert W. *Kansas: A Land of Contrasts*. 3d edition. Arlington Heights, Ill.: Forum Press, 1989.

Ritzenthaler, Robert E., and Frederick A. Peterson. *The Mexican Kickapoo Indians*. Milwaukee: Milwaukee Public Museum Publications in Anthropology, 1956.

Ronda, James P., and James Axtell. *Indian Missions: A Critical Bibliography*. Bloomington: Indiana University Press, 1978.

Satz, Ronald N. *American Indian Policy in the Jacksonian Era*. Lincoln: University of Nebraska Press, 1975.

Schoolcraft, Henry R. *Information respecting the History, Condition and Prospects of the Indian Tribes of the United States*. 6 vols. Philadelphia: Lippincott, Grambo & Company, 1851–1857.

Schultz, George A. *An Indian Canaan: Isaac McCoy and the Vision of an Indian State*. Norman: University of Oklahoma Press, 1972.

Sheehan, Bernard W. *Seeds of Extinction: Jeffersonian Philanthropy and the American Indian*. New York: W. W. Norton & Company, 1974.

Skinner, Alanson. *Observations on the Ethnology of the Sac Indians*. Westport, Conn.: Greenwood Press, 1970.

Skinner, Grace C., and Elmer L. Skinner. *History Stories of New Baltimore*. New Baltimore, Mich.: New Baltimore Public Library, 1979.

Spicer, Edward H. *Cycles of Conquest: The Impact of Spain, Mexico, and the United States on the Indians of the Southwest, 1533–1960*. Tucson: University of Arizona Press, 1962.

Steffen, Jerome O. *William Clark: Jeffersonian Man on the Frontier*. Norman: University of Oklahoma Press, 1977.

Stull, Donald D. *Kiikaapoa: The Kansas Kickapoo*. Horton, Kans.: Kickapoo Tribal Press, 1984.

Stull, Donald, and James Divney. *Discussion Leader's Guide for* Neshnabek: The People. Lawrence: Kansas University Printing Service, 1980.

Stull, Donald D., and Jean J. Schensul, eds. *Collaborative Research and Social Change: Applied Anthropology in Action*. Boulder, Colo.: Westview Press, 1987.

Sturtevant, William C., ed. *Handbook of North American Indians*. 20 vols. Washington, D.C.: Smithsonian Institution, 1978– .

Sweet, William W. *Religion on the American Frontier, 1783–1840*. Vol. 4: *The Methodists: A Collection of Source Materials*. Chicago: University of Chicago Press, 1946.

Szasz, Margaret. *Education and the American Indian: The Road to Self-Determination, 1928–1973*. Albuquerque: University of New Mexico Press, 1974.

Tatum, Lawrie. *Our Red Brothers and the Peace Policy of President Ulysses S. Grant*. Introduction by Thomas C. Battey. Philadelphia: John C. Winston & Company, 1899.

Thwaites, Reuben Gold, ed. *Early Western Travels, 1748–1846*. 32 vols. Cleveland: Arthur H. Clark Company, 1904–1907.

Tibbles, Thomas Henry. *Buckskin and Blanket Days*. Garden City, N.Y.: Doubleday, 1957.

Trennert, Robert A., Jr., *Alternative to Extinction: Federal Indian Policy and the Beginnings of the Reservation System, 1846–1851*. Philadelphia: Temple University Press, 1975.

Unrau, William E. *The Emigrant Indians of Kansas: A Critical Bibliography*. Bloomington: Indiana University Press, 1979.

———. *The Kansa Indians: A History of the Wind People, 1673–1873*. Norman: University of Oklahoma Press, 1971.

Unrau, William E., and H. Craig Miner. *Tribal Dispossession and the Ottawa Indian University Fraud*. Norman: University of Oklahoma Press, 1985.

Utley, Robert M. *The Indian Frontier of the American West, 1846–1890*. Albuquerque: University of New Mexico Press, 1984.

Vandergriff, James H., ed. *The Indians of Kansas*. Emporia, Kans.: Teachers College Press, 1973.

Van Deusen, Glyndon G. *The Jacksonian Era, 1828–1848*. New York: Harper & Row, 1963.

Van Every, Dale. *Disinherited: The Lost Birthright of the American Indian*. New York: Avon Books, 1967.

———. *The Final Challenge: The American Frontier, 1804–1845*. New York: William Morrow and Company, 1964.

Viola, Herman J. *Diplomats in Buckskins: A History of Indian Delegations in Washington City*. Washington, D.C.: Smithsonian Institution, 1981.

———. *Thomas L. McKenney, Architect of America's Early Indian Policy: 1816–1830*. Chicago: Swallow Press, 1974.

Wallace, Ernest. *Ranald S. Mackenzie on the Texas Frontier*. Lubbock: West Texas Museum Association, 1964.

Washburn, Wilcomb E. *The Assault on Indian Tribalism: The General Allotment Law (Dawes Act) of 1887*. Edited by Harold M. Hyman. Philadelphia: J. B. Lippincott Company, 1975.

Weslager, C. A. *The Delaware Indians: A History*. New Brunswick, N.J.: Rutgers University Press, 1972.

———. *The Delawares: A Critical Bibliography*. Bloomington: Indiana University Press, 1978.

Whitney, Ellen M., ed. *The Black Hawk War, 1831–1832*. 3 vols. Springfield: Illinois State Historical Library, 1970.

Zornow, William Frank. *Kansas: A History of the Jayhawk State*. Norman: University of Oklahoma Press, 1957.

ARTICLES

Abel, Anna H. "Indian Reservations in Kansas and the Extinguishment of Their Title." *Kansas State Historical Society Collections* 8 (1903–1904): 72–109.

Anderson, Duane. "Iowa Ethnohistory: A Review." *Annals of Iowa* 41 (Spring 1973): 1228–1241 (part 1); 42 (Summer 1973): 41–59 (part 2).

Anderson, Gary Clayton. "Joseph Renville and the Ethos of Biculturalism." In *Being and Becoming Indian: Biographical Studies of North American Frontiers*, pp. 59–81. Edited by James A. Clifton. Chicago: Dorsey Press, 1989.

Anonymous. "The Prairie Potawatomie Resistance to Allotment." *Indian Historian* 9 (Fall 1976): 27–31.

Anson, Bert. "Variations of the Indian Conflict: The Effects of the Emigrant Indian Removal Policy, 1830–1854." *Missouri Historical Review* 59 (Oct. 1964): 64–89.

Axtell, James. "Forked Tongues: Moral Judgments in Indian History." American Historical Association *Perspectives* 25 (Feb. 1987): 10–13.

Banks, Dean. "Civil-War Refugees from Indian Territory, in the North, 1861–1864." *Chronicles of Oklahoma* 41 (Autumn 1963): 286–298.

Barnes, Lela. "Journal of Isaac McCoy for the Exploring Expedition of 1828." *Kansas Historical Quarterly* 5 (Aug. 1936): 227–277.

———. "Journal of Isaac McCoy for the Exploring Expedition of 1830." *Kansas Historical Quarterly* 5 (Nov. 1936): 339–377.

Barr, Thomas P. "The Pottawatomie Baptist Manual Labor Training School." *Kansas Historical Quarterly* 43 (Winter 1977): 377–431.

Barry, Louise, ed. "Scenes in (and en route to) Kansas Territory, Autumn, 1854: Five Letters by William H. Hunter." *Kansas Historical Quarterly* 35 (Autumn 1969): 312–336.

Bee, Robert L. "Potawatomi Peyotism: The Influence of Traditional Patterns." *Southwestern Journal of Anthropology* 22 (Summer 1966): 194–205.

Berryman, Jerome C. "A Circuit Rider's Frontier Experiences." *Kansas State Historical Society Collections* 16 (1923–1925): 177–226.

Brice, J. Y. "Some Experiences in the Sac and Fox Reservation." *Chronicles of Oklahoma* 4 (Dec. 1926): 307–311.

Byers, O. P. "When Railroading Outdid the Wild West Stories." *Kansas State Historical Society Collections* 17 (1926–1928): 339–348.

Caldwell, Martha B., ed. "Records of the Squatter Association of Whitehead District, Doniphan County." *Kansas Historical Quarterly* 13 (Feb. 1944): 16–35.

Callender, Charles. "Fox." In *Handbook of North American Indians*. Vol. 15: *Northeast*, pp. 648–655. Edited by Bruce G. Trigger. Washington, D.C.: Smithsonian Institution, 1978.

———. "Great Lakes–Riverine Sociopolitical Organization." In *Handbook of North American Indians*. Vol. 15: *Northeast*, pp. 610–621. Edited by Bruce G. Trigger. Washington, D.C.: Smithsonian Institution, 1978.

———. "Sauk." In *Handbook of North American Indians*. Vol. 15: *Northeast*, pp. 636–647. Edited by Bruce G. Trigger. Washington, D.C.: Smithsonian Institution, 1978.

Callender, Charles, Richard K. Pope, and Susan M. Pope. "Kickapoo." In *Handbook of North American Indians*. Vol. 15: *Northeast*, pp. 656–667. Edited by Bruce G. Trigger. Washington, D.C.: Smithsonian Institution, 1978.

Calloway, Colin G. "Simon Girty: Interpreter and Intermediary." In *Being and Becoming Indian: Biographical Studies of North American Frontiers*, pp. 38–58. Edited by James A. Clifton. Chicago: Dorsey Press, 1989.

Carman, J. Neale, and Karl S. Pond. "The Replacement of the Indian Languages of Kansas by English." *Transactions of the Kansas Academy of Science* 58 (Summer 1955): 131–150.

Carriker, Robert C. "Joseph M. Cataldo, S.J.: Courier of Catholicism to the Nez Percés." In *Churchmen and the Western Indians, 1820–1920*, pp. 109–139. Edited and with an introduction by Clyde A. Milner II and Floyd A. O'Neil. Norman and London: University of Oklahoma Press, 1985.

Clifton, James A. "Alternate Identities and Cultural Frontiers." In *Being and Becoming Indian: Biographical Studies of North American Frontiers*, pp. 1–37. Edited by James A. Clifton. Chicago: Dorsey Press, 1989.

———. "Potawatomi." In *Handbook of North American Indians*. Vol. 15: *Northeast*, pp. 725–742. Edited by Bruce G. Trigger. Washington, D.C.: Smithsonian Institution, 1978.

———. "Sociocultural Dynamics of the Prairie Potawatomi Drum Cult." *Plains Anthropologist* 14 (May 1969): 85–93.

Connelley, William E. "The Prairie Band of Pottawatomie Indians." *Kansas State Historical Society Collections* 14 (1915–1918): 488–570.

Conway, Thomas G. "Potawatomi Politics." *Journal of the Illinois State Historical Society* 65 (Winter 1972): 395–418

Cruise, John D. "Early Days on the Union Pacific." *Kansas State Historical Society Collections* 11 (1909–1910): 529–549.

Custer, Milo. "Kannekuk or Keeanakuk: The Kickapoo Prophet." *Illinois State Historical Society Journal* 2 (Apr. 1918): 48–56.

Danziger, Edmund J., Jr. "The Office of Indian Affairs and the Problem of Civil War Indian Refugees in Kansas." *Kansas Historical Quarterly* 35 (Autumn 1969): 257–275.

Duignan, Peter. "Early Jesuit Missionaries: A Suggestion for Further Study." *American Anthropologist* 60 (Aug. 1958): 725–732.

Dunbar, John, and Samuel Allis. "Letters Concerning the Presbyterian Mission in Bellevue, Nebraska, 1831–1841." *Kansas State Historical Society Collections* 14 (1915–1918): 570–784.

Edmunds, R. David. " 'Designing Men Seeking a Fortune': Indian Traders and the Potawatomi Claims Payment of 1836." *Indiana Magazine of History* 77 (June 1981): 109–122.

———. "Indians as Pioneers: Potawatomis on the Frontier." *Chronicles of Oklahoma* 65 (Winter 1987/88): 340–353.

Ewers, John C. "Thomas Easterly's Pioneer Daguerreotypes of Plains Indians." *Bulletin of the Missouri Historical Society* 24 (July 1968): 329–339.

Ferris, Ida M. "The Sauks and Foxes in Franklin and Osage Counties, Kansas." *Kansas State Historical Society Collections* 11 (1909–1910): 333–395.

Fixico, Donald. "The Black Hawk–Keokuk Controversy." In *Indian Leaders: Oklahoma's First Statesmen*, pp. 64–78. Edited by H. Glenn Jordan and Thomas M. Holm. Oklahoma City: Oklahoma Historical Society, 1979.

Garraghan, Gilbert J. "The Kickapoo Mission." *St. Louis Catholic Historical Review* 4 (Jan.–Apr. 1922): 25–50.

Gates, Paul Wallace. "A Fragment of Kansas Land History: The Disposal of the Christian Indian Tract." *Kansas Historical Quarterly* 6 (Aug. 1937): 227–240.

———. "Indian Allotments Preceding the Dawes Act." In *The Frontier Challenge: Responses to the Trans–Mississippi West*, pp. 141–170. Edited by John G. Clark. Lawrence: University Press of Kansas, 1971.

Gilstrap, Harry B., Jr. "Colonel Samuel Lee Patrick." *Chronicles of Oklahoma* 46 (Spring 1968): 58–63.

Glick, George W. "The Drought of 1860." *Kansas State Historical Society Collections* 9 (1905–1906): 480–485.

Goddard, Ives. "Delaware." In *Handbook of North American Indians*. Vol. 15: *Northeast*, pp. 213–239. Edited by Bruce G. Trigger. Washington, D.C.: Smithsonian Institution, 1978.

Hagan, William T. "Justifying Dispossession of the Indian: The Land Use Argument." In *American Indian Environments: Ecological Issues in Native American History*, pp. 65–80. Edited by Christopher Vecsey and Robert W. Venables. Syracuse, N.Y.: Syracuse University Press, 1980.

Hamilton, Kenneth G. "Cultural Contributions of Moravian Missions among the Indians." *Pennsylvania History* 18 (Jan. 1951): 1–15.

Harrington, M. R. "Sacred Bundles of the Sac and Fox Indians." *University of Pennsylvania Anthropological Publications* 4 (1914): 125–262.

Herring, Joseph B. "The Chippewa and Munsee Indians: Acculturation and Survival in Kansas, 1850s–1870." *Kansas History* 6 (Winter 1983/84): 212–220.

———. "Cultural and Economic Resilience among the Kickapoo Indians of the Southwest." *Great Plains Quarterly* 6 (Fall 1986): 263–275.

———. "Indian Intransigency in Kansas: Government Bureaucracy vs. Mokohoko's Sacs and Foxes." *Western Historical Quarterly* 17 (Apr. 1986): 185–200.

———. "Presbyterian Ethnologists among the Iowa and Sac Indians, 1837–1853." *American Presbyterians: Journal of Presbyterian History* 65 (Fall 1987): 195–203.

———. "The Prophet Kenekuk and the Vermillion Kickapoos: Acculturation without Assimilation." *American Indian Quarterly* 9 (Summer 1985): 295–307.

———. "The Vermillion Kickapoos of Illinois: The Prophet Kenekuk's Peaceful Resistance to Indian Removal, 1819–1833." *Selected Papers in Illinois History 1983* (1985): 28–38.

Horsman, Reginald. "American Indian Policy and the Origins of Manifest Destiny." *University of Birmingham Historical Journal* 11 (Dec. 1968): 128–140.

———. "Scientific Racism and the American Indian in the Mid–Nineteenth Century." *American Quarterly* 27 (May 1975): 152–168.

House, R. Morton. " 'The Only Way' Church and the Sac and Fox Indians." *Chronicles of Oklahoma* 43 (Winter 1965/66): 443–466.

Howard, James H. "The Kenakuk Religion: An Early 19th Century Revitalization Movement 140 Years Later." *Museum News* 26 (Nov.-Dec. 1965): 1–49.

———. "When They Worship the Underwater Panther: A Prairie Potawatomi Bundle Ceremony." *Southwestern Journal of Anthropology* 16 (Summer 1960): 217–224.

Hubbard, Gurdon S. "A Kickapoo Sermon." *Illinois Monthly Magazine* 1 (Oct. 1831): 473–476.

"Incidents of Frontier Life." *Journal of the Illinois State Historical Society* 32 (Dec. 1939): 529.

Iverson, Peter. "Building toward Self-Determination: Plains and Southwestern Indians in the 1940s and 1950s." *Western Historical Quarterly* 16 (Apr. 1985): 163–173.

Jacobs, Hubert, ed. "The Potawatomi Mission 1854." *Mid-America* 36 (Oct. 1954): 220–248.

Jones, Dorothy V. "A Preface to the Settlement of Kansas." *Kansas Historical Quarterly* 29 (Summer 1963): 122–136.

Kelsey, Harry. "William P. Dole and Mr. Lincoln's Indian Policy." *Journal of the West* 10 (July 1971): 484–492.

Kelly, Lawrence C. "The Indian Reorganization Act: The Dream and the Reality." *Pacific Historical Review* 44 (Aug. 1975): 291–312.

King, James. " 'A Better Way': General George Crook and the Ponca Indians." *Nebraska History* 50 (Fall 1969): 239–256.

King, Joseph B. "The Ottawa Indians in Kansas and Oklahoma." *Kansas State Historical Society Collections* 13 (1913–1914): 373–378.

Klopfenstein, Carl G. "Westward Ho: Removal of Ohio Shawnees, 1832–1833." *Bulletin of the Historical and Philosophical Society of Ohio* 15 (Jan. 1957): 3–31.

Lewis, James R. "Shamans and Prophets: Continuities and Discontinuities in Native American New Religions." *American Indian Quarterly* 12 (Summer 1988): 221–228.

Lonn, Ella. "Ripples of the Black Hawk War in Northern Indiana." *Indiana Magazine of History* 20 (Sept. 1924): 288–307.

Lutz, J. J. "The Methodist Missions among the Indian Tribes in Kansas." *Kansas State Historical Society Collections* 9 (1905–1906): 160–235.

McDermott, John Francis, ed. "Isaac McCoy's Second Exploring Trip in 1828." *Kansas Historical Quarterly* 13 (Aug. 1945): 400–462.

Meyer, Roy W. "The Iowa Indians, 1836–1885." *Kansas Historical Quarterly* 28 (Autumn 1962): 273–300.

Miles, William. " 'Enamoured with Colonization': Isaac McCoy's Plan of Indian Reform." *Kansas Historical Quarterly* 38 (Autumn 1972): 268–286.

Morrison, T. F. "Mission Neosho." *Kansas Historical Quarterly* 4 (Aug. 1935): 227–234.

Nicholson, William. "A Tour of Indian Agencies in Kansas and the Indian Territory in 1870." *Kansas Historical Quarterly* 3 (Aug. 1934): 289–326.

Ortiz, Alfonso. "Indian/White Relations: A View from the Other Side of the 'Frontier.' " In *Indians in American History*, pp. 1–16. Edited by Frederick E. Hoxie. Arlington Heights, Ill.: Harlan Davidson, 1988.

Pate, J'Nell L. "Ranald S. Mackenzie." In *Soldiers West: Biographies from the Military Frontier*, pp. 177–192. Edited by Paul Andrew Hutton. Introduction by Robert M. Utley. Lincoln and London: University of Nebraska Press, 1987.

Philp, Kenneth R. "Stride toward Freedom: The Relocation of Indians to Cities, 1952–1960." *Western Historical Quarterly* 16 (Apr. 1985): 175–190.

Prucha, Francis Paul. "American Indian Policy in the 1840s." In *The Frontier Challenge: Responses to the Trans-Mississippi West*, pp. 81–110. Edited by John G. Clark. Lawrence: University Press of Kansas, 1971.

———. "Andrew Jackson's Indian Policy: A Reassessment." *Journal of American History* 56 (Dec. 1969): 527–539. Reprinted in *The Indian in American History*, pp. 67–74. Edited by Francis Paul Prucha. Hinsdale, Ill.: Dryden Press, 1971.

———. "Indian Removal and the Great American Desert: Visions of Reform." *Indiana Magazine of History* 59 (Dec. 1963): 299–322.

———. "Thomas L. McKenney and the New York Indian Board." *Mississippi Valley Historical Review* 48 (Mar. 1962): 635–655.

Remsburg, George J. "Some Notes on the Kickapoo Indians." *The Philatelic West* 36 (Apr. 1907): 325–326.

Ritzenthaler, Robert E. "The Potawatomi Indians of Wisconsin." *Bulletin of the Public Museum of the City of Milwaukee* 19 (Feb. 1953): 99–174.

Rogers, E. S. "Southeastern Ojibwa." In *Handbook of North American Indians*. Vol. 15: *Northeast*, pp. 760–771. Edited by Bruce G. Trigger. Washington, D.C.: Smithsonian Institution, 1978.

Romig, Joseph. "The Chippewa and Munsee (or Christian) Indians of Franklin County, Kansas." *Kansas State Historical Society Collections* 11 (1909–1910): 314–323.

Ronda, James P. "The European Indian: Jesuit Civilization Planning in New France." *Church History* 41 (Sept. 1972): 385–395.

Root, George A., ed. "No-ko-aht's Talk: A Kickapoo Chief's Account of a Tribal Journey from Kansas to Mexico and Return in the Sixties." *Kansas Historical Quarterly* 1 (Feb. 1932): 153–159.

Schultz, George A. "Kennekuk, the Kickapoo Prophet." *Kansas History* 3 (Spring 1980): 38–46.

Sibley, George C. "Extracts from the Diary of Major Sibley." *Chronicles of Oklahoma* 5 (June 1927): 196–200.

Skinner, Alanson. "The Mascoutens or Prairie Potawatomi Indians." *Bulletin of the Public Museum of the City of Milwaukee* 6 (Jan. 1927): 327–411.

———. "Societies of the Iowa, Kansa, and Ponca Indians." *Anthropological Papers of the American Museum of Natural History* 9 (1915): 683–740.

———. "A Summer among the Sauk and Ioway Indians." *Yearbook of the Public Museum of the City of Milwaukee* 2 (Aug. 1923): 6–22.

Socolofsky, Homer E. "How We Took the Land." In *Kansas: The First Century,* vol. 1; pp. 281–306. Edited by John D. Bright. New York: Lewis Historical Publishing Company, 1956.

"Some Contemporary References to St. Mary's Mission." *Mid-America* 17 (Apr. 1935): 84–103.

Steffen, Jerome O. "William Clark." In *Soldiers West: Biographies from the Military Frontier,* pp. 11–24. Edited by Paul Andrew Hutton. Introduction by Robert M. Utley. Lincoln and London: University of Nebraska Press, 1987.

Stuart, Benjamin F. "The Deportation of Menominee and His Tribe of Pottawattomie Indians." *Indiana Magazine of History* 18 (Sept. 1922): 255–265.

Stull, Donald D., Jerry A. Schultz, and Ken Cadue, Sr. "In the People's Service: The Kansas Kickapoo Technical Assistance Project." In *Collaborative Research and Social Change: Applied Anthropology in Action,* pp. 33–54. Edited by Donald D. Stull and Jean J. Schensul. Boulder, Colo.: Westview Press, 1987.

———. "Rights without Resources: The Rise and Fall of the Kansas Kickapoo." *American Indian Culture and Research Journal* 10, 2 (1986): 41–59.

Sturm, John A. "Letters from Westport: To Kansas by Difficult Ways," copy of an unpublished manuscript in my possession.

Thomas, Peter A. "Contrastive Subsistence Strategies and Land Use as Factors for Understanding Indian-White Relations in New England." *Ethnohistory* 23 (Winter 1976): 1–18.

Trennert, Robert A. "The Business of Indian Removal: Deporting the Potawatomi from Wisconsin, 1851." *Wisconsin Magazine of History* 63 (Autumn 1979): 36–50.

Unrau, William E. "The Council Grove Merchants and Kansa Indians, 1855–1870." *Kansas Historical Quarterly* 34 (Autumn 1968): 266–281.

———. "George Sibley's Plea for the 'Garden of Missouri' in 1824." *Bulletin of the Missouri Historical Society* 27 (Oct. 1970): 3–13.

———. "The Ottawa Indian University: C. C. Hutchinson, the Baptists, and Land Fraud in Kansas." *Arizona and the West* 25 (Autumn 1983): 229–244.

———. "Removal, Death, and the Legal Reincarnation of the Kaw People." *Indian Historian* 9 (Winter 1976): 3–9.

Van Quickenborne, Charles F. "Relations d'un voyage fait chez les tribus indiennes situées à l'ouest du missouri." *Annales de la propagation de la foi* 9 (Sept. 1836): 88–103.

Voget, Fred W. "The American Indians in Transition: Reformation and Accommodation." *American Anthropologist* 58 (Apr. 1956): 249–263.

Wallace, Anthony F. C. "Prelude to Disaster: The Course of Indian-White Relations Which Led to the Black Hawk War of 1832." In *The Black Hawk War, 1831–1832,* 1:36–38. 3 vols. Edited by Ellen M. Whitney. Springfield: Illinois State Historical Library, 1970.

———. "Revitalization Movements." *American Anthropologist* 58 (Apr. 1956): 264–281.

Wallace, Ernest, and Adrian S. Anderson. "R. S. Mackenzie and the Kickapoos: The Raid into Mexico in 1873." *Arizona and the West* 7 (Summer 1965): 105–126.

Wallace, Paul A. W. "The Moravian Records." *Indiana Magazine of History* 48 (June 1952): 143–144.

Waltmann, Henry G. "Circumstantial Reformer: President Grant and the Indian Problem." *Arizona and the West* 13 (Winter 1971): 323–342.

Washburn, Wilcomb E. "Indian Removal Policy: Administrative, Historical, and Moral Criteria for Judging Its Success or Failure." *Ethnohistory* 12 (Summer 1965): 274–278.

———. "The Moral and Legal Justification for Dispossessing the Indians." In *Seventeenth Century America: Essays in Colonial History*, pp. 15–32. Edited by James Morton Smith. New York: W. W. Norton & Company, 1972.

Weslager, C. A. "Enrollment List of Chippewa and Delaware Munsies in Franklin County, Kansas, May 31, 1900." *Kansas Historical Quarterly* 40 (Summer 1974): 234–240.

Willner, Ann Ruth, and Dorothy Willner. "The Rise and Role of Charismatic Leaders." *Annals of the American Academy of Political and Social Science* 358 (Mar. 1965): 77–88.

Wilmeth, Roscoe. "Kansa Village Locations in Light of McCoy's 1828 Journal." *Kansas Historical Quarterly* 26 (Summer 1960): 152–157.

Young, Mary E. "Indian Removal and Land Allotment: The Civilized Tribes and Jacksonian Justice." *American Historical Review* 64 (Oct. 1958): 31–45.

INDEX

25,10